THE YEAR-ROUND BULB GARDEN

THE YEAR-ROUND BULB GARDEN

Brian Mathew

SOUVENIR PRESS

ISBN 0 285 62787 2

Typeset by CCC, printed and bound in Great Britain by
William Clowes Limited, Beccles and London

CONTENTS

Acknowledgements   6
List of Colour Plates   7
Introduction   II

1   THE BULB GARDEN IN AUTUMN: September–
    November   2I
    The Autumn-Flowering Bulbs
      Allium, Amaryllis, Colchicum, Crinum, Crocus, Cyclamen, Galanthus,
      Leucojum, Lilium, Nerine, Scilla, Sternbergia, Zephyranthes

2   THE BULB GARDEN IN WINTER: December–February   36
    The Winter-Flowering Bulbs
      Anemone, Arum, Crocus, Cyclamen, Eranthis, Galanthus, Iris,
      Leucojum, Narcissus, Scilla

3   THE BULB GARDEN IN SPRING: March–May   5I
    The Spring-Flowering Bulbs
      Allium, Anemone, Arisarum, Arum, Bulbocodium, Calochortus,
      Chionodoxa, Colchicum, Corydalis, Crocus, Cyclamen, Eranthis,
      Erythronium, Fritillaria, Galanthus, Hermodactylus, Hyacinthus,
      Ipheion, Iris, Ixiolirion, Leucojum, Muscari, Narcissus, Ornithogalum,
      Puschkinia, Romulea, Scilla, Tecophilaea, Trillium, Tulipa

4   THE BULB GARDEN IN SUMMER: June–August   93
    The Summer-Flowering Bulbs
      Acidanthera, Allium, Anemone, Anomatheca, Arisaema, Brodiaea,
      Camassia, Cardiocrinum, Crinum, Crocosmia, Curtonus, Cypella,
      Dierama, Dracunculus, Eucomis, Freesia, Galtonia, Gladiolus, Iris,
      Ixia, Lilium, Moraea, Nectaroscordum, Nomocharis, Ornithogalum,
      Polianthes, Rhodohypoxis, Scilla, Sparaxis, Tigridia, Tulipa, Watsonia,
      Zantedeschia, Zigadenus

Bulb Nurseries and Specialist Societies   I37
Further Reading   I39
Index of Bulb Names   I40
General Index   I44

Acknowledgements

As usual I am indebted to Maggie for converting the heap of chaos on my desk into a readable typescript, and this is also an appropriate place to say thank you to my son Paul for capturing the hundreds of scarlet beetles which threaten my lilies each year! I must also thank Pat Halliday for preparing the line drawings and John Ingham for the use of the photograph of *Sternbergia lutea*.

LIST OF COLOUR PLATES

Between pages 16 and 17

1. *Acidanthera bicolor* (= *Gladiolus callianthus*), sweetly scented, from Africa.
2. *Allium aflatunense* with grey Mallow and Helichrysum.
3. *Allium christophii* (*albopilosum*), also good for dried decorations.
4. *Allium karataviense*, a striking Onion relative from Central Asia.
5. *Allium moly* in grass, also good under shrubs.
6. *Allium sphaerocephalon* with grey Helichrysum.
7. *Allium stipitatum* with white Honesty.
8. *Amaryllis belladonna* requires a warm sunny border.
9. *Anemone apennina* is good for naturalising.
10. *Anemone blanda* 'Atrocaerulea' in a woodland setting.
11. *Anemone blanda* 'Radar', the most vividly coloured variety.
12. *Anemone nemorosa* (Wood Anemone) with *Podophyllum* leaves.

Between pages 32 and 33

13. *Anemone nemorosa* 'Robinsoniana', one of the best Wood Anemones.
14. *Anemone ranunculoides*, a yellow Wood Anemone for semi-shade.
15. *Anomatheca laxa* (*Lapeirousia*), an easy summer-flowering bulb.
16. *Arum italicum* 'Pictum' leaves in winter with Snowdrops.
17. *Brodiaea* (*Triteleia*) *hyacinthina*, an Onion relative from America.
18. *Calochortus luteus*, gorgeous but not easy to grow.
19. *Camassia quamash*, a large Squill-like bulb for a damp spot.
20. *Cardiocrinum* (*Lilium*) *giganteum*, an astonishing Lily from the Himalaya.
21. *Chionodoxa gigantea*, a Turkish relative of Scilla.
22. *Chionodoxa luciliae*, the best 'Glory of the Snow'.
23. *Colchicum agrippinum* flowers in the early autumn.
24. *Colchicum byzantinum*, a very free-flowering autumn bulb.
25. *Colchicum speciosum* in grass.
26. *Colchicum speciosum* 'Album', the lovely white form, easy to grow.
27. *Colchicum* 'The Giant' with grey-leaved plants.
28. *Colchicum* 'Waterlily', the largest double Colchicum.
29. *Corydalis solida*, a good early bulb for the rock garden.
30. *Crinum powellii* 'Album' for late summer or early autumn.
31. *Crocosmia* 'Emily McKenzie', a striking Montbretia relative.
32. *Crocosmia masonorum*, a stately plant for the herbaceous border.
33. *Crocus angustifolius* (*susianus*), the 'Cloth of Gold' Crocus.
34. *Crocus banaticus* with the grass *Molinia caerulea* 'Variegata'.

35. *Crocus chrysanthus* 'Lady Killer', one of the most striking varieties.
36. *Crocus chrysanthus* 'Snow Bunting', the best pure white variety.

Between pages 48 and 49
37. *Crocus imperati* 'De Jager' has a yellowish outside to the flowers.
38. *Crocus nudiflorus*, a good autumnal Crocus in grass.
39. *Crocus ochroleucus* in grass with *Cotinus* leaves in autumn.
40. *Crocus sieberi* 'Violet Queen', an easy free-flowering spring species.
41. *Crocus sativus*, the source of saffron.
42. *Crocus tommasinianus* with Snowdrops in late winter.
43. *Crocus tommasinianus* 'Ruby Giant' with *Cornus stolonifera* stems.
44. *Crocus tournefortii* keeps its flowers open in dull weather.
45. *Crocus vernus* 'Pickwick' naturalised in grass. One of the Large Dutch varieties.
46. *Crocus* 'Yellow Dutch' ('Yellow Giant', 'Golden Yellow') in grass.
47. *Cyclamen coum* and its white form, a true winter flowering species.
48. *Cyclamen hederifolium* under deciduous shrubs in autumn.
49. *Cyclamen pseudibericum* in spring, for a sheltered position.
50. *Cyclamen repandum*, the hardiest of the spring-flowering species.
51. *Cypella herbertii*, a curious summer bulb from Argentina.
52. *Dierama pulcherrimum*, the 'Angel's Fishing Rod'.
53. *Eranthis* x *tubergenii* 'Guinea Gold' in the rock garden.
54. *Erythronium dens-canis*, the Dog's Tooth Violet.
55. *Erythronium* 'Pagoda' is ideal for a semi-shaded position.
56. *Erythronium revolutum* in a peat garden.
57. *Erythronium* 'White Beauty', perhaps the best of the Dog's Tooth Violets.
58. *Eucomis comosa*, a South African species but very hardy.
59. *Fritillaria camtschatcensis* likes a cool soil, rich in humus.
60. *Fritillaria imperialis* 'Lutea Maxima', a striking yellow 'Crown Imperial'.

Between pages 64 and 65
61. *Fritillaria meleagris*, the Snakeshead Lily, is good in grass.
62. *Fritillaria pallidiflora*, a lovely species from Central Asia.
63. *Fritillaria persica* needs low-growing companions to accentuate its stature.
64. *Galanthus caucasicus* 'Hiemale', a truly winter-blooming Snowdrop.
65. *Galanthus elwesii* has bold grey leaves and large flowers.
66. *Galanthus ikariae* (*latifolius*), unusual with its glossy green leaves.
67. *Galanthus nivalis* with Hellebores and Crocus.
68. *Galanthus nivalis* and Crocus in grass.
69. *Galanthus nivalis* 'Atkinsii', probably the best variety of Snowdrop.
70. *Galtonia candicans*, a tall stately Cape bulb for the summer border.
71. *Gladiolus byzantinus* with tall bearded Iris. A hardy species.
72. *Hyacinthus orientalis* with greyish Rosemary. One of the 'Multiflora' varieties.

Between pages 80 and 81
73. *Ipheion uniflorum* in a woodland in spring.
74. *Iris* (English) *latifolia* (*xiphioides*), a good summer border plant.
75. *Iris* (Spanish) *xiphium* var. *lusitanica* is just one of many varieties.
76. *Iris* (Dutch) 'Golden Harvest' with variegated Ivy.
77. *Iris* (Dutch) 'White Excelsior' with grey foliage and Quaking Grass.
78. *Iris* (Juno) *bucharica*, an unusual bulbous Iris.

79. *Iris* (Juno) *graeberiana* for the connoisseur's garden.
80. *Iris* (Juno) *magnifica* looks best with a dark background.
81. *Iris* (Reticulata) *danfordiae* with grey Dianthus leaves.
82. *Iris* (Reticulata) *histrioides* in grass. Also good for the rock garden.
83. *Iris* (Reticulata) *reticulata* with the grey conifer, *Abies koreana*.
84. *Leucojum aestivum* (Summer Snowflake) in grass, enjoys damp places.

Between pages 96 and 97
85. *Leucojum autumnale* in the rock garden in autumn.
86. *Leucojum vernum*, the Spring Snowflake, for a damp soil.
87. *Lilium auratum*, the Golden-Rayed Lily of Japan.
88. *Lilium* 'Bright Star', an easily cultivated Lily for the garden or patio.
89. *Lilium candidum*, the Madonna Lily.
90. *Lilium dauricum*, a dwarf Lily for the rock garden.
91. *Lilium* 'Fire King' in front of purplish-leaved *Rosa rubrifolia*.
92. *Lilium* 'Golden Splendour', a superb Trumpet Lily hybrid.
93. *Lilium henryi* can reach three metres when growing well.
94. *Lilium martagon*, a good deep pink form of the Martagon Lily.
95. *Lilium monadelphum*, an unusual species from the Caucasus.
96. *Lilium pumilum* (*tenuifolium*), a delicate but easily-grown Lily.
97. *Lilium* 'Red Night' with *Corydalis ochroleuca* on a wall behind.
98. *Lilium regale*, one of the best of all Lilies, strongly fragrant.
99. *Lilium tigrinum* (*L. lancifolium*) 'Splendens', a good form of the much-loved Tiger Lily.
100. *Moraea huttonii*, a South African relative of Iris.
101. *Muscari armeniacum* 'Blue Spike' with *Viola* 'Prince John'.
102. *Muscari azureum* in the rock garden.
103. *Muscari azureum* 'Album' shows the unconstricted flowers of this Grape Hyacinth.
104. *Muscari comosum*, the Tassel Hyacinth with its crown of sterile flowers.
105. *Muscari tubergeniana* is one of the best Grape Hyacinths.
106. *Narcissus bulbocodium* in grass at Wisley Garden.
107. *Narcissus* 'Dove Wings' with early Primulas and Tulips.
108. *Narcissus* 'February Gold' with *Anemone nemorosa* in grass.

Between pages 112 and 113
109. *Narcissus* 'Minnow', a miniature Tazetta Narcissus.
110. *Narcissus pseudonarcissus* subsp. *abscissus* with its straight trumpets.
111. *Narcissus pseudonarcissus* subsp. *alpestris* with Pulsatilla. An unusual form of Daffodil.
112. *Narcissus* 'Tête-à-Tête', a delightful dwarf Cyclamineus hybrid.
113. *Narcissus* 'Thalia' is one of the best of the Triandrus hybrids.
114. *Narcissus triandrus* 'Albus' for a rock garden or peat bed.
115. *Nectaroscordum siculum* (*Allium siculum*) is good in winter for dried decoration.
116. *Nerine bowdenii* against a warm wall in autumn.
117. *Ornithogalum balansae*, a good dwarf species for the rock garden.
118. *Ornithogalum nutans* in grass. Also good under shrubs.
119. *Ornithogalum thyrsoides* with a greyish background.
120. *Ornithogalum umbellatum* ('Star of Bethlehem') and Forget-me-Nots.
121. *Puschkinia scilloides*, a Scilla-relative from Turkey.
122. *Rhodohypoxis baurii*, a dwarf hardy summer bulb from Natal.
123. *Romulea ramiflora* in grass. Also suitable for a rock garden.

124. *Scilla bithynica* in a rock garden; also good for naturalising.
125. *Scilla campanulata* (*S. hispanica*), the Spanish Bluebell.
126. *Scilla siberica* 'Spring Beauty', a superb Squill from Russia.
127. *Scilla tubergeniana* pushes through at the first hint of spring.
128. *Sternbergia lutea* is one of the few yellow autumn bulbs.
129. *Tecophilaea cyanocrocus*, the Chilean Blue Crocus, an expensive connoisseur's plant.
130. *Tigridia pavonia*, the Mexican Tiger Flower, a striking summer bulb.
131. *Tigridia pavonia* 'Alba', the pure white form of the Tiger Flower.
132. *Tigridia pavonia* 'Lutea', a yellow form of the Tiger Flower without blotches.

Between pages 128 and 129
133. *Trillium grandiflorum* in a damp semi-wild setting.
134. *Trillium grandiflorum* 'Flore Plena' in a peat garden.
135. *Trillium sessile* 'Rubrum', a lovely foliage plant for a cool spot.
136. *Tulipa* (Lily Flowered) 'China Pink' with *Silene dioica* at Kew.
137. *Tulipa fosteriana* 'Orange Emperor' is superb with back-lighting.
138. *Tulipa* (Darwin Hybrid) 'Golden Apeldoorn' with Forget-me-Nots and Bowles' Golden Grass.
139. *Tulipa greigii* 'Red Riding Hood' has striking leaves and flowers.
140. *Tulipa kauffmanniana* 'Stresa', one of the varieties of the early Water Lily Tulip.
141. *Tulipa linifolia*, a wild species from Central Asia. Needs a hot sunny position.
142. *Tulipa tarda* in a rock garden. One of the dwarfest species.
143. *Tulipa* (Lily Flowered) 'West Point' with *Brunnera macrophylla* at Kew.
144. *Zephyranthes candida* in a warm sunny bed in autumn.

INTRODUCTION

As a small child (so I am told) I used to dig up the Daffodil bulbs in my own small plot once a week, scrub them, and put them back again. I use this story not to evoke uncontrollable mirth among my horticultural friends but to illustrate what I think is behind the fascination which so many people feel for bulbous plants. No other plants encapsulate themselves in such a neat package, which can be dug up, dried off for months, put into the post, forgotten on the potting shed bench for a week or two and then planted, only to burst into activity once more as if nothing had happened. In fact some, like Daffodils and Hyacinths, will flower perfectly well if you give them a glass of water on the windowsill, such is the efficiency of the package in storing a complete plant in miniature surrounded by its fleshy food scales. Encompassed by the loose term 'bulb' we find a whole world of plants which are brought together in books, by specialist nurseries and in people's gardens, not because of any technical reason such as belonging to the same plant family, but because of this perfect storage system which they have in common, enabling the plants to overcome a period of adversity.

In the following pages we shall be looking at bulbs through the different seasons of the year, mainly from the point of view of their garden value and the ways in which they may be used in association with other plants for the best effect. Recommendations about cultivation should be taken as a guide only, for, as we all know, each garden has its own characteristics of soil and microclimate and what is true for one site may be entirely wrong in another garden with a different aspect a few miles along the road. It is primarily a book for outdoor gardening, dealing mainly with hardy species, although such subjects as Gladiolus, which require lifting and storing for the winter, are also included since they are such an important part of summer bulb gardening. Very rare and unobtainable species are not mentioned since they mostly require rather specialised treatment with protection, and in any case it is very frustrating for the keen gardener to read about plants he cannot acquire! With certain groups, for example Narcissus and Tulips, there are thousands of selections and hybrids and I make no attempt to provide a catalogue of these. The selection given is a personal one based on what is known to be available in current nurserymen's lists.

The main part of the book consists of four seasonal chapters, each taking a look at the various bulbs which flower at that time and the way in which they may be incorporated into the garden scene. It may at first seem curious to start with the autumn chapter rather than spring, but in the world of bulbs this is the most important time of the year, when the great majority of bulbs are purchased and planted, ready to make their new roots for the seasons to come. There is no doubt that for many bulbous plants, and therefore for the bulb gardener, the autumn is the first season of the year.

In the specialist bulb nursery catalogue you can find a wide range of plants representing a dozen or so different families, although the main three are the monocotyledon families Liliaceae (Lilies, Tulips and their relatives), Amaryllidaceae (*Narcissus, Amaryllis*, etc.) and Iridaceae (*Iris, Crocus* and their kin). There are others belonging to the dicotyledons, in a quite separate part of the plant kingdom, for example the Ranunculus family (*Anemone*, Winter Aconite) which have tubers, *Cyclamen* in the Primula family and so so. So, if these plants are unrelated botanically, what is it that groups them together, apart from the swollen appearance of their 'rootstock' and their ability to withstand several months out of the ground? The linking factor is the natural environment in which they have developed in the wild over tens of thousands of years, adapting slowly to the changing conditions, and if we trace on a map of the world where the majority of bulbous plants occur we find that it is not an entirely haphazard arrangement but a rather well-defined pattern. If we look further at the climates in those regions we find that they are, in most of the bulb-rich areas, rather similar. Two factors combine to produce the 'right' conditions for plants to evolve with a swollen storage system: a long, dry summer period, usually hot as well, and a well defined damp, usually cooler, autumn-to-spring period during which there is rapid growth, with flowering and seeding taking place before the next dry spell. The Mediterranean and Middle East regions provide such a climatic pattern and indeed there are a great many bulbous plants in this area; most of the hardy bulbs we have in our gardens originate somewhere in southern Europe or Western Asia, such as *Narcissus, Tulipa, Crocus,* bulbous *Iris, Scilla* and *Hyacinthus*. There are other regions where a similar type of climate exists and here, too, we find a considerable number of bulbs; for example, in the western States of North America (e.g. *Erythronium*), the S.W. Cape region of South Africa (very many bulbous groups although few are hardy in Britain), and temperate South America (e.g. *Ipheion, Tecophilaea*).

There are also a few regions with a climate which is the opposite of this, that is the summer is damp and the winter dryish, and here, too, some bulbs have evolved, but with the reverse growth pattern, growing and flowering in summer and dormant in winter. The Himalaya and China, with a summer monsoon-type climate, provide such conditions and it is here that many of the best Lilies have their origins, while in the Eastern Cape region of South Africa there is a considerable number of exciting 'bulbous' plants which are of importance in our gardens, notably *Gladiolus*. In the Americas, Mexico has a summer rainfall climate and here there are many bulbs which are unfortunately tender in Britain, but they include the spectacular *Tigridia pavonia* which is a fine and dramatic plant for the summer bulb garden.

WHAT IS A 'BULB'?

As mentioned above, this book deals with a motley collection of plants, loosely termed 'bulbs' because there is no other suitable collective term for plants with swollen storage systems. Thus true bulbs, corms, tubers and a few rhizomatous

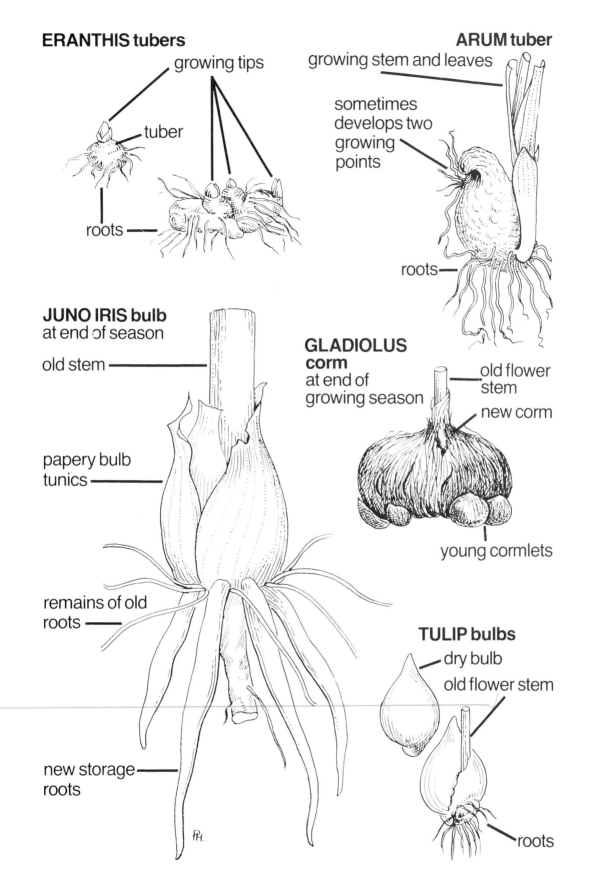

ERANTHIS tubers

growing tips

tuber

roots

ARUM tuber

growing stem and leaves

sometimes develops two growing points

roots

JUNO IRIS bulb
at end of season

old stem

papery bulb tunics

remains of old roots

new storage roots

GLADIOLUS corm
at end of growing season

old flower stem

new corm

young cormlets

TULIP bulbs

dry bulb

old flower stem

roots

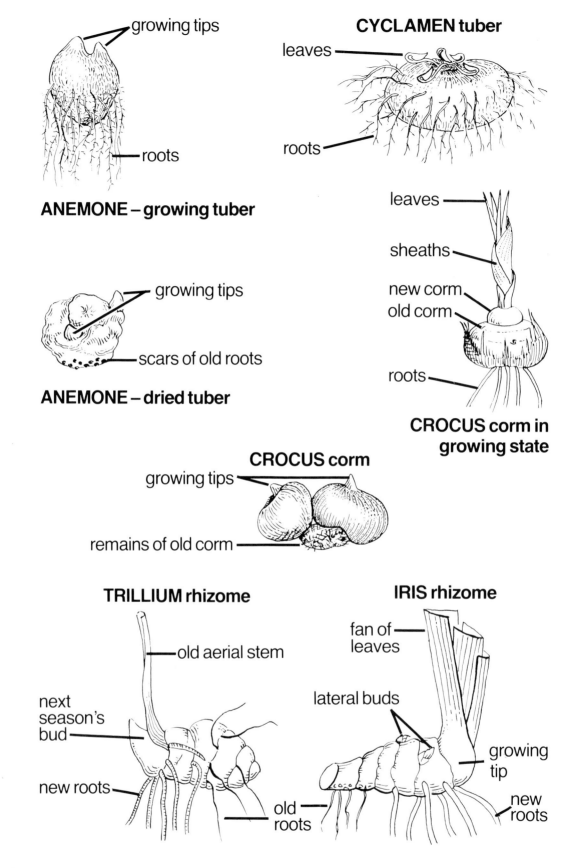

growing tips

roots

ANEMONE – growing tuber

CYCLAMEN tuber

leaves

roots

growing tips

scars of old roots

ANEMONE – dried tuber

leaves

sheaths

new corm
old corm

roots

CROCUS corm in growing state

CROCUS corm

growing tips

remains of old corm

TRILLIUM rhizome

old aerial stem

next season's bud

new roots

old roots

IRIS rhizome

fan of leaves

lateral buds

growing tip

new roots

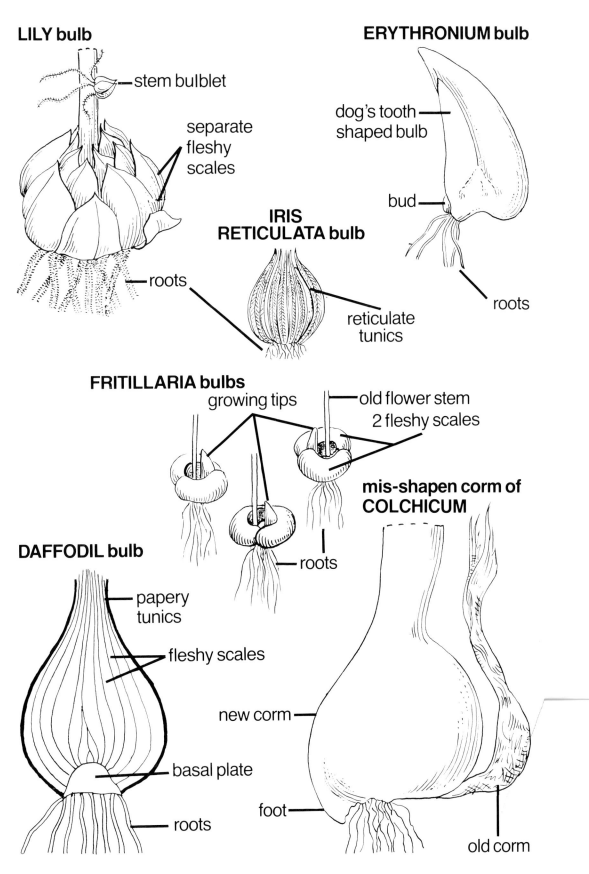

LILY bulb

stem bulblet

separate
fleshy
scales

roots

ERYTHRONIUM bulb

dog's tooth
shaped bulb

bud

roots

**IRIS
RETICULATA bulb**

reticulate
tunics

FRITILLARIA bulbs

growing tips

old flower stem
2 fleshy scales

roots

**mis-shapen corm of
COLCHICUM**

new corm

foot

old corm

DAFFODIL bulb

papery
tunics

fleshy scales

basal plate

roots

plants are included, although the last are mainly excluded on the grounds that you cannot lift them and dry them off in the same way as the others, so they are generally not found in nurserymen's bulb catalogues. The accompanying line drawings show the main characteristics of some of the different types of storage organ and, incidentally, which way up to plant them, which is not always obvious.

True bulbs usually consist of several fleshy scales wrapped around the growing point, like an onion, although there are a few, such as those of Fritillaries, which possess only one or two scales. These are attached to a basal plate, and the whole bulb is usually covered with a tunic or coat which can be papery as in Daffodils or, in a few less well-known cases, fibrous. Some bulbs are naked with no coverings, for example Lilies and Fritillaries, and it is well to remember that those without protection of this kind should not be dried off to quite the same extent as heavily jacketed ones. A bulb is very different from a corm in that it is permanent, the same individual going on year after year producing new leaves and flowers then dying back, whereas a corm is replaced every year by a new one on top of the old. Corms are solid structures, not scaly, with their main growing point at the apex, but there may be other secondary buds around the circumference capable of producing shoots and new corms, which is important for propagation purposes.

Tubers are also solid structures without covering tunics, but unlike corms they are not usually replaced by new ones each year. Some tubers, like those of Cyclamen, have a growing point at the top and no supplementary ones lower down, so that they may be interpreted as modified roots; others, in addition, produce lateral buds, or 'eyes' as they are called in the potato, and these are undoubtedly modified stems. The rhizome of an Iris is a form of the latter type which has taken to creeping along the surface of the soil. The normal process of development in this case is that an apical fan of leaves produces a flower stem in the first season after planting, followed shortly afterwards by the sprouting of two lateral buds each of which gives rise to a fan of leaves, thus producing two flower stems the next year, and so on, if conditions are ideal. Rhizomes can be very thin and elongated, such as those of *Anemone nemorosa* and *Convallaria* (Lily-of-the-Valley) or they can be very fat and chunky like a bearded Iris or Trillium.

These, then are the main types of swollen storage system, but within each type there are many variations, each one often so characteristic that it is usually possible to tell what genus a plant belongs to just by looking at its 'bulb'. In some cases, for example in Crocus, the species themselves have different types of tunic covering the corm and here it is often an easy job to identify the individual species, if you know your Crocuses well.

CULTIVATION AIMS

Whatever their shape and structure, these organs all do roughly the same job: they store food reserves. Half of our aim in the successful cultivation of bulbs is to obtain as large a reserve as possible ready for the next growing season, and the other half is to provide the right conditions for those reserves to produce healthy growth and flowers; the two are nearly inseparable, of course, forming a continuous cycle if the bulb is kept for an indefinite period. The first year after purchase is usually taken care of by the nurserymen, for they are experienced in building up large-sized bulbs

1 *Acidanthera bicolor (= Gladiolus callianthus)*, sweetly scented, from Africa. **2** *Allium aflatunense* with grey Mallow and Helichrysum. **3** *Allium christophii (albopilosum)*, also good for dried decorations. **4** *Allium karataviense*, a striking Onion relative from Central Asia. **5** *Allium moly*, in grass, also good under shrubs. **6** *Allium sphaerocephalon* with grey Helichrysum.

7 *Allium stipitatum* with white Honesty.   8 *Amaryllis belladonna* requires a warm sunny border.   9 *Anemone apennina* is good for naturalising.   10 *Anemone blanda* 'Atrocaerulea' in a woodland setting.   11 *Anemone blanda* 'Radar', the most vividly coloured variety.   12 *Anemone nemorosa* (Wood Anemone) with *Podophyllum* leaves.

which perform well, often storing them at the correct temperatures so that buds form and are already inside when they arrive. Flowers will be produced in this first season almost (but not quite!) regardless of what you provide in the way of conditions; it is the next and subsequent seasons that will suffer if the conditions are not suitable for proper growth.

DRAINAGE

Perhaps the single most important factor in the cultivation of bulbs is drainage; even species which require dampish soils do not thrive in sour, waterlogged conditions, and you will find in the following pages the frequent mention of coarse, gritty sand and humus as a means of improving such soils. Once the bulbs in the garden have flowered it is easy to forget all about them, but they require just as much attention as your vegetables or prize lawn if they are to go on performing well year after year, even when they are dormant.

DORMANT BULBS

At the so-called dormant stage, although there may be no visible activity, the bulb is actually laying down its future in the form of a miniaturised bud; whether this bud contains a flower or just leaves is largely up to you, the grower. Most bulbs require a dry period when their top growth and roots have died back, and with many species this period should also be relatively warm. So, clearly, a bulb which is sitting in a damp, dark corner during its period of rest is unlikely to thrive and will probably not flower and most likely dwindle and die. Obviously this is a generalisation and there are exceptions, and we all know that Snowdrops, for example, are woodland plants which enjoy semi-shade, although here again, cold, waterlogged soils are unsuitable. So the general rule is to keep the area where the bulbs are growing free from weeds so that the sun can warm up the soil. You will find that I have often mentioned companion plantings for bulbs in order to enhance their appearance. This does not mean that the whole site should be covered with other plants in order to hide the bare patches: by all means place other attractive subjects nearby, but make sure they do not cast too much shade on the resting bulbs.

PLANTING DEPTHS

I have included details of planting depths in the comments on cultivation for each group of bulbs; this depth refers to the distance between the soil surface and the top of the bulb, so it follows that with a recommended planting depth of, say, 10 cm for a bulb 3 cm long, a hole at least 13 cm deep will be required. Although it is true that some bulbs (by no means all, however) are capable of pulling themselves down to their correct working depth, it is not good practice to plant them shallowly and leave them to do the rest. In a bad winter they may well perish by being frozen before they have pulled themselves down. Furthermore, a bulb can use a considerable amount of its food reserves in forming contractile roots and, with shallowly-planted bulbs, this may result in a lack of flowers while they build up strength again. When lifting old-established clumps, do bear in mind that the bulbs of some species of, for example, *Colchicum*, *Tulipa* and *Erythronium* pull themselves down to considerable depths and you may have a major excavation on your hands!

BULBS IN GROWTH

While they are in growth bulbs also need some attention. Firstly, they must not dry out or they may decide to go prematurely dormant, and in extreme drought may abort their flower buds. Secondly, they may require feeding, just like your tomatoes, roses or grass. The production of good, healthy leaves is another key factor in their life cycle and the outcome of a good crop of foliage is normally a fine bulb below. It is best to choose potash-rich fertilisers for this purpose and, to assist in this, the makers of proprietary brands of mixed plant foods quote on their packets their N:P:K ratio (Nitrogen:Phosphate:Potash); a good ratio for bulbs which I use is 15:15:30, but any figures near to this will be suitable. The best time to apply this is when the bulbs are pushing vigorously into growth near the beginning of their growing season, for this is when the roots are at their most active. Small bulbs will need only two or three applications, preferably watered on, at roughly two-weekly intervals, whereas large ones, such as Lilies in pots, will need a weekly feed right through their growing and flowering period. If this is too troublesome, a light dressing of a pelleted fertiliser scattered on the surface of the soil will filter down during rain or watering; this need not be repeated for small bulbs but larger ones like Lilies would benefit from two repeat applications at monthly intervals. Having achieved this good crop of leaves they must then be allowed to die down naturally, first turning yellowish, then withering to brown, dry crisps. Any attempt to dry off bulbs too soon, before the leaves are fully mature, may well result in less well-developed bulbs for the coming season. This also applies to the practice of tying Daffodil leaves into knots to tidy them up, which has been shown to have much the same effect on the bulbs as actually cutting off the green leaves.

In short, the most important factors in healthy bulb cultivation are:
(a) *Drainage:* must be good.
(b) *Water:* plenty for the flowering and growing season.
(c) *Food:* potash-rich fertiliser for good foliage.
(d) *Dry off:* warm, dry rest period to encourage flower bud production.

BULB TROUBLES

I have made little mention in the following pages of the pests and diseases that attack bulbs. This is partly because they are, by and large, fairly trouble-free subjects when growing well, and I must stress the 'growing well', for it is very important. Given good growing conditions, strong bulbs should result, much better able to cope with life than weak ones, which are more likely to succumb to infections. Firstly, make sure that you have the conditions right; then, if there are problems, you at least have a strong plant which can stand up to a certain amount of damage.

Most pests are fairly obvious and there will be a large arsenal of weapons to wage chemical warfare on these at your local garden shop. In general, it is better first to use the least drastic means of disposing of them, such as the hand-picking of slugs, snails, caterpillars, lily beetles, etc., but it will almost certainly be necessary to resort to sprays or dusts sooner or later, and the best advice is to follow the maker's instructions carefully, remembering that many of these sprays are very dangerous chemicals.

Most of the common pests are perhaps more easily dealt with than diseases, since you can squash them, stamp on them, trap them or throw them into the neighbour's garden. Diseases are for most people less easy to see and identify and may well have quite a hold before their effects are noticeable. Virus diseases are, for most of us, incurable and the only thing to be done is to burn infected plants and reduce the chances of the disease spreading by controlling the aphides which act as the dispersal agents. The most common signs of viruses are yellowish-streaked leaves, streaks and splashes of colour on flowers and distorted growth. Many species of bulbs seem to be more or less virus-free, but certain groups, such as Lilies, are very vulnerable.

Fungal diseases are often the result of poor cultivation, for example Grey Moulds (Botrytis) may arise because of damp, still air, where plants are over-crowded. However, even the best growers cannot avoid certain problems and a trip to the weapons factory will probably be necessary from time to time. In the bulb-growers' world the advent of the systemic fungicides based on benomyl (e.g. Benlate) has been a blessing since this, used in solution as a dip for the dormant bulbs, prevents a number of nasty problems, such as 'Ink Disease' of bulbs of the *Iris reticulata* group. There are some good pest and disease books on the market to assist in the identification of any troubles which occur and, having pinpointed the problem, it is then much easier to find a cure among the many proprietary brands of chemicals. In particular I can recommend the book *Collins' Guide to the Pests, Diseases and Disorders of Garden Plants* by Buczacki and Harris, published by Collins in 1981, and *Diseases of Bulbs* published by Her Majesty's Stationery Office. The Royal Horticultural Society, Wisley, Surrey, runs an excellent advisory service for its members and the Royal Botanic Gardens, Kew, Surrey, has an enquiry unit which will assist in identification. The local Horticultural and Agricultural Colleges (most counties have one) are often willing to help out with advice.

Anyway, enough of morbid thoughts! Let us now delve into the more optimistic side of gardening and look at the ways in which we can enjoy, season by season, the fascinating range of bulbous plants available to us, and how we can use them to the best advantage in various garden situations.

1

THE BULB GARDEN IN AUTUMN

(September–November)

The autumn bulbs are a very important part of the garden flora, for they flower at a time when nearly everything else is at an end and the main display is provided by berries or by the coloured autumn foliage of deciduous trees and shrubs. In fact, these and the bulbs can be complementary and splendid effects can be obtained by underplanting, for example, a shrub which has brilliant autumn tints, with a drift of blue *Crocus speciosus* or purple-pink *Colchicum speciosum*. The beautiful white form of *Colchicum speciosum* is much improved if a few autumn leaves, whether brown or more highly coloured, have fallen amongst the large white goblets. Areas of rough lawn which were bright with Daffodils, Crocus and other spring bulbs in the early part of the year, then mown for the summer, can now be full of interest again with a variety of autumn Crocuses and Colchicums which, because of their leafless nature, look much better spearing through turf than they do in a bare, weed-free area of border. In addition, the grass provides some support for the flowers and protection from mud splashes in wet or windy weather.

Some of the less hardy autumn bulbs, such as Amaryllis and Nerine, require a warm, sunny bed at the foot of a south-facing wall or fence if they are to flower well, and if several of these are planted in a clump they make a fine feature with their bold, satiny-pink flowers. These are leafless at flowering time and it is a good plan to place some low-growing silver or grey plants alongside, for these two colours make a very delicate combination and the foliage of the accompanying plants hides the somewhat naked appearance of the bulbs.

A similar warm, sunny position is ideal for the brilliant yellow Crocus-like *Sternbergia lutea* which lights up the dull autumnal days, and the lovely-sounding *Zephyranthes*, with its upright, white wineglass-shaped flowers, also responds to this sort of treatment. Clearly, a south-facing wall is a treasured site, not for wasting on plants that will grow perfectly well in the open garden.

For the connoisseur, there are some unusual autumn bulbs which will lift the overall interest of any garden, such as a patch of Snowdrops in full flower in October! The miniature wild Cyclamen never fail to catch the eye, flowering for a long period through the autumn, then following with attractive silvery-zoned leaves for the winter. Easily cultivated, hardy, beautiful and relatively inexpensive, it is hard to imagine why they are not in every garden.

So, far from regarding the autumn as an end to the garden year, the bulb gardener can view it as a beginning when, after a period of rest in a semi-dormant state, many of the bulbs are bursting into growth like an alternative spring.

These autumn-flowering bulbs are an interesting group of plants which bloom at this time of year for a variety of different reasons. Some are simply late summer flowerers that carry over into September—good examples are certain lilies, such as *L. speciosum* and *L. auratum*, which are tall plants, taking a long time to develop through the summer and often not starting to flower before August. The true autumn-flowering bulbs, however, are plants that have lain dormant through the summer and are then stimulated into growth by the falling temperatures and higher humidity. The majority originate from areas with a Mediterranean type of climate, with most of the annual rainfall coming between autumn and spring, followed by a warm and dry summer. Examples of bulbous plants with this type of life cycle are *Amaryllis belladonna* from South Africa, *Zephyranthes candida* from Argentina and *Sternbergia lutea* from several Mediterranean countries, showing just how geographically widespread is this particular growth form. Although these three examples all belong to the same family, the Amaryllidaceae, there are many other autumn-blooming bulbs in other families such as *Crocus* (Iris family), *Colchicum* (Lily family) and *Cyclamen* (Primula family).

Within this overall group of true autumn-flowering bulbs there are also some different patterns of growth, mainly depending upon the harshness of the winters in their countries of origin. Certain species have chosen to burst into activity at the onset of autumn but have confined the development to flowers alone, so that no leaves appear above ground. Many of the autumn *Colchicum* and *Crocus* behave in this way. The flowers die away having been pollinated and, above ground at least, the plant appears to go into a state of dormancy again for the winter. In early spring, when the worst of the frosty weather is over, the leaves are pushed up, together with the developing fruits, and these last through until the start of the summer dry period. The ripe seeds are dispersed and the annual growth cycle is complete.

Other species, however, mostly from regions which have wet but not excessively cold winters, produce their leaves together with the flowers and these remain green right through winter and spring, dying down when the drier weather arrives. Some of these quickly produce seeds in the autumn (e.g. *Nerine*) but quite a lot of species delay their fruiting stage until spring (*Crocus serotinus*, *C. longiflorus*). Crocus is an interesting group since it contains many species which are spring-flowering, several autumn ones which have no leaves at flowering time and are mostly from cold winter districts, and some autumnal ones which do have leaves at flowering time, these being mostly from areas where mild winters are encountered. In countries such as England which has a fairly equable climate bulbs of all these groups can be cultivated satisfactorily in the open garden but in cold areas it may be possible to grow only those which are leafless in winter.

The Autumn-Flowering Bulbs

ALLIUM

The Onions have little importance in the autumn garden, being mostly spring or summer subjects, but there is one tiny species from southern Greece and Crete which might amuse the enthusiast with a rock garden or raised bed. It is *A. callimischon* which makes tufts of bulbs, producing thread-like leaves and small umbels of papery white flowers spotted with dark red, reaching at most about 10 cm in height when in flower in October or November. Although not at all showy, it is a charming little plant of interest for its unusual flowering season.

CULTIVATION *A. callimischon* is best planted in spring 3–4 cm deep in a gritty, well-drained soil in full sun, preferably in a raised position where it is most obvious to the eye. Its size makes it ideal for a rock garden, a sink or trough, or a double wall which has planting space for small alpines and rock plants. From time to time it is worth lifting the clumps and dividing them into smaller groups.

AMARYLLIS

The one species in this South African genus, *A. belladonna*, is a must for the autumn garden since it is undoubtedly one of the most spectacular of all. It should not be confused with the South American Hippeastrums which are frequently cultivated as house plants and sold in pre-packs under the name 'Amaryllis'. The Cape Belladonna Lily produces its large flowers in September or October, before the leaves appear, on stout purple-tinted stems about 50–90 cm in height. They are funnel-shaped and bright pink, shading to white at the centre, with the tips of the segments flaring outwards to give a spread of up to 15 cm, and are carried in an umbel of two or six or sometimes more. There is also a bonus in the form of a delicate perfume. Soon after the flowers have faded the bright green, strap-like leaves appear and these remain in evidence until the following summer when the aerial growth dies down completely for an apparent rest period, although this is actually the time when the large bulbs form new buds for the coming autumn and is an important stage in the cultivation.

In addition to the usual pink form there are other named varieties, although these are seldom available from nurseries. 'Purpurea Major' is a deeper pink and 'Hathor' is a white version which is unfortunately rarely seen in cultivation.

CULTIVATION Although not particular as to the type of soil, it is important that the large Amaryllis bulbs, which are usually sold in spring, are planted in as hot and sunny a place as possible, with shelter from cold winds. The planting depth needs to be about 10 cm to the top of the bulbs so that they are below the level of hard frosts, although in cold districts the ground can of course freeze solid to a greater depth than this and in such areas it may be difficult to grow the plant at all. In most areas of Britain a choice site up against a south wall of the house is ideal and gives enough protection, as does a sunny border alongside a heated greenhouse. If the soil is very heavy it is best at planting time to lighten it with coarse, gritty sand and leafmould, but otherwise any ordinary garden soil is suitable.

The other danger point for Amaryllis is during cold winters when heavy frosts can kill off the leaves, thus interrupting the growth cycle, although I find that, when this has happened, as soon as warm spring weather arrives the leaves start to develop again. Frost damage can be prevented to a large extent by covering the leaves with a loose layer of bracken or evergreen twigs such as conifer trimmings pushed into the ground, to make a protective umbrella until spring arrives.

In early spring a feed of bonemeal is worthwhile, encouraging plenty of leaf development before the summer dormancy. Good flowering depends largely upon plenty of warmth reaching the bulbs and if the summer is not sunny and dry it pays to place a slanting pane of glass over the site to warm up the soil.

The long, leafless stems of *Amaryllis belladonna* may not appeal to some gardeners but careful companion planting can help to improve this. The main thing to avoid is having plants which will grow over the bulbs and shade them in summer, thus discouraging bud formation. In a sunny border by the house, which can be devoted to autumn bulbs like *Amaryllis*, *Zephyranthes*, *Sternbergia*, *Iris unguicularis* and *Nerine*, the clumps can be separated by low-growing foliage plants such as the purple and silver-leaved versions of Sage (*Salvia officinalis*), the grey rock garden plant *Aethionema* 'Warley Rose', *Dianthus* varieties and *Alyssum saxatile*, all of which will provide colour at other times of the year.

The only practical method of propagation

of Amaryllis is by lifting established clumps of bulbs and dividing them, preferably in late summer and before new growth begins. This should be carried out infrequently since the bulbs are really best left undisturbed to form groups and they will not flower freely if they are dug up every year or two.

COLCHICUM

These Crocus-like plants are actually more closely related to the Lilies than Crocuses, but in their growth pattern they do resemble the latter. Most of the well-known species of Colchicum flower in the autumn and these are often erroneously known as 'Autumn Crocus', although the name 'Meadow Saffron' is also used for the common *C. autumnale*. There are also a few spring-flowering Colchicums, just as there are autumn and spring Crocus, but these are mostly rather small-flowered, not easy to grow outdoors, and are thus of limited garden value. On the whole the autumn ones have much larger flowers than Crocus, although they are of similar goblet shape, and come in various shades of pink and purple whereas Crocus tend to the bluish and violet end of the spectrum; some species have strongly chequered (tessellated) flowers and there is a range of hybrids which also show this feature. Nearly all the commonly available species and garden varieties are of the type which flower before any leaves appear, these mostly staying below ground until the spring. In view of the fact that the leaves are often rather wide and coarse, Colchicums need careful placing so that their foliage does not swamp other smaller plants when it expands in the spring. The corms of Colchicums have a very distinctive appearance, rather elongated with an off-centre downward-projecting 'toe' at the base, and the whole corm is covered with a papery to leathery, brown or blackish tunic.

CULTIVATION All the species and vari-eties mentioned below are satisfactory in well-drained, sunny situations in deeply cultivated soil, since the corms need to be planted at a depth of about 10–15 cm. They are equally at home in acid or alkaline conditions and seem to do particularly well on sandy soils. Some of the species are suitable for planting in semi-shade under deciduous shrubs to provide autumn colour and others, especially *C. autumnale*, will do well in grass. Species such as the very easy pinkish-purple *C. speciosum* are ideal for planting in a drift beneath shrubs which will be in their yellow autumn tints when the Colchicums are in bloom, and the lovely white form of this species is very effective where russet, orange or red autumn leaves will fall among the blooms. *C. agrippinum*, an unusual small-flowered, strongly tessellated species, is better in a warm, sunny border and, as its foliage is not gross, can be planted effectively in association with various grey or silver-leaved plants such as Alyssum, Dianthus, Lavender and Nepeta (Catmint).

The corms of Colchicums are normally available from late summer onwards and are best obtained as early as possible and planted straight away in August. Occasionally it is mentioned that Colchicums will flower on the windowsill without any water or soil and, although this is quite true, they are doing it at the expense of food stored in the old corm and if they are to survive for another year they must be planted out in the garden in order to make roots and leaves to build up reserves and form a new corm for the next season. Most of the autumn species increase naturally by corm division so that, for propagation purposes, it is simply a case of lifting the clumps in late summer and dividing them up. Seeds are produced in large capsules amid the leaves in spring, but it is an extremely slow matter to raise them to flowering-sized corms.

C. agrippinum. This is one of the smaller-flowered autumnal Colchicums, probably a hybrid, with rather funnel-shaped flowers in pinkish-purple, conspicuously chequered darker, with somewhat pointed segments and with purple stems. The leaves appear much later and are quite small and somewhat wavy at the margins. It is an attractive plant, increasing rapidly by corm division when growing well in a sunny situation and is particularly good on alkaline soils. A surprisingly effective association I once achieved by mistake was a planting of this in front of a golden-yellow conifer.

C. autumnale. The commonest species, known as the Meadow Saffron, although it has no connection with the Saffron Crocus and is in fact a poisonous plant. Each corm produces several pale pinkish-lilac flowers about 15 cm high in September, long before the leaves which do not really expand fully until spring. It is a very easily grown species, European in origin, which can be grown in an open, sunny border, beneath shrubs in semi-shade or in a piece of rough grass. Personally I prefer to see it in grass, for the flowers have a long, slender, rather weak tube, giving a rather naked appearance when growing in open borders, and during wet weather they fall over and become mud-splashed; in grass there is some support for the flowers and protection from soil splashes. This applies even more to the double forms of the species, which are very 'top heavy'. In addition to the normal single pinkish one there is a single white 'Album', a double pink 'Roseum Plenum' and a double white, 'Album Plenum'. The white forms are rather effective planted near the autumn-blooming shrub *Ceratostigma willmottianum* which at this time of year has deep blue flowers and reddish-tinted foliage.

C. bivonae (C. sibthorpii, C. bowlesianum). There are various forms of this beautiful plant, which originates mainly from Greece and Turkey, and it may be found in catalogues under any of these names. It flowers in early autumn, usually September, and is leafless but with a strong tube to the flower, so that it is not so susceptible to wind and rain damage as *C. autumnale.* The flowers are very colourful, being strongly chequered purple on a pale pink ground, and the stamens are purple, not yellow as in most species. This distinctive colouring has also been imparted to several hybrids which have *C. bivonae* as one of the parents.

This rather choice species is easily cultivated but it is worth finding a sheltered, sunny corner since it can be damaged by severe frosts.

C. byzantinum. This is an old plant in cultivation whose origins are obscure but, this aside, it is an excellent garden plant with pale pinkish-lilac, unchequered flowers slightly larger and more robust than those of *C. autumnale*, but flowering at about the same time in late August to September. It will grow in any reasonable soil in sun or semi-shade and soon increases by corm division into clumps.

C. cilicicum. The free-flowering habit and large, bright rose-coloured flowers, produced in September or October, make this Turkish species a worthwhile subject for an open, sunny border, but it produces large leaves so careful siting is necessary. It associates well with grey-leaved shrubs such as *Senecio laxifolius* and some of the *Cistus* species which also prefer full sun. It is one of the most floriferous species, with a long succession of flowers from each corm.

C. speciosum. The best of the non-chequered Colchicums is undoubtedly this Turkish and Caucasian species. It produces only one or two flowers per corm, but they are large with very sturdy perianth tubes, so will stand up to almost any amount of adverse weather. The usual colour is a mid rosy-lilac, but there is quite a bit of variation in colour to deep reddish purple, and some forms have a large white centre. 'Album' is a beautiful pure white form and is one of the best of all autumn bulbs.

It flowers in September or October, slightly later than *C. autumnale* and, because of the robust stature of the blooms, is a very suitable plant for open borders and underplanting shrubs, although it also grows well in grass.

There are few more attractive autumnal displays than a patch of this lovely Colchicum, especially in its white form, mixed with fallen coloured leaves.

Garden Varieties. In addition to the species mentioned above, there are a lot of named varieties of Colchicum, many of which are undoubtedly hybrids. Few of these are on general sale in bulb nurseries but some of the more specialised firms stock some from time to time. The most likely ones to be found are 'The Giant', a large rosy-lilac, 'Conquest', a strongly tessellated purple, 'Darwin', deep purple, 'Princess Astrid', with large purple flowers with a white centre, 'Atrorubens', a deep reddish-purple including the tube, 'Violet Queen', large, deep purple throughout with no pale throat, and 'Water Lily', with enormous double lilac flowers.

CRINUM

The beautiful Crinums are members of the family Amaryllidaceae and are related to *Amaryllis belladonna* although distinguishable from it at a glance by having leaves present at flowering time and by the slightly longer tubes to the flowers. Although there are perhaps one hundred or more species from many tropical and warm temperate parts of the world, only one, *C. × powellii*, is reliably hardy and readily obtainable. This is thought to be a hybrid between two South African species which occur in the Eastern Cape summer rainfall region and, like its parents, this successful garden plant is dormant in winter and makes its vigorous growth through the summer, flowering in late summer or early autumn.

It has extremely large, club-like bulbs with a very long neck, and these first produce broad, bright green fleshy leaves followed by a stout flower stem up to a metre in height alongside the rosette of leaves, not from its centre. In vigorous plants the umbel may carry as many as ten of the pink funnel-shaped flowers which have a long arching tube and

segments which reflex a little at their tips. There is also an attractive white form, known as 'Album'.

CULTIVATION *Crinum powellii* bulbs are usually sent out by nurseries in spring, whilst still in their semi-dormant state, and require planting straight away before they have dried out too much. Any good garden soil is satisfactory providing it is well supplied with water in summer and, if it is inclined to be dry, it pays to dig in a liberal amount of well-rotted manure or compost, very deeply, at least two spades' depth. Mature bulbs are very long and bottle-shaped and it is necessary to plant them with the top of the neck about level with the surface, so that a deep hole will probably be required, possibly as much as 60–80 cm depending upon the size of the bulb. Once planted, they should be left undisturbed for many years, providing they are doing well and flowering, for they take a long time to settle in again once dug up and moved. If propagation is desired, it will be found that the young offsets which are produced around the parent bulbs can be detached when the clumps are lifted.

C. powellii is a good plant for the herbaceous border but requires a position where it will not be swamped by other taller late-summer plants. At the same time it is a good idea to plant some shorter subjects in front which will cover the rather unattractive leaves of the *Crinum*. A dark background is advantageous, especially for the white-flowered form.

CROCUS

It is often not realised that there are a lot of true autumn Crocus species in addition to the larger and unrelated Colchicums which are often referred to as 'Autumn Crocuses'. It is easy to tell the difference, for Crocuses have only three stamens while Colchicums have six, and the latter never have the very narrow leaves with a whitish stripe along the centre which are such a familiar feature of the true crocuses. Within Crocus there is a wide range of species, about ninety in all, flowering between August and April, so this is a very important group when considering a succession of flowering bulbs for the cooler months. They are all, whatever the species, unmistakably crocuses with their wineglass- or goblet-shaped flowers, sometimes opening out rather more widely in the sunshine; but within this basic recognisable form there is a tremendous range of variation in size, shape and colour, even within the autumn-flowering group.

The winter and spring flowering species are dealt with elsewhere and in this chapter it is only the autumnal ones which concern us, but even here there is wide choice. Some produce their flowers before any leaves show through the ground, others send up flowers and leaves together, and the flowers may be white, lilac or purple in colour, with or without prominent stripes on the outside. Looking more closely inside the flower may reveal yellow or white stamens and a great intricacy of form and colour of stigma, from simply three-branched to much-dissected into a mass of thread-like branches, and varying from pale yellow to deep red. The crocuses are certainly a group of plants which call for closer inspection if they are to be appreciated to the full, although certain autumnal species such as *C. speciosus* are also well worth planting in quantity, to be viewed for their mass effect in the distance.

CULTIVATION The species recommended below are all relatively easy to cultivate but are not all the same in their requirements. The majority, however, are suitable for open, sunny situations in well-drained soils, acid or alkaline; they are hardy subjects without any need for extra protection in winter and, if the drainage is good, should receive a sufficiently dry summer rest period for the corms. Their size means that they are of course ideal for a rock garden, but such a feature is not essential for their well-being and they can be grown in any open, sunny border where there is not too much disturbance in the form of cultivation. The front of a sunny shrub border is, for example, ideal and here they can be left to increase at will.

The exceptions among those mentioned below are *C. banaticus* and *C. nudiflorus* which need a semi-shaded or moist site where their corms will not become too hot and dry in summer. The former is an unusual and beautiful plant which does very well growing between heathers and rhododendrons, or on a peat bed, while *C. nudiflorus* is particularly suitable for an area of rough grass such as one might have around apple trees. I have also found *C. ochroleucus* and *C. speciosus* to be successful in grass.

Crocuses appear in the autumn bulb catalogues and should be obtained and planted as soon as possible, from August onwards, generally about 5 cm deep except in the case of *C. sativus* which needs to be at least 10 cm deep in rich 'vegetable garden' type of soil.

Propagation of most of these autumn Crocuses is either taken care of naturally by corm division or by the production of seeds which can be left to scatter themselves or can be gathered and sown separately in pots during the following autumn. This should give rise to young corms which can be planted out about a year after germination for flowering in two to three years' time.

C. banaticus. A rare, unusual Crocus from Rumania, whose lilac-blue flowers have three large outer segments and three small inner ones, somewhat Iris-like; the stigma is beautifully dissected. It is leafless at flowering time in October or November. A moist soil is best, in partial shade.

C. cancellatus. This Turkish species has slender flowers in pale lilac, striped darker on the outside, and is leafless at flowering time which is in September or October. It is usually sold as var. *cilicicus*. It needs full sun.

C. goulimyi. Although coming from southern Greece, this is surprisingly hardy, ideal for a sunny, sharply drained soil. The graceful, long-tubed, pale lilac flowers appear with the leaves in October or November.

C. hadriaticus. Another Greek species, with white flowers zoned yellow in the centre. It is related to the Saffron Crocus and therefore has the three red stigma branches which are characteristic of this group. The leaves appear at or before flowering time in September or October. It prefers a hot, sunny position.

C. kotschyanus (C. zonatus). This is one of the earliest of the autumnal species to flower, long before the leaves emerge, usually in September. The colour is pale lilac-pink with a deep yellow zone in the centre and whitish stamens. A variation of it known as *leucopharynx*, which has a white throat lacking the yellow marks, is sometimes wrongly listed as *C. karduchorum*, a related but distinct and very rare species. *C. kotschyanus* increases rapidly and prefers a sunny situation which is, however, not too hot and dry.

C. laevigatus. I have described this in the Winter Section (page 40) since it flowers very late in December or January, but sometimes the first blooms may appear in November.

C. longiflorus. An unusual species, usually obtainable from at least a few of the bulb nurseries each year. It comes from southern Italy and Sicily and therefore, as one might expect, needs a sunny, sheltered site, but is not a difficult species to grow. The strongly fragrant flowers appear in October, together with the leaves, and are lilac with prominent stripes on the outside and striking red stigma branches.

C. medius. An Italian species, flowering in October before the leaves appear, usually with rather deep purplish-lilac flowers which are made more colourful by a frilly, bright orange stigma. An open, well-drained situation is all it requires.

C. niveus. An uncommon beautiful Greek species with large white or soft lavender yellow-throated flowers appearing with the leaves in November. It needs full sun with

good drainage and the corms should be planted 8–10 cm deep.

C. nudiflorus. A very unusual species from the Pyrenees which produces stolons from its corms and is thus capable of forming patches. Its long-tubed, leafless flowers appear in October and are deep purple with orange stigma branches which were probably used in England at one time as an alternative to *C. sativus* as a source of Saffron. It should be planted in a moist situation where it can be left undisturbed to increase by its stolons, and is good in rough grass.

C. ochroleucus. Although rather small-flowered, this Lebanese species is late-flowering, in October or November, and quite attractive. The flowers are creamy white with a yellow throat, produced with or just before the leaves. It prefers an open situation which is not too hot and dry and I have found that it does well in grass.

C. pulchellus. A very easily grown species from Greece and Turkey which increases well by corm division and seed in almost any sunny or semi-shaded situation. The pale bluish-lilac, delicately veined flowers have a yellow throat and white stamens and are produced in September or October before the leaves. 'Zephyr' is a garden form with very large, pale lilac flowers.

C. sativus. This is the true *Saffron* Crocus, the spice being obtained from the dried three red stigma branches which are a striking feature of the large lilac flowers. These have darker veins and a dark purple eye in the centre and are produced in October together with the leaves. The large corms should be planted very deeply (10–15 cm) in a sunny place in rich soil and fed with sulphate of potash in autumn and spring; replant and divide every second or third August after planting.

C. serotinus. Various different forms of this Spanish species appear in nursery catalogues, sometimes listed as *C. salzmannii* and *C. asturicus*. The flowers appear with or just before the leaves in October and come in various shades of pale lilac or deeper violet, with or without a touch of yellow in the throat. It is an easily grown, free-flowering species, suitable for any sunny, well-drained site.

C. speciosus. Perhaps one of the best-known autumnal Crocus, with rather elegant, long-petalled flowers produced before the leaves in September or October. It is a widespread plant in the wild, from eastern Europe to the Caucasus and Iran, and is very variable so that in cultivation there are a number of named varieties in different shades of lilac and purple-blue, and a lovely pure white. The coloured forms have a delicate network of darker veining and sometimes a deeper speckling on the exterior, or a silvery wash on the three outer segments. *C. speciosus* is also attractive for its much-dissected orange stigma. It is an easy species to cultivate, suitable for naturalising in sun or semi-shade under shrubs or in grass and, when well settled in, is likely to seed itself. Named forms are 'Aitchisonii', a very large, pale lavender form, 'Artabir' with pale inner and dark blue outer segments, 'Oxonian', deep violet-blue, and 'Albus', pure white.

C. tournefortii. This is a lowland species from the Greek islands, requiring a sunny, sheltered position to protect the late autumn blooms which remain open even on rainy days. The flowers, which are pale lilac-blue with a yellow throat, have white stamens and beautiful large, much-dissected orange stigmas which are a prominent feature of this species. It usually flowers in October or November, sometimes even later, and produces its leaves at the same time or before. Since this lovely Crocus can overlap two seasons, I have included it also in the Winter Section on page 40.

CYCLAMEN

In this small but beautiful group of tuberous-rooted plants there are species which flower in autumn, winter and spring, which makes them particularly valuable as garden plants, although not all are hardy. The very tender *C. persicum*, for example, is a greenhouse plant from which all the large-flowered florists' cyclamen have been raised, and several other species will only grow well in an unheated greenhouse or frame which provides a little protection from the worst of the winter weather. They are all natives of southern Europe, eastwards to Iran, and therefore occur in a 'winter-rainfall' region with a dryish summer dormancy period. All are of dwarf stature, producing mainly heart-shaped or rounded leaves which have attractively patterned leaves in the form of silvery or light and dark green zones and are thus quite handsome for their foliage. The flowers, which are carried singly on stalks overtopping the leaves, are in all the species of typical Cyclamen shape in being nodding with reflexed petals, but the range of form within this basic shape is enormous; some have long, slender, pointed petals, others short, broad, rounded ones, some are twisted, some have swellings around the mouth of the flower, and so on. There is also quite a colour range in the pink, carmine and magenta shades, with or without a dark purple stain at the base around the mouth, and some are white-flowered. Certain species have a delicious fragrance which makes them ideal as alpine house plants, where they can be appreciated at close quarters, but the scent is somewhat lost in the open garden. Even in the fruiting stage Cyclamen are fun to watch, because their flower stalks coil like a watch spring and drag the seed pod down to ground level where the sticky seeds are carried off by ants, an effective method of dispersal.

The most commonly available, easiest to grow, and hardiest species is undoubtedly the Mediterranean *C. hederifolium* (*C. neapolitanum*) which has leaves not unlike those of Ivy, with attractive silvery-green, angular patterns, but they are extremely variable and the various forms can look completely different in their shape and markings. The flowers, too, vary quite a lot in intensity of the pinkish purple colouring, but the most usual form is rather pale with a slightly darker stain towards the mouth. Perhaps even more garden-worthy is the pure white form 'Album', which shows up extremely well. The flowers usually appear in September or October, sometimes at the same time as the leaves unfurl but more often just before there is any real sign of leaf development. *C. hederifolium*, in its usual commercial form, is unscented, but in the wild, fragrant-flowered plants can be found.

It is a very long-lived plant with old tubers reaching up to 15 cm in diameter when fully grown, but when purchased from a nursery they are likely to be not more than about 5–7 cm, which is a good flowering size. Each corm can produce a large quantity of flowers— fifty is not an exceptional number for a large corm—all opening within a few days of each other but lasting for a week or two so that the whole display can be very impressive.

C. purpurascens (*C. europaeum*), on the other hand, produces its highly fragrant lilac to purple-red flowers a few at a time over a long period, at any time from July to December. This eastern European mountain species is thus a rather less showy plant but very distinct and worth having for the delicious scent. The leaves are usually more rounded than those of *C. hederifolium* and often less conspicuously marked, but even so there is a zone of silvery markings.

C. cilicium from southern Turkey is a smaller-flowered, delicate-looking species with pale pinkish flowers that have a dark purple stain around the mouth or 'nose', as it is sometimes called. The leaves are usually heart shaped, with a silvery or light green zone, but it is such a variable species that it is difficult to generalise about these markings. Very similar to it and of much the same garden value is *C. mirabile*, a species which has received much publicity in conservation circles in recent years because it has been dug up and imported in large quantities from Turkey.

The flowers differ slightly from those of *C. cilicium* in having conspicuously toothed edges to the petals.

Most of the other species of autumn-flowering Cyclamen are either not very hardy, coming from North Africa or Cyprus, or require very hot, sunny situations in order to be encouraged to flower, conditions which often do not arise in northern countries away from their Mediterranean homelands. *C. graecum* falls into this category, a charming plant with flowers rather like those of *C. hederifolium* but with beautiful satiny green leaves, variously zoned with silvery green and dark green. Although in the wild it often grows with *C. hederifolium*, it is a much more difficult plant to grow and encourage into flower and really needs to be kept in a pot in an alpine house or frame where its tubers can be dried off and sunbaked in summer.

CULTIVATION The tubers of Cyclamen can usually be obtained in the autumn just before they start to grow. Often these have been dug up in the wild and are frequently either damaged or over-dried, in which case they do not always survive, or may take more than a year to recover. Some of the better specialist bulb nurseries, however, grow their own tubers and send these out, either in the autumn packed in peat or as growing plants in pots at any time of the year. It is well worth any extra expense involved in getting nursery-grown tubers and of course discourages the deplorable practice of destroying the wild colonies of these lovely plants.

Cyclamen tubers should be planted just below the surface—2–3 cm is sufficient—in leafmould-rich soil which is freely draining and in a situation which receives dappled or partial sunlight, at least for all the more easily grown species mentioned above. They are equally good on alkaline or acid soils as long as it is not too extreme and somewhere just on either side of neutral should be aimed at. After the leaves have died away in summer, a thin top dressing of well-decayed leafmould over the tubers is beneficial.

Their small size makes Cyclamen ideal subjects for a rock garden where they fit in very well with other shade-loving plants such as Hepatica (*Anemone hepatica*), dwarf Hostas and various Primulas, adding colour at a time when these other plants have finished their displays. Used in some quantity, *C. hederifolium* is also a glorious sight in a drift beneath colouring autumn shrubs, like the Smoke Bush, *Cotinus coggygria*, or the purple-leaved *Rosa rubrifolia*, either in mixed pink and white forms or in pure stands of either colour.

Propagation is easy by seed which is produced rather readily by most species, the capsules on their coiled stalks being ripe at some time during late spring or early summer. It is important to keep an eye on them while ripening, since ants will remove the seeds quickly once the capsules have split open. If left to their own devices, Cyclamen will produce self-sown seedlings, but it is probably better to collect the seeds and raise new plants for planting out in chosen situations rather than haphazardly sown ones which may turn out to be in undesirable positions.

Ideally the seeds should be sown as soon as gathered, before they have had time to dry out, since this may delay germination for a considerable period. Sown straight away in summer, they may well germinate the following autumn or spring. They are best sown thinly in pots or boxes of a seed-sowing compost, then covered with grit before watering and placed outside for the rest of the summer; after this they are kept just moist, never dried out completely. When the young leaves appear it is best to give some protection in a cold frame or greenhouse for the rest of the winter, since at this stage they are likely to be susceptible to frost; but as soon as spring has arrived they can be placed outside in the open air once more and kept growing for as long as possible by watering with a liquid feed once a fortnight. Even when the foliage dies away in summer, these young seedlings should not be dried out too much, for they can shrivel and die. After one growing season there should be a small tuber which can be handled in early autumn and pricked out into larger pots or boxes of leafmould-rich soil ready for starting into growth for the autumn. Alternatively a seedling bed of similar soil can be made up in the open ground and the young tubers planted directly into this. They will flower in two to four years depending upon the species.

GALANTHUS

When considering suitable bulbs for planting up for an autumn display one does not readily think of Snowdrops, since these really epitomise the coming of spring. There is, however, one Snowdrop from southern Greece which can be relied upon to produce its leafless flowers in October—in fact at one time it was called *G. octobrensis*, although this is not the correct name and it should really be known as *G. reginae-olgae*.

In its flowers this is almost indistinguishable from an ordinary spring *G. nivalis* but the leaves look a little different in being dark green with a grey stripe along the centre, instead of wholly greyish-green. However slight these differences, from a garden viewpoint the autumnal flowering is enough to make this a distinct and valuable plant which is well worth seeking in the specialist catalogues. The acquisition of a bulb or two may be fairly expensive, but if a suitable position is chosen, *G. reginae-olgae* is not slow to increase and it should not take too long to build up a small patch.

CULTIVATION This autumnal Snowdrop is of very easy cultivation if given a little more sun than is usual for the spring varieties, and some shelter from really cold winds. The drainage of the soil should be reasonably good and if not it is best to mix in some sharp sand and leafmould to improve matters since the summer rest period needs to be reasonably dry. A sunny pocket on a rock garden or the front of a sunny border will provide suitable conditions and, for a companion, choose something which will not grow over the Snowdrop and shade it but will provide some contrasting evergreen foliage nearby. *Iris unguicularis*, for example, is a suitable associate and this will carry on the interest by flowering after the Galanthus has finished its display. *G. reginae-olgae* will also mix well with *Cyclamen hederifolium* if the latter is growing in a partially sunny, sheltered spot, and they should be in flower at about the same time. The planting depth should be 5 cm or slightly deeper (to 8 cm) if the soil is very light.

Normally this autumn Snowdrop will increase vegetatively, so that from time to time the bulbs can be lifted and divided, preferably in spring when the foliage is about to die down. Seeds are often produced and these should be sown immediately or in the following autumn.

LEUCOJUM

These little white-flowered plants known as Snowflakes are close relatives of the Snowdrops and, like them, belong to the Amaryllis family but are easily distinguished from the Snowdrops by having their six perianth segments all equal in size, not three large outer ones and three small inner ones. There are two groups of species, the well known Spring and Summer Snowflakes, both of which are spring-flowering in spite of the name of the latter, and the less well-known autumnal ones which are much smaller plants with narrow, thread-like leaves.

L. autumnale, from the western Mediterranean region, is the one most frequently encountered, with one to four tiny white bells on slender stems 10–15 cm tall, which are produced just before the leaves, usually in September; in fact it is one of the first of all the true autumn bulbs to appear. Occasionally

one can find in specialist bulb catalogues the similar but shorter *L. roseum* which has delicate pink flowers, but being so small and also slightly tender, this is not really a plant for outdoor cultivation.

CULTIVATION *Leucojum autumnale* does best in a fully sunny situation in sandy soil, so if the garden soil is naturally on the heavy side it is best to work in a liberal amount of sand before planting in mid to late summer. The planting depth should be about 5 cm. With its slender, diminutive proportions, it needs to be placed carefully or it will be lost among other larger plants and the ideal situation is on a sunny pocket of a rock garden, preferably backed by a darkish rock or dark evergreen shrub which will give it some protection from cold winds in winter and provide a suitable background to show up the small white flowers. It usually increases quite rapidly by bulb division and when clumps have built up it is of course a much more noticeable plant and can be quite effective planted in quantity as an edging along the front of a warm, sunny border. If other dwarf plants are growing nearby, care must be taken that they do not shade the resting bulbs in summer for, like so many bulbous plants, they rely on receiving all the available warmth from the sun to ripen their bulbs and produce flower buds.

LILIUM

The Lilies are, naturally enough, dealt with in considerable detail in the Summer Section on pages 110 to 128, since most of them flower between June and August; a few, however, start to bloom later and may well be at their peak in September. Especially late and certainly worthy of consideration for the autumn garden are the Japanese Golden Rayed Lily, *L. auratum*, and its gorgeous relative *L. speciosum*, both of which are plants for acid leafmould-rich conditions. The common Tiger Lily, *L. tigrinum*, and its variants are also

13

14

15

16

17

18

13 *Anemone nemorosa* 'Robinsoniana', one of the best Wood Anemones. **14** *Anemone ranunculoides*, a yellow Wood Anemone for semi-shade. **15** *Anomatheca laxa (Lapeirousia)*, an easy summer-flowering bulb. **16** *Arum italicum* 'Pictum' leaves in winter with Snowdrops. **17** *Brodiaea (Triteleia) hyacinthina*, an Onion relative from America. **18** *Calochortus luteus*, gorgeous but not easy to grow.

19 *Camassia quamash*, a large Squill-like bulb for a damp spot.   20 *Cardiocrinum (Lilium) giganteum*, an astonishing Lily from the Himalaya.   21 *Chionodoxa gigantea*, a Turkish relative of Scilla.   22 *Chionodoxa luciliae*, the best 'Glory of the Snow'.
23 *Colchicum agrippinum* flowers in the early autumn.   24 *Colchicum byzantinum*, a very free-flowering autumn bulb.

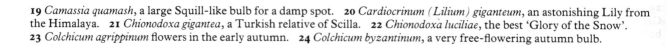

25

26

27

28

29

30

25 *Colchicum speciosum* in grass.　**26** *Colchicum speciosum* 'Album', the lovely white form, easy to grow.　**27** *Colchicum* 'The Giant' with grey-leaved plants.　**28** *Colchicum* 'Waterlily', the largest double Colchicum.　**29** *Corydalis solida*, a good early bulb for the rock garden.　**30** *Crinum powellii* 'Album' for late summer or early autumn.

31 *Crocosmia* 'Emily McKenzie', a striking Montbretia relative. **32** *Crocosmia masonorum*, a stately plant for the herbaceous border. **33** *Crocus angustifolius (susianus)*, the 'Cloth of Gold' Crocus. **34** *Crocus banaticus* with the grass *Molinia caerulea* 'Variegata'. **35** *Crocus chrysanthus* 'Lady Killer', one of the most striking varieties. **36** *Crocus chrysanthus* 'Snow Bunting', the best pure white variety.

late-summer flowering and may still be giving a fine display in September. All of these are described in full in the Summer Section, with details of their cultivation requirements and suggestions for siting and plant associations.

NERINE

The only really frost-hardy species in this southern African genus is *N. bowdenii*, which can be cultivated successfully without protection in most parts of the country in much the same way as its cousin *Amaryllis belladonna*. The bulbs are about the size of a daffodil bulb, producing first, between September and November, a flowering stem about 45–70 cm in height, followed by strap-shaped leaves which overwinter and die down the following summer. The flowers, usually about three to nine, are carried in an umbel and consist of six narrow, widely-spreading, bright pink segments which are somewhat wavy at the margins and curled back, leaving the purplish stamens protruding. Variations include 'Pink Triumph' which has deeper pink flowers and 'Fenwick's Variety', a very robust form; both of these are sometimes offered, but the white form 'Alba' is a very rare plant in cultivation.

In addition to *N. bowdenii* there are many lovely species and varieties, some very dwarf, but they are really plants for a cool greenhouse and will not survive outdoors except in very mild districts.

CULTIVATION Like *Amaryllis*, *Nerine bowdenii* needs a sheltered, sunny situation if it is to grow and flower well, so a protected bed against a south-facing wall is ideal. The bulbs are sometimes on sale in early autumn and sometimes in spring, and when obtained should be planted immediately, without drying out. The main part of the bulb needs to be well covered by soil but the top of the neck should be level with the surface. The type of soil is not too important, but if very heavy it pays to lighten it before planting with coarse, gritty sand and leafmould. The bulbs will probably take a season or two to settle in and flower, so once planted they should be left undisturbed for as long as possible, the only care necessary being an annual feed of bone-meal in early spring, or a potash-rich fertiliser such as 'Tomorite' or sulphate of potash. Clearly, so long as the clumps are flowering well it is better to leave them alone, but if propagation is desired they can be lifted and divided in late summer before coming into growth.

I commented under *Amaryllis belladonna* about the somewhat naked appearance of some of these leafless autumn bulbs and how a few dwarf plants nearby might improve this. The point to watch out for is that the dormant bulbs are not overgrown in summer, thus preventing the sun from reaching them, for it is the warmth that helps to encourage bud formation inside the resting bulbs. Small shrubby plants like *Genista lydia* are useful for this purpose, since they have slender stems and small leaves and therefore cast only slight shade; or compact, grey-leaved subjects such as *Dianthus* can be planted in front of the clumps of Nerine bulbs to attract attention away from the bare stems.

SCILLA

One does not usually associate the Squills with autumn, but there is one tiny species, *S. autumnalis*, which is actually native to Britain as well as to much of southern Europe and the Mediterranean region. It is not a showy plant, only 10 cm in height at most, with racemes of small, starry lilac flowers produced before the leaves in very early autumn, usually in late August or September. The leaves appear shortly afterwards and are very narrow, almost thread-like.

CULTIVATION The small bulbs, rather like those of a Grape Hyacinth, are obtained in autumn and should be planted 3–4 cm deep in a sunny well-drained, preferably sandy soil. In view of its size it needs to be planted among other compact plants which will not swamp it, and carpeting species such as Thyme (*Thymus serpyllum*) are ideal, providing a little protection for the bulbs in severe winters but not too coarse to prevent the Scilla flowers pushing through in the autumn. For propagation purposes the bulbs usually split up to form clumps which can be lifted and divided, and seeds are produced very freely. These can be sown in spring or autumn and will produce flowering-size bulbs in only two to three years.

STERNBERGIA

Although Crocus-like in overall shape, these yellow-flowered autumn bulbs are actually members of the Amaryllis family and are sometimes sold in garden centres as Autumn Daffodils although they bear no resemblance in flower to the Daffodil. The bulbs are, however, somewhat Daffodil-like and produce narrow strap-shaped leaves either at or before flowering time, or quite a while after the flowers have finished. Only one species, the Mediterranean *S. lutea*, is generally available and this is the best garden plant of them all. It has dark green leaves contrasting with the brilliant golden-yellow, goblet-shaped flowers, which are carried on 10–15 cm stems just above the leaves and are somewhat larger than the average Crocus. In southern Italy, Greece and western Turkey there is a more dwarf version of this with narrower leaves, known as *S. sicula* (*S. lutea* var. *sicula*, *S. sicula* var. *graeca*), which is sometimes offered by specialist nurseries; this is well worth seeking for it is sometimes more free-flowering in gardens, as is the plant known as *S. lutea* 'Angustifolia' which may be a form of *S. sicula*. These narrow-leaved Sternbergias differ slightly from *S. lutea* in having dark green leaves with a greyish band along the centre.

The Turkish *S. clusiana* is also offered from time to time, and this is distinguished by having upright wax-like yellow goblets on short stems, larger than those of *S. lutea* and produced before the leaves appear. When the leaves do emerge they are greyish-green and up to 2 cm wide. All these Sternbergias flower in September or October.

In addition to the autumn-flowering species, there are two attractive spring-flowering ones, the yellow *S. fischeriana* and white *S. candida*, but these are not for cultivation outdoors in most areas, requiring a long, dry, warm summer before they will produce flowers, so they are best grown in a frame or cool greenhouse.

CULTIVATION   *S. lutea* and *S. sicula* are the easiest species to grow providing that a warm, sunny and sheltered position is available, such as a south-facing bed at the foot of a wall—in fact the sort of place where one would plant *Iris unguicularis*, *Amaryllis belladonna*, *Nerine bowdenii* and *Zephyranthes candida*. If there is such a choice position in the garden it is worth planting small groups of these autumn bulbs, separated by compact-growing foliage plants such as sage (*Salvia officinalis*) in its grey- and purple-leaved forms, Lavender (*Lavandula*), dwarf grey *Hebe* 'Pagei' or silvery *Santolina chamaecyparissus*. Care must be taken, however, that the associating plants do not overlap the groups of bulbs so that they are shaded in summer, for this will discourage flowering.

The soil needs to be freely draining but apart from that the condition and type is fairly unimportant, although Sternbergias are particularly good in alkaline soils. The bulbs are normally sold in early autumn and must be planted straight away, at a depth of about 10 cm, and watered in if the soil is dry, but after this they are best left undisturbed for as long as they go on flowering well. They increase quite rapidly by bulb division and it may be necessary after a few years to lift crowded clumps and divide them, since such groups sometimes become shy of flowering.

This can be done in late summer or in late spring while the leaves are still green; if they are to be planted back into the same site, dig over the soil, working in a dressing of bonemeal or a potash-rich fertiliser such as 'Tomorite', and old bonfire ash is also suitable. Propagation is, of course, simply a matter of dividing crowded clumps such as this. *S. lutea* and *S. sicula* should flower well if the site is warm and sunny but if they do not, it is worth trying a light feed of sulphate of potash in autumn and again in early spring, since this tends to encourage flower production in the following autumn.

S. clusiana, although a beautiful plant, is not generally such a satisfactory garden plant. It is, however, certainly worth a try in a sheltered, sunny border at the foot of a wall, especially if the soil is chalky or limy, for in some gardens it does settle in and is a fine, unusual autumn bulb.

ZEPHYRANTHES

This latin name, meaning 'Flower of the West Wind', is as pleasant on the ear as the plant is on the eye, for it is a beauty in any of its species, although only one of them is at all well known in cultivation. This is *Z. candida* which comes from Argentina. It is a species that has only a partial rest in summer and then bursts into new activity in the early autumn with upright, goblet-shaped white flowers on short stems up to about 15 cm in height, carried amid green, rush-like leaves. Although Crocus-like, it is not a member of the same family, being more closely related to *Amaryllis* and *Narcissus* and not unlike the Mediterranean *Sternbergia* which is also autumn-flowering. The pink *Z. grandiflora* and yellow *Z. citrina* are occasionally offered in catalogues, but these are more tender than *Z. candida* and will only survive in really mild winters.

CULTIVATION   The bulbs, which resemble small Daffodil bulbs, can usually be obtained in spring for immediate planting about 8–10 cm deep in a sheltered, sunny place; in fact they are suitable companions for any other bulbs requiring a hot, dryish summer period, such as *Amaryllis belladonna* and *Iris unguicularis*. The white flowers show up best if given some dark foliage nearby for contrast, and one might choose, for example, the fairly compact purple-leaved version of Sage (*Salvia officinalis*) as a companion. *Z. candida* seems to prefer light sandy soils, but any reasonably well-drained, sunny situation will do, with the protection of a wall or fence in colder districts. When growing well, its bulbs divide up naturally and clumps are soon formed which can be lifted and divided for propagation purposes; this is best carried out in late summer, just before growth begins again. Any tendency to be shy-flowering may be rectified by lifting and dividing old clumps, or by feeding with sulphate of potash in autumn and spring.

2

THE BULB GARDEN IN WINTER
(December–February)

Needless to say, the garden is a fairly drab place in the winter months as far as flowering plants are concerned; it is mainly attractive foliage and coloured twigs that provide most of the interest at this time of year, save for the Winter Heathers and a few flowering trees and shrubs, such as the Viburnums, the Witch Hazels (*Hamamelis*), Winter Jasmine (*Jasminum nudiflorum*), Winter Sweet (*Chimonanthus*) and some shrubby Honeysuckles (*Lonicera*). In December it is hard to find any bulbous plant whose natural flowering time coincides with these cold, short days, but there are always a few and it is well worth capitalising on them and making a few plantings near the house, preferably combined with some other winter subject so that there is a winter focal point to attract attention. A few Crocus can be relied upon to produce some very late blooms, so a patch of these can be placed in front of *Viburnum farreri* or between clumps of *Erica carnea*. A few varieties of Snowdrop produce their flowers before Christmas and, although not in every nursery catalogue, they can certainly be obtained and are well worth the extra inevitable expense caused by their scarcity.

The miniature *Cyclamen coum* usually starts to produce a few flowers around Christmas in all but very severe winters and this, too, associates beautifully with Winter Heathers; it is certainly a good plan to find a sunny, sheltered spot within view of the main windows, where a few corms of this can be placed together with an early variety of Snowdrop.

Although a rhizomatous rather than a bulbous plant, I think I may be forgiven for mentioning the winter Algerian Iris, *I. unguicularis*, in view of the paucity of material for this chapter! This will push up flowers at any time from about November onwards, whenever the weather allows, but although it is nice to see them out in the garden, they give much better value if picked in the bud stage for opening in a vase indoors, where the blooms and their delicate scent can be appreciated. A good winter corner can be arranged on a south-facing wall or fence by training Winter Jasmine along it, with Snowdrops and *Cyclamen coum* below, and a quite spectacular effect can be achieved by a planting of an early Snowdrop around a shrub of the scarlet-twigged Dogwood, *Cornus alba* 'Sibirica'.

With December gone, the picture brightens considerably. With lengthening days, it requires only a few mild spells to trigger off *Crocus tommasinianus*, more varieties of Snowdrop and the Hellebores with which these two associate so beautifully, while by February most parts of the country will expect plenty of dwarf bulbs to be 'on the move' and the early bees out, setting about their business whenever the sun appears. Few of the Narcissus make it in time to be classified as winter flowerers, although one or two of the unusual miniature species can be relied upon. Even the superb *N. cyclamineus* hybrid 'February Gold' does not live up to its name, and as far south as Surrey I have not yet had it in flower in my garden earlier than 1st March. Doubtless, however, in the milder counties, this and many other early spring bulbs would squeeze into our winter category of December to February.

Nearly all the hardy winter-flowering bulbs for our gardens come from the mountain regions around the Mediterranean or western Asia—in fact I can think of no exceptions. They are either low-altitude plants which naturally flower at this time, when moisture is available before their native haunts become sunbaked, or are normally spring flowering mountain plants which, because of our relatively mild maritime climate, bloom rather earlier than they would in the wild. In the first category comes *Crocus laevigatus*, a common plant of the lower hill slopes in the Greek islands where it can be found in flower at any time between October and February. A good example of the second category is *Cyclamen coum* which, in its mountain home in Turkey, often does not flower before March or April but when cultivated in our low, relatively mild gardens, is tempted into bloom a month or two earlier.

All of these winter-flowering bulbs are easily cultivated and do not call for any special treatment, requiring only a reasonably well-drained position in sun or semi-shade, in soil which is well-supplied with leafmould to retain some moisture in spring and summer, for several of them, such as the Cyclamen, Snowdrops and Winter Aconites, are naturally woodland plants. *Iris unguicularis* is the exception and this does need a sunbaked bed at the foot of a fence or wall if it is to flower well. Without exception they are also lime tolerant—in fact I would go farther and say that they are better on alkaline soils, if leafmould is added to give a degree of moisture-retaining humus.

Being summer-dormant, most of these plants are obtainable as dry bulbs through nurserymen in the early autumn, along with all the spring-flowering species. Some groups, however, for example Snowdrops and Cycla-

men, do not take too kindly to being dried off and some nurseries now sell Snowdrops 'in the green' during spring, soon after flowering time but before the leaves have died down. *Cyclamen coum* can often be purchased growing in pots, but is likely to be more expensive than if sold in the dried state. Good nurseries are aware of the fact that Cyclamen should not be over-dried and will send them out packed in peat, but if dried tubers are bought then my advice is to get them as early in autumn as possible and plant them straight away, so that they have as long as possible to make new roots before the cold, damp weather sets in. Some people recommend first 'plumping up' over-dried bulbs and tubers in damp sand or peat before planting out, but the drawback here is that a move is required and any young roots that are developing might be damaged. A twenty-four hour soak in water before planting, with a systemic fungicide added if they do not look too healthy, sometimes proves to be a worthwhile treatment to break dormancy, and I always do this with Winter Aconites since the tubers usually arrive from nurseries looking like pieces of dead wood.

The Winter-Flowering Bulbs

ANEMONE

Most of these delightful members of the Ranunculus family are fibrous-rooted plants, either spring- or summer-flowering, but there are a few early-flowering tuberous-rooted species, the earliest and most notable of which is *A. blanda*. This eastern Mediterranean plant is one of the first spring flowers on its native hillsides and in gardens may emerge any time from February onwards. The rounded tubers give rise to dissected leaves, about 10 cm in height at most, and these are soon overtopped by the many-petalled flowers about 3–5 cm in diameter, which in the most usual form are mid blue but may be deep bluish-violet, pink, carmine or white, all with a central cluster of yellow stamens. They are frequently offered as mixed collections, but can also be obtained in their named varieties such as 'Atrocaerulea' (dark blue), 'White Splendour' (white), 'Rosea' (pink), 'Radar' (bright magenta with a white centre), and 'Charmer' (reddish-pink).

CULTIVATION *A. blanda* is a plant for dappled sunlight such as deciduous shrubs and trees will provide, where its flowers can receive all the available sunshine early in the year but later on, when dormant, the tubers will be partially shaded. The tubers are on sale in autumn and, if very dry, may to advantage be soaked overnight before planting. Good drainage is necessary for *A. blanda* and some leafmould or old compost worked in thoroughly should provide this and help with moisture retention in summer, but the acidity or alkalinity of the soil is unimportant and almost any type of soil will suffice, providing it is freely draining and humus-rich. The tubers are placed shallowly in the soil, about 3–4 cm deep being quite sufficient. Once established, they are best left undisturbed, save for weeding the area, and when growing happily will start to seed about to form large colonies. The only attention necessary is an annual top dressing of leafmould in the autumn through which they will grow in spring. Apart from seedlings, they also increase by division of the tubers, so this is an easily propagated plant, simply by lifting clumps and dividing them; this may be carried out in early autumn or in spring after the flowers have finished, replanting straight away without drying them out.

A. blanda associates very well with other late winter and early spring bulbs such as Snowdrops and Winter Aconites and, since these all enjoy partial shade, it is worth devoting an area to them beneath and near deciduous trees and shrubs. The winter bark of Silver Birch, for instance, makes an excellent setting for these lovely early bulbs, as do the yellow and red coloured twigs of *Cornus stolonifera* and *Cornus alba*. The pink varieties of *A. blanda* look particularly attractive when planted near grey-leaved subjects and if you have a shrub of something such as *Senecio laxifolius*, greyish *Cistus, Hebe* 'Pagei' or Lavender, try a group of 'Rosea', 'Charmer' or 'Radar' in front or alongside. Shrubs such as these will normally be growing in rather hot, sunny places and the Anemones may not naturalise as well as they would in the dappled shade of deciduous shrubs, but they are fairly cheap to buy and new ones can be planted every now and again to achieve this rather attractive effect. Since *A. blanda* will flower well into the spring, it is also included with the other spring-flowering Anemones on page 53.

ARUM

One species of Arum, the Lords and Ladies or Cuckoo Pint, which is invaluable in the winter garden, is *A. italicum* in its variety 'Pictum'. This could in fact be mentioned in the Autumn, Winter or Spring sections since its delightful arrow-shaped leaves with their prominent creamy veins are produced in the autumn and last in good condition right through to early summer. It is as a foliage plant that this is really most useful, although it does also produce greenish spathes in spring and spikes of bright red berries in summer. The leaves are excellent for cutting for flower arrangements and in the garden will associate with almost any of the winter-flowering subjects.

CULTIVATION *A. italicum* 'Pictum' does best when planted in a semi-shaded situation in soil well-supplied with moisture. The tubers are obtained either dormant in the autumn or in spring in the growing state and placed at least 10 cm deep in the soil. A position where they can be left undisturbed should be chosen so that in time a colony can build up to form a mat of foliage. Propagation is thus simply a matter of digging up these established clumps and dividing them, but remember that the tubers may well have pulled themselves down to a considerably greater depth than the original 10 cm. I find that the best time to do this is in the spring while the foliage is still visible.

A. italicum 'Pictum' is a splendid associate for Snowdrops, Winter Aconites and Hellebores to make a colourful winter corner near the house. Further mention of this excellent garden plant will be found on page 55 of the Spring Section.

CROCUS

Although the Crocuses are associated mainly with spring there are quite a number which flower in the autumn and a few which can be regarded as truly winter-flowering, although only one of these, *C. laevigatus*, is easy to obtain. *C. tommasinianus* can be relied upon to appear as soon as there is any sign of a let-up in the cold weather in January, but in cold winters and in the more northern districts it may be February before it makes a move. Similarly *C. flavus* (*C. aureus*), which is usually grown in the form of its larger garden variety 'Dutch Yellow' or 'Golden Yellow', can also appear during mild spells and in some years coincides with *C. tommasinianus*, giving a very colourful display. If there is a particularly sheltered, sunny spot in the garden near the house, it is also worth trying some *C. sieberi*, for a little winter sunshine may well trigger off growth in those as well.

CULTIVATION   The Crocuses mentioned are all easy to cultivate in any well-drained garden soil, preferably in full sun, although *C. tommasinianus* will take dappled shade under shrubs. *C. laevigatus* will need a sheltered, sunny place since it flowers at such an inclement season, and a site should be chosen where there is protection from the worst of the wind and rain. Conifers provide ideal shelter, and a dense-foliaged one like the silvery *Chamaecyparis* 'Boulevard' gives such a service, while also supplying a perfect backdrop for the purplish Crocus. A sunny, south-facing wall bed is also suitable for *C. laevigatus* which is likely to flower on and off at any time from November to January. It is a tough little plant which has even taken to growing in a grassy patch in my own garden, throwing a few flowers whenever there are a few mild days.

C. tommasinianus is a very hardy, tolerant plant for sun or semi-shade which, once established, is likely to seed freely in any undisturbed place, especially along the edges of paths and drives and between paving stones. Although it can make almost solid patches of growth, it seldom becomes a nuisance for it dies down very quickly in spring and its welcome sheet of early flowers more than makes up for the slightly inconvenient mass of grassy leaves which follow. *C. flavus* enjoys similar sunny conditions where it can be left to increase at will, so it follows that these are not plants for a herbaceous border where disturbance of the soil is fairly regular. They are best planted informally, along the front of shrub borders or places where hardy perennials such as Hellebores, Hostas and Pulmonarias are grown, plants which also require little disturbance. One might consider, for example, creating a winter border with a winter-flowering shrub or two, such as *Viburnum tinus* and *Garrya elliptica*, to give evergreen shelter from the cold winds for a planting of Crocuses, Hellebores, *Cyclamen coum* and *Scilla tubergeniana*; such a site may tend to become hot and dry in summer, so a top dressing of leafmould would be beneficial after the bulbs have died down. *Crocus flavus* ('Dutch Yellow') will also do extremely well in grass, and any patch of lawn which can be left unmown for a while, until the Crocus leaves have died down, is suitable. Again, a sunny, sheltered spot is more likely to encourage them into early flower.

C. ancyrensis. Although small-flowered,

this Turkish Crocus is a good bright orange-yellow and, in its variety 'Golden Bunch', produces several flowers in succession from each corm. In mild winters these may appear in January or February, so it is worth planting a group near the house in the hope of some late winter colour. A position in full sun is necessary, and well-drained soil, but given these two conditions it is a perfectly easy little Crocus and increases well.

C. flavus. This Balkan species is only commonly seen in gardens in its large Dutch form which is sold under various names—'Large Yellow', 'Dutch Yellow', 'Yellow Giant', etc.—and is a much more substantial plant than the wild form. The colour is a good, deep yellow with a certain amount of dark veining towards the base on the outside. The large corms are covered with tunics which have a fibrous appearance, the fibre strands running lengthways and quite different from the netted tunics of the large hybrid purple-and-white spring Crocuses and from the *C. chrysanthus* varieties with their eggshell-like coats which separate off into rings at the bottom. Thus it is quite easy to distinguish the dried corms of these three groups of Crocus when they are on sale in the autumn. *C. flavus* is the earliest yellow of the commonly available Crocuses and well worth planting in quantity since it is fairly cheap. It is usually sterile, so will not seed itself around, but does increase quickly into clumps which can be lifted in autumn and divided.

C. laevigatus. The name of this Greek species means 'smooth' and refers to the corm which has a very hard, smooth tunic covering it. It is a true winter-flowering plant and will produce a succession of flowers over a long period any time between November and January, depending upon the weather. For this reason it is an extremely useful plant and, although slightly more expensive than the common varieties, is a 'must' for the gardener who is trying to bring a little interest into the garden at this time of year. It needs only a

sunny well-drained spot and is very good on alkaline soils. The most commonly available form is 'Fontenayi', a good lilac with prominent stripes on the outside.

C. sieberi. Although this is a spring-flowering species, in mild winters and in sheltered, sunny spots it will often open its first flowers during February. These are lilac with a conspicuous yellow throat and have a delicious honey-like scent which attracts the first bees on fine sunny days when they are fully open. There is a rich violet form known as 'Violet Queen' which is often to be seen in catalogues, and occasionally the purple-and-white blotched 'Hubert Edelsten' may be found, both of which are interesting variations worth having. Like *C. laevigatus*, it is a Greek species and is appreciative of well-drained soils, alkaline or acid.

C. tommasinianus. The first starry flowers of this Yugoslavian species appear at any time between January and March depending upon the weather and, in its most common form, are lavender with a silvery outside. However, it varies greatly and a number of selections have been made, including 'Whitewell Purple' (purple), 'Albus' (white) and 'Ruby Giant' which is a very vigorous purple variety, probably of hybrid origin. Although *C. tommasinianus* prefers semi-shade, it will do well in a variety of situations and, when settled in, is likely to seed itself freely, especially along the edges of paths and in rock gardens. If a few of each of the different varieties are planted initially, these are likely to cross in time, giving a whole range of different shades. This is a good species for naturalising under shrubs where it can remain undisturbed to form large colonies.

C. tournefortii. This beautiful close relative of *C. laevigatus* is sometimes available in nurseries and is a plant to be treasured. Although originating in the Greek islands it is surprisingly hardy and its requirements are not too exacting. A well-drained soil in full sun, acid or alkaline, suits it admirably, and preferably with some protection from the north by a dense conifer, fence or wall to break the colder winds. The flowers come in October or November, together with the leaves, and are a lovely shade of soft lavender-blue with a yellow throat, but the most noteworthy feature is the large orange style, dissected into a mass of stigma branches. Another unusual and useful attribute is that the flowers stay wide open on dull days and even in the rain, so it is worthwhile having a cloche or pane of glass nearby to cover them in really bad weather and so keep them in good condition. Mention of *C. tournefortii* is also made on page 29 of the Autumn Section.

CYCLAMEN

The only reliably winter-flowering species in this delightful group of plants is *C. coum*. In most gardens it will flower at or soon after Christmas but in cold areas may be delayed until February. It is fortunate for gardeners that this widespread plant, which grows in Turkey, the Caucasus, Lebanon and Bulgaria, is a very variable one so that it is possible to have many different forms, all of equal garden value, but unfortunately such variation has led to a multiplicity of names and in consequence much confusion. It may be found in catalogues under the names *C. vernum*, *C. orbiculatum*, *C. ibericum* and *C. atkinsii*.

The smallish rounded tubers produce leaves and flower buds in late autumn, at first tightly folded and pressed to the upper surface of the tuber, then later the nearly circular leaves unfurl and are raised above the soil on short stems. Following these, in December if you are lucky, but usually January or February in cold districts, the flower stems carry aloft miniature Cyclamen flowers, unscented in this case, although several of the other species mentioned in the Autumn and Spring Sections are beautifully fragrant. The great range of variability in both flowers and leaves means that it is possible to have white, pink or deep carmine-coloured forms, each colour combined with either plain deep green or attractively silvery-zoned leaves. In all colour forms, around the 'nose' of the flower there is a much darker stain, usually with a white zone as well.

Individual flowers last a long time so that there is a display for several weeks, and the foliage remains until late spring when the tubers go into their summer rest period. If produced, the seed heads can be seen on the surface of the soil, pulled down by the stems which coil after flowering, like watch springs.

CULTIVATION *Cyclamen coum* is a very easily cultivated plant for semi-shade or full sun provided the soil and site do not become too sun-baked in summer. The drainage should be good and, whatever the type of soil, it is advantageous to mix in plenty of leafmould to at least 15 cm deep. The tubers are usually obtained and planted in early autumn but some nurserymen sell them individually as pot plants at any time of the year. It is a common practice to plant them with the tubers at or just below the soil surface, as is the case with greenhouse pot-grown Cyclamen. For the hardy ones, however, this is not a good idea, for it makes them vulnerable to severe frosts, and they may become sunburnt and over-dried in summer. The tubers are best covered by 2–3 cm of loose, leafy soil and a top dressing of a leafmould-rich mixture every autumn. Fertiliser should not normally be necessary, but in poor soils, or if the plants look starved at any time, bonemeal is a good all-round feed, again given in autumn when active growth commences.

C. coum is fairly tolerant of sun or shade, given the correct cultural conditions. The main dislikes are heavy, waterlogged soils and very hot dry ones, but both of these can be improved by the addition of organic matter. The size of the plant demands that it must be placed near the front of borders or in raised positions such as on a rock garden or in a double wall with other low-growing plants. It associates well with the Winter Heathers, *Erica carnea*, and some attractive plantings can be made using the white form of *Cyclamen coum* between pink or purple Heathers (e.g. 'Winter Beauty', 'King George') or carmine *Cyclamen coum*, among white Heather ('Springwood', 'Snow Queen'). Care must be taken that the Heathers do not smother the Cyclamen after a few years of growth. Snowdrops also go well with Cyclamen and a small bed of these mixed together near the house provides a welcome winter scene. Using larger numbers of tubers, which is possible if you propagate your own from seed, *C. coum* is an ideal plant for carpeting open areas in front of and between Rhododendrons, for they enjoy the same humus-rich soils and are natural neighbours in the mountains of Turkey.

Propagation is by seed which is best sown as soon as it is collected, while still sticky; in fact it must be collected as soon as the pods burst open (usually early summer) or ants will carry it off to some unknown destination. Sow it thinly in pots or boxes of any proprietary seed compost, cover with fine grit and leave it outside until germination takes place, watering as necessary. Once the young leaves have appeared (usually during the first autumn and winter after sowing) the seedlings should be protected from any severe frosts, preferably in a cold frame or greenhouse. After one whole growing season the tiny dormant tubers can be moved on into boxes of leafmould-rich compost, preferably in late summer; at no time should they be allowed to become excessively dry, even when dormant. Flowering normally begins in about two to four years after germination.

ERANTHIS

The Winter Aconite is perhaps a little more promising in its vernacular name than it is in its actual behaviour, for it is at best late winter before it emerges, February being the most likely month. However, that aside, it is a superb plant in any of its forms with the lovely cup-like bright yellow flowers just overtopping deeply cut leaves and surrounded by a ruff of leaf-like bracts. There are two species usually to be found in catalogues, the common *E. hyemalis* from European woodlands and the Turkish *E. cilicica* which is very similar and scarcely different in its garden value. There is, however, a hybrid between them which has relatively enormous flowers of deep gold with distinctly bronze-tinted foliage, and this is well worth obtaining. It is *E.* x *tubergenii* 'Guinea Gold', named after the firm of Van Tubergen of Haarlem which was responsible for the raising and introduction of many fine bulbous plants. Like some of the Anemones, which also belong to the Ranunculus family, Winter Aconites have a solid, rather misshapen tuber which becomes very hard when dried out. They are usually sold dried in the autumn, fortunately fairly cheaply since they often do not grow very well. It is best to soak them overnight before planting, or put them in a tray of moist peat for a week or two. Occasionally it is possible to buy them in the growing state and this gives a much better chance of success. Reputable bulb firms, however, should be aware that over-drying can damage the tubers and, if selling in the autumn, will seek to avoid this and send them out packed in peat.

CULTIVATION *Eranthis hyemalis* is a woodland plant which likes cool growing conditions beneath deciduous trees and shrubs. The soil is relatively unimportant providing it is not waterlogged and stagnant or, at the other extreme, very dry. Some leafmould incorporated at planting time is beneficial but after this they are best left completely undisturbed when they will probably begin to seed around and form colonies. *E. cilicica* and the hybrid 'Guinea Gold' do not increase in this way in cultivation, but they do multiply vegetatively, so can be dug up after flowering and divided from time to time. They will take more sun than *E. hyemalis* and are suitable for a humus-rich pocket on the rock garden or front of a sunny border. The tubers should be planted fairly shallowly, at about 5 cm deep.

The common Winter Aconite associates very well with Snowdrops since they like similar cool, moist soils, acid or alkaline, and adds a welcome splash of bright yellow to a late winter border composed of purple and white Hellebores and Snowdrops.

GALANTHUS

Nearly all the species and varieties of the much-loved Snowdrop are winter- or early spring-flowering, except for one curiosity, *G. reginae-olgae*, which produces its leafless flowers in autumn. Although there is a very large number of named varieties, these are mostly in the hands of a few specialist enthusiasts and are not generally obtainable from nurseries. However, there is quite a range available, providing a spread of flowering time, and some interesting variations on the usual Snowdrop theme. All are of the easiest cultivation and, when growing healthily, will soon increase into clumps which can be divided.

Snowdrops are, of course, instantly recognisable by their white pendent flowers arising on slender stems from between a pair of narrow, often greyish-green leaves. Like most bulbous plants, the flowers have six parts and in this case there are three large outer segments and three smaller inner ones forming a cup, which is tipped with green. In some species there are also green marks at the base of the cup. The closely related Snowflakes (Leucojum—see pages 32 and 72) can be easily distinguished by having flowers with six equal segments. A few Snowdrops have bright green leaves which set off the white flowers rather well and give these species a very distinct appearance.

CULTIVATION Snowdrops are naturally plants of woodlands or cool mountain meadows and it follows that in gardens they must not be given hot, dry conditions. The planting depth should be 5 cm in heavy soils, up to 8 cm in light, sandy ones. The type of soil does not matter too much—acid or alkaline, light or heavy—and in fact they thrive on heavy, chalky soils. However, in gardens which have very well-drained, sandy conditions it is necessary to incorporate plenty of moisture-retaining organic matter in the soil in the form of leafmould or well-rotted compost. Dappled shade suits them best and they mix very well with Hellebores for a showy display from late January or early February onwards. They also look well beneath shrubs or between Rhododendrons and a good winter corner can be made by planting drifts of Snowdrops around such shrubs as *Viburnum farreri*, *Mahonia japonica* and Witch Hazels, *Hamamelis*, and especially the purple leafless *Daphne mezereum*.

The very early Snowdrops, such as *G. reginae-olgae* and *G. caucasicus* 'Hiemale' are likely to be more difficult to find, and consequently more expensive, but are well worth the effort so that the flowering season can be extended almost continuously from November through to March. I usually reckon to have at least one clump in full flower before Christmas and, even in the bad winter of 1984–85, *G. caucasicus* was blooming in November. It was buried by snow in January but emerged to go on flowering in March. Such varieties are best placed in a spot where you can see them easily from the most frequented part of the house or beside a path or drive which is used daily.

Snowdrops are obtainable either as dried bulbs in the autumn or as growing plants in spring, just after flowering. The latter is certainly the best time to get them, although they may be a little more expensive. The dried bulbs do not always give such good results, especially if they have been over-dried, and they may take a year or two to settle down, so the extra expense of buying 'green' plants is worthwhile. Some of the specialist bulb nurseries which have the more unusual varieties will only sell them in the growing state. Propagation is also best carried out in spring, the clumps being lifted while in full growth, divided into single bulbs and replanted straight away before they have had time to dry out. Seeds are also produced and, although it is not necessary to increase Snowdrops in this way, it can be fun to see if any interesting new variations crop up, since they hybridise readily. The seeds should be sown as soon as ripe in spring, either in pots which are then kept watered and cool for the summer, or directly into a seed bed in a partially shaded place where they can be left to grow undisturbed until they reach flowering size.

G. elwesii. This is often called the Giant Snowdrop. It is a native of western Turkey and is imported in large numbers to be sold cheaply in European markets. The bold leaves are grey-green, rather broad and wider towards the apex; the flowers, which have green marks at the base and apex of the inner segments, are somewhat larger than those of the common Snowdrop.

G. caucasicus. The Caucasian Snowdrop is well worth growing for its bold, wide grey leaves which are very similar to those of *G. elwesii*, but it may be distinguished by having only one green mark on each of the inner segments. The early flowering forms are the most valuable, either offered as 'Early Form' or 'Hiemale' and with me these are usually open just before Christmas, or soon after.

G. ikariae (G. latifolius). This is very different in general appearance from most Snowdrops because of its bright green, glossy leaves. The flowers have rather rounded segments and green marks only at the apex of the cup. It is a native of the Caucasus and the Aegean Islands.

G. nivalis. The Common Snowdrop. In its most frequent form this has narrow grey-green leaves and the flowers are somewhat smaller than those of most other species, with green marks at the apex of the cup. There are,

however, many different varieties, among them some very fine garden plants.

'Atkinsii' is one of the best of all, with tall stems and long graceful flowers.

'Flore Plena' has tightly double flowers.

'Scharlockii' is curious in having two green leaf-like spathes sticking up like rabbit's ears above the flower.

'Viridapicis' has green marks on the tips of the outer segments as well as the inner.

'Lutescens' is a rare variety in which the flowers have yellow markings instead of green. It is small and not as robust a grower as most of the others.

'Magnet' has large flowers carried out away from the stem on long, slender stalks, giving it a distinctive appearance.

G. reginae-olgae. The main difference in appearance between this and *G. nivalis* is the distinctive white stripe along the centre of each leaf, for in other respects it is much the same. More important from the gardener's point of view, however, is the flowering time which, depending upon the variety, is from about October through to early spring. Var. *reginae-olgae* from southern Greece is the earliest, blooming even before the leaves emerge (see Autumn Section, page 31) but var. *corcyrensis* from Corfu (*G. corcyrensis*) is a little later, usually November, and has short leaves at flowering time. I find that these require rather more sun than other Snowdrops, with protection from a wall or fence to shield them from some of the inclement weather that is to be expected at this time.

IRIS

Two different groups of Iris can be considered for the winter garden, the Algerian Iris (*I. unguicularis*) in all its forms, and the bulbous Reticulate Irises. The species of the latter group are essentially early spring-flowering but some of the species will bloom in February in most winters and even in the 1984–85 winter, when my garden experienced lengthy periods of cold down to $-15°C$, *I. danfordiae* and *I. histrioides* had faded by the second week of March.

I. unguicularis (I. stylosa) needs little description for there are few gardeners, I am sure, who do not know its long-tubed lilac-purple flowers and tufts of untidy grassy leaves. This is a rhizomatous type, increasing to form a mat of knobbly rhizomes which are nearly hidden by the tough evergreen leaves. At any time from November through to March the buds can push up, in long succession when the plants are doing really well. If the weather is mild these can be left on the plant to open, which they do as soon as the day is warm enough. In frosty weather, however, it is much better to pick them for a vase indoors since they are not at all frost resistant and will be ruined overnight. In a warm room the buds open in a very short space of time and emit a subtle fragrance suggestive of Primroses.

There are many forms of *I. unguicularis*, the most common of which is a mid-lavender colour. 'Alba' has white flowers with a yellow central line on the falls, 'Mary Barnard' is a deeper purple, 'Walter Butt' a large pale silvery-blue and 'Cretensis' a dwarf form with narrow leaves which is not as free flowering and needs a very sheltered position.

CULTIVATION   Pot-grown plants can be planted out at almost any time, making sure that the rhizomes are only just beneath the surface, in fact the top side of the rhizome should be visible. September is a good month to plant if there is a choice, and old clumps can be divided at this time of year, although they may take a year or so to settle down and begin to flower. A very hot, sunny position should be chosen, such as a south-facing wall or fence, since these Irises only flower well if their rhizomes receive a hot dry period in summer; after a dull damp summer, flowering may be rather poor the following winter. For this reason, too, there must be no tall plants

nearby which will grow up and shade them. Some people recommend trimming back the leaves in summer to allow the sunlight to fall on the rhizomes, but I have not found this to be helpful and it looks rather odd, to say the least. The soil for *I. unguicularis* is not too important, so long as it is reasonably well drained, and may be acid or alkaline. Fertilisers are normally unnecessary, and it will grow perfectly well on very poor soils, but I think it does encourage flowering to give a light dressing of sulphate of potash in spring and autumn. Propagation is by division of established clumps, since seeds are rarely produced and take a long time to produce flowering-sized plants.

Reticulata Irises. These are the dwarf species whose bottle-shaped bulbs are covered with a coarsely netted jacket and whose narrow leaves are (in nearly all the species) four-angled in cross-section. Being only about 10–15 cm high when in flower, and enjoying sunny positions, they are ideally suited to the rock garden or the front of borders where they will be among the first of the early bulbs to flower. The variety within this fairly small group of species is enormous, from the deep yellow *I. danfordiae* to rich blue *I. histrioides*, with a wide range of purple, blue and violet shades in *I. reticulata* itself. *I. danfordiae*, a Turkish mountain plant, does not vary and is a good rich yellow with a tinge of green, blackish spotted on the falls. There is one other yellow-flowered reticulate Iris, the rare Caucasian *I. winogradowii*, which has larger flowers in pale primrose spotted with green and, although obtainable, is rather expensive by comparison with *I. danfordiae*. Nevertheless it is a beautiful plant and well worth the initial expense of a bulb or two. *I. histrioides* is known in the wild from only one mountain in Turkey but has become quite common in cultivation in one form or another, for there has been a certain amount of selection of seedlings giving rise to several named cultivars. There is, however, not a great deal of difference between them, and from the garden point of view all are good, varying slightly in the intensity of blue and in the amount of dark and light blotching on the falls; all have a conspicuous yellow stripe in the centre of the falls. For those with an eye for the unusual there are hybrids between *I. histrioides* and *I. winogradowii* which have taken on the pale yellow of the latter as a background colour, overlaid with a bluish hue and veining from *I. histrioides*; of these hybrids, the first and most likely to be encountered at present is 'Katharine Hodgkin'.

I. reticulata, a widespread species from Turkey, the Caucasus and Iran, is the most variable in the group and obtainable in a great range of named colour variants, most of which flower slightly later than *I. histrioides* and usually have their leaves developed a little more; in *I. histrioides* the foliage is barely visible when the flowers are at their peak. The ordinary commercial form of *I. reticulata* is a strong violet with a yellow ridge in the centre of the falls. 'Cantab' is a less vigorous plant with smaller flowers in pale blue, 'Harmony' and 'Joyce' are darker sky-blue, both with a yellow stripe on the falls, and 'Clairette' is bicoloured with sky-blue standards and deeper blue falls. In the purplish and violet shades there are 'Hercules' and 'J. S. Dijt', both reddish-purple with yellow crests on the falls, 'Pauline', an unusual dusky violet with a white zone on the falls, and 'Jeannine', in purple with an orange stripe. Rather more conspicuously blotched is 'Springtime' which has a dark blue tip to the falls and paler blue standards. Some of these, especially the ones with white-zoned or dark-tipped falls, are probably hybrids with the related *I. bakeriana* which has markings of this type in shades of blue. The most obvious difference between it and *I. reticulata* is in the leaves which, instead of being squarish, are nearly round in cross-section and the hybrids may show intermediate characteristics with more than four ribs to the leaves.

Occasionally it is also possible to obtain the very early *I. histrio* var. *aintabensis*, also Turkish, which has smallish pale blue flowers blotched darker, but *I. histrio* itself, although very striking, with the most conspicuous markings of them all, is not generally available and flowers rather too early, often in December or January, to be satisfactory as an outdoor plant. Heavy frosts damage the fragile blooms but those of var. *aintabensis* are later and more resistant, so it can be grown without protection.

CULTIVATION All the Reticulata Irises mentioned require sunny positions in well-drained soil, which may be acid or alkaline although the latter is preferable. The bulbs are obtained in autumn and should be planted straight away at a depth of about 5–8 cm, except in the case of *I. danfordiae* which is best if it has at least 10 cm of soil above the top of the bulb. This species has a reputation for flowering the first year but then splitting up into small non-flowering bulbs thereafter. However, deep planting discourages this and it is possible to maintain a flowering group year after year. Their size makes them perfect for the front of a sunny border or rock garden, either mixed with other late-winter bulbs such as Crocus and Scillas, or as isolated groups associated with foliage plants, and it is worth experimenting with various combinations to see what might be successful. I find that the steely, violet flowers of *I. reticulata* look excellent alongside a silvery spiky-leaved dwarf conifer and a group of the yellow *I. danfordiae* is enhanced by the grey rosettes of Dianthus. One surprise has been *I. histrioides*, doing extremely well and increasing in a patch of rough grass.

When growing well these Irises need little in the way of attention and they can increase to form clumps of bulbs which need division from time to time in late summer. A light dressing of sulphate of potash is beneficial, as with other Irises, and in the case of Reticulatas is best given in early spring just after flowering, when the leaves are about to make their maximum growth. The main causes of failure are likely to be poorly drained soils or the disease known as 'Ink Disease' which can attack and destroy whole colonies of bulbs in a short space of time. Drainage can be improved in heavy soils by digging in deeply some sharp gritty sand and moss peat or leafmould. If a rock garden is being built, then drainage becomes less troublesome since the pockets are raised above general soil level and can be filled with a well-drained soil mixture. 'Ink Disease' can be prevented by dipping the bulbs at planting time in one of the systemic fungicides based on the substance Benomyl, or watering this into the soil rather than disturb established patches of bulbs.

Propagation of these Reticulate Irises is usually a simple matter of lifting the bulbs in late summer and dividing the clumps, or removing any small offsets prior to replanting. The offsets can be grown on separately in similarly prepared soil, or planted back in the freshly prepared site with the parent bulbs, spaced out to give each some growing room. Seeds are produced in some years, in fat capsules sitting at ground level, and these can also be grown on to produce flowering bulbs in about three or four years. This, of course, gives the possibility of raising new varieties, so, although it may be much slower, it can be more interesting.

LEUCOJUM

The Snowflakes, although only a small group, provide us with interest in the autumn, winter and spring and will be found in each of these seasonal chapters. I have described *L. vernum*, the Spring Snowflake, fully in the Spring Section since it is usually March when its large pendent white bells appear, but in sheltered areas or mild winters it may be as early as

February, along with the Snowdrops. In the most frequently seen variety the six petals are tipped with green, but there is also a yellow-tipped variation known as var. *carpathicum*. In its bulb and leaves *L. vernum* resembles a small Daffodil, except that the foliage is bright glossy green; the height of the flower stems is usually about 15–20 cm and it carries one, or less frequently two, bells.

CULTIVATION   *L. vernum* bulbs are best obtained in spring whilst in leaf if possible for, like Snowdrops, they seem to transplant better at this time of year. A few of the specialist nurseries deal with them in this way, but most of the larger firms sell dried bulbs in the autumn; this does not matter unduly, provided they have not been over-dried. The best site is in a cool, semi-shaded spot where there is plenty of moisture available where the soil will not become too sun-baked in summer. The addition of plenty of humus will help with moisture retention. Like Snowdrops, they seem to thrive on heavy alkaline soils, so don't be deterred if you garden on a sticky clay, for this is the type of soil in which they grow in the wild. The bulbs should be planted about 5–7 cm deep.

The Spring Snowflake associates well in a semi-shaded border with Hellebores and is also suitable, because of its compactness, for a cool pocket on the rock garden.

Propagation is simply a matter of division of clumps, after flowering.

NARCISSUS

The many species and hybrids of Daffodil are dealt with mainly in the Spring Section since they are mostly in bloom from March onwards. There are, however, just a few of the smaller Narcissus which can be in flower earlier and are hardy enough to be tolerant of outdoor cultivation, but some of the small mid-winter species, such as the white Hoop Petticoat Daffodil, *N. cantabricus*, are really too fragile for anywhere but a cold greenhouse (alpine house) or frame where the worst of the weather is excluded. A close relative of this, *N. bulbocodium* var. *romieuxii*, is a little tougher and can be grown in the milder counties, producing its lovely widely flaring trumpets of pale lemon in February. These tiny species of the Bulbocodium type are only about 8–12 cm in height and very different in appearance from other more well-known types of Narcissus, forming a distinct group of their own. The six perianth segments (corolla) are very small and narrow compared with the corona which is widely funnel-shaped, quite unlike that of the trumpet Daffodils or the small cup-like coronas of the Jonquils and Tazettas. In all these other groups the perianth segments are wide, petal-like and showy, forming a significant part of the flower. There are many different varieties of *N. bulbocodium*, in all shades from pale sulphur to deep golden yellow and with a wide range of flowering times, but the North African var. *romieuxii* is usually the earliest, with most of the Spanish forms coming a little later, in March. They all have very narrow, thread-like green leaves, much more slender than in most of the other species in which they are usually flattened and very often greyish-green.

A miniature trumpet Narcissus species which may sometimes also flower in February in mild winters is *N. asturiensis*, a native of northern Spain. This grows to only 10 cm high, with narrow, grey strap-shaped leaves and perfect tiny Daffodil flowers in deep yellow, with a trumpet only 1.5–2 cm long. Similar to this, but slightly larger and flowering regularly in January or February, is the excellent *N.* 'Cedric Morris' which really qualifies as a first-rate winter-flowering plant. It is named after its discoverer, a famous Suffolk gardener and is, I am glad to say, slowly becoming distributed around in cultivation. There are a few other trumpet Daffodils which flower early and, during average winters, may well produce their first flowers during late winter, in particular the Spanish species, *N. cyclamineus*, and its hybrids such as 'Dove Wings', 'February Gold' and 'Peeping Tom'. The species was given its name because of the way in which the perianth segments reflex in Cyclamen fashion, leaving the trumpet protruding prominently. This feature is carried through to the hybrids which are mostly larger versions of the species, as a result of crossing with the more robust trumpet Daffodils, and it gives them a most distinctive and graceful appearance. The wild species has deep yellow flowers with a trumpet about 2 cm long and reaches a height of not more than about 15 cm, whereas the hybrids may be 30–40 cm tall.

Another dwarf hybrid which is one of the first to flower and of very strong constitution is 'Tête-a-Tête'. This has *N. cyclamineus* as one parent, and the 'swept-back', deep yellow corolla clearly shows this, with the taller, cluster-headed *N. tazetta* as the other parent. The result is that this excellent little 15–20 cm-tall hybrid produces more than one flower on each stem and is thus in bloom over a long period.

CULTIVATION   All the above-mentioned *Narcissus* species and hybrids prefer open, sunny sites with good drainage, but *N. cyclamineus* and its hybrids will not do so well in very hot, dry situations and are a better choice for damper, heavier soils. 'February Gold', for instance, is excellent for planting in damp, rough grass around apple trees, where it will flower much earlier than the standard Daffodil varieties, thus extending the season considerably. The wild species *N. cyclamineus* is a good plant for cool, semi-shaded situations where it can be left to naturalise without disturbance, along with other moisture-loving bulbs such as *Erythronium* and *Anemone blanda*. Deciduous trees and shrubs provide ideal cover for such bulbs, allowing the winter sun through early in the year, but giving shade from the scorching sun in summer.

37 *Crocus imperati* 'De Jager' has a yellowish outside to the flowers.   **38** *Crocus nudiflorus*, a good autumnal Crocus in grass.
39 *Crocus ochroleucus* in grass with *Cotinus* leaves in autumn.   **40** *Crocus sieberi* 'Violet Queen', an easy free-flowering spring
species.   **41** *Crocus sativus*, the source of saffron.   **42** *Crocus tommasinianus* with Snowdrops in late winter.

43 *Crocus tommasinianus* 'Ruby Giant' with *Cornus stolonifera* stems.   **44** *Crocus tournefortii* keeps its flowers open in dull weather.   **45** *Crocus vernus* 'Pickwick' naturalised in grass. One of the Large Dutch varieties.   **46** *Crocus* 'Yellow Dutch' ('Yellow Giant', 'Golden Yellow') in grass.   **47** *Cyclamen coum* and its white form, a true winter-flowering species.
48 *Cyclamen hederifolium* under deciduous shrubs in autumn.

49

50

51

52

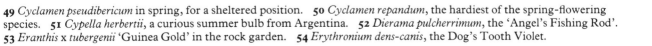

53

54

49 *Cyclamen pseudibericum* in spring, for a sheltered position.   **50** *Cyclamen repandum*, the hardiest of the spring-flowering species.   **51** *Cypella herbertii*, a curious summer bulb from Argentina.   **52** *Dierama pulcherrimum*, the 'Angel's Fishing Rod'.
53 *Eranthis* x *tubergenii* 'Guinea Gold' in the rock garden.   **54** *Erythronium dens-canis*, the Dog's Tooth Violet.

55

56

57

58

59

60

55 *Erythronium* 'Pagoda' is ideal for a semi-shaded position.　**56** *Erythronium revolutum* in a peat garden.　**57** *Erythronium* 'White Beàuty', perhaps the best of the Dog's Tooth Violets.　**58** *Eucomis comosa*, a South African species but very hardy. **59** *Fritillaria camtschatcensis* likes a cool soil, rich in humus.　**60** *Fritillaria imperialis* 'Lutea Maxima', a striking yellow 'Crown Imperial'.

N. bulbocodium and its varieties all like very good drainage and are best on the sunny rock garden where their bulbs will dry out whilst dormant, but they must have plenty of moisture available in spring and a peaty soil mixture will assist in this. The early-flowering forms should be given a site where they receive some shelter from icy winds, and a dense evergreen shrub such as a conifer can provide such protection, with the bulbs planted on its south side. A carpeting plant such as an alpine Phlox can be used for a ground cover for these early bulbs which push up through without difficulty and are protected from mud splashes.

N. asturiensis and *N.* 'Cedric Morris' are both easily cultivated in a sunny, well-drained situation and are ideal for a rock garden or front of a border where there is to be little disturbance.

The planting depth varies from 5 cm for the small species such as *N. bulbocodium* and *N. asturiensis* up to 10 cm for the more robust varieties like 'February Gold'.

All of those mentioned will increase naturally to some extent by bulb division, so that propagation is purely a matter of digging up clumps and splitting them in the autumn. The *N. cyclamineus* hybrids are particularly vigorous in this respect, and need lifting about every three years to prevent the clumps from becoming too congested. Seeds are also produced, especially by the species, and these can be collected and sown separately in pots in the autumn. When the young bulbs are large enough to handle, after one or two growing seasons, they can be planted out into the open ground, but may take two or three more years to flower. It is fun to try crossing Narcissus species if you have the time and patience to wait for the results, but *N. bulbocodium* will not, apparently, hybridise with the trumpet Daffodils.

SCILLA

Apart from one or two autumn-flowering species, the Squills are associated with early spring, but a few of them can be early enough to brighten up the late winter and are sometimes in flower in February, or even late January, with the help of a few mild days. They are nearly all blue-flowered but are far from uniform in their appearance, for the depth and shade of colour varies widely and the shape of the flowers can be anything from flat and starry to bell-like, sometimes only one per stem but in most species several in a raceme. The three species which might be tried for the winter garden are the Iranian *S. tubergeniana* (sometimes found under its correct but impossibly difficult synonym *S. mischtschenkoana*!), *S. siberica* and *S. bifolia*. The first has very pale blue, relatively large, cup-shaped flowers with darker blue stripes along the centre of each segment. This begins to open its flowers immediately it pushes through the ground and continues flowering over a period of several weeks as the stem elongates, but it never exceeds more than about 10 cm, even when fully developed. Its soft blue colour associates very well with grey foliage such as is provided by some of the spurges like the dwarf *Euphorbia myrsinites* or bush-like *E. characias*, and a drift of *Scilla* around an established plant of the latter is a charming combination. Rosemary (*Rosmarinus officinalis*) is another good companion plant.

Similar, but with bell-shaped flowers in dark vivid blue, is *S. siberica*, which inhabits the Crimea, Turkey, the Caucasus and Iran. It is usually sold in its variety 'Spring Beauty' which has very intense blue flowers, but there are other named variants such as 'Alba', white, and 'Taurica', a paler blue. The deep blue form is rather striking when planted with *Cyclamen coum* which, although starting to flower earlier than the Scilla, is long-lasting and usually still blooming in February and March. *S. siberica* is also effective when providing a splash of blue among the Winter Heathers.

S. bifolia, from eastern Europe and Turkey,

is a very different plant with a pair of basal leaves and short racemes of small, starry, deep mauve-blue flowers in the common form, but there are also white ('Alba') and pink ('Rosea') varieties in cultivation. It is an attractive little species, good for naturalising under deciduous shrubs or for planting among such subjects as Hellebores in perennial borders where there is little disturbance and it can increase freely.

CULTIVATION   These three Scillas are all of the easiest cultivation, preferring sites which are not too hot and sunny and which have plenty of moisture available in spring, although not waterlogged. In very heavy soils it is best to mix in some humus in the form of leafmould or peat, and some sharp sand when planting. The bulbs should be planted about 5 cm deep in heavy soils, 7–8 cm in sandy soils. A position in dappled shade beneath deciduous shrubs or trees is ideal and preferably one which is not frequently cultivated, apart from weeding. Once established they are best left undisturbed, so long as they are growing well, and the only attention needed is an annual top dressing of leafmould or old compost in the summer or autumn. Propagation is easiest by division of established clumps in the autumn before root growth commences. Seeds can be gathered and sown in pots but this is a much slower method and the efforts are better reserved for the more unusual bulbs which do not increase naturally.

3

THE BULB GARDEN IN SPRING
(March–May)

One of the highlights of the garden year is, of course, the early spring when there is a great awakening in the garden, spear-headed by the bulbous plants which are waiting, buds ready formed, for the first few warm days to trigger off new growth. The great majority of the hardy spring-flowering bulbs suitable for growing outside in our gardens originate in the Mediterranean region and Western Asia, and a few from similar latitudes in North America. Hardly any of the multitude of amazing South African spring bulbs are frost-hardy and, since they need to be grown in a slightly heated greenhouse, they are not considered here as subjects for the spring garden. The same applies to South American bulbs, although there are one or two attractive hardy species which are well worth growing, including the prolific *Ipheion uniflorum* and the stunning Chilean Blue Crocus, *Tecophilaea*.

Like the autumn-flowering bulbs, the spring ones are mainly plants from areas which receive most of their rainfall in autumn, winter and spring which is then followed by a warm, dry period, during which time the bulbs ripen and form buds for the coming season. Some species have evolved to flower immediately the cooler, damper weather arrives, that is they are autumn-flowering, while others make root growth but keep their shoots below ground until the worst of the winter is past, then produce flowers and leaves together in spring. A few, mostly from low altitudes (e.g. some Scillas, Ornithogalums and Muscari) produce leaves in the autumn but delay flowering until spring.

Thus the method of growing most spring bulbs is similar to that for the autumn bulbs. They are purchased and planted in early autumn, ready for the coming cool, damp growing season and, on the whole, they need a sunny position in well-drained soil which will dry out in summer, enabling the bulbs to ripen in the same way as they do in nature. As with all groups of plants, there are exceptions to the general rules, and certain species such as the Dog's Tooth Violets (*Erythronium*) and our own native Bluebells, are woodland plants which, although dying down in summer and becoming somewhat dry because the tree roots have removed most of the available moisture, do not become sun-baked like those on exposed Mediterranean hillsides or rocky mountain slopes.

Most of the spring bulbs are dwarf plants, flowering soon after emerging from the ground, in contrast to the summer ones which are mostly rather tall, with a long growing season before flowering. This makes them ideal for rock gardens, the front of borders beneath deciduous shrubs, and for planting in areas of rough lawn, since they flower when the grass is short and are almost over before it becomes necessary to start mowing the lawn for the summer. There is, in fact, such a diversity of spring bulbs that species can be chosen which are suitable for almost any site and situation in the garden. In open spaces in shrub borders, a great array of Anemones, Scillas, Chionodoxas, Muscari, Crocus and Narcissus can be planted to accompany Helle-bores, which are at about their best in March or early April, along with blue and red Pulmonarias, to give lovely splashes of colour which will give way later on to the flowering shrubs behind. On the whole it is best to keep spring bulbs out of the herbaceous border, since in the latter the plants require a certain amount of cultivation and rich diet, with frequent lifting and dividing if their vigour is to be maintained. This sort of treatment is not good for the majority of bulbs which prefer to remain undisturbed to increase at will, al-though there is always a place for groups of the larger Daffodils and Tulip hybrids among herbaceous plants.

For rock gardens there is a similar wide choice of subjects, the sunny well-drained pockets being ideal for such treasures as the dwarf Tulip species, miniature Narcissus, Cyclamen, Crocus and Reticulata Irises, while the cooler semi-shaded corners make perfect homes for the lovely Trilliums and Erythron-iums. For those with peat gardens containing dwarf Rhododendrons and other ericaceous plants, these two last-mentioned genera are perfect and will revel in the moister, shadier conditions provided by such a home.

For grassy places where the mowing can be left until May or June, there is again a wide choice of suitable spring bulbs which will flourish and possibly naturalise if a period of at least five to six weeks is allowed between flowering and cutting the grass. This should be sufficient time for the leaves to mature and at least partially die down, thus strengthening the bulb for the next season, and in some cases it may be enough time for the seed pods to ripen as well. If a naturalising colony is to build up, self-sown seedlings must be encour-aged, so in this case it pays to avoid cutting the grass until the seeds are shed. Cutting the foliage down while it is still green may not do much damage in one year, but will lead to poor flowering and eventually to the death of the bulbs. It is fun experimenting with a variety of bulbs in grass, apart from the obvious Daffodils. In a small patch of rough grass I have had success with various *Allium*, *Crocus*, *Muscari*, *Ornithogalum*, *Scilla*, *Fritil-laria*, *Iris histrioides*, *Tulipa* and *Leucojum* species which give a range of flowering times through March and April; after this I have avoided any later bulbs so that some tidying up can be done before the grasses and weeds begin to flower and seed. One can, of course, given a little extra space, keep a section of rough grass for the whole year round in which summer and autumn bulbs, and other plants, can be incorporated.

These dwarf spring bulbs are also very suitable for growing in raised beds and in sink or trough gardens such as one might place on a terrace in view of the house. Double walls, with planting space between, also give ideal sharply-drained conditions, and small alpines can be planted to spread the interest through the season. In such situations the very smallest of bulbs can be tried, without the danger of losing them in the open border among other coarser plants, and of course they are much easier to view at close quarters, which is the only way to appreciate the minuscule beauty of some of them.

The Spring-Flowering Bulbs

ALLIUM

Only a few of the enormous number of bulbous species of 'Onion' are spring-flowering, and the most striking ones from an ornamental point of view are undoubtedly the large summer-flowering 'drumstick' types which will be found in the chapter on the Bulb Garden in Summer. In late spring, in May, there are some species just starting their display, and in particular I must mention the Asiatic *A. karataviense*, for it is such an extraordinary plant. At ground-level it produces broad, flat leaves which are greyish-green tinted purple, and between these in late spring arises a large spherical umbel, some 15–20 cm in diameter on a stout 15 cm stem, so that the head of pinkish flowers almost rests on the leaves. May also sees the start of flowering of one of the best rock garden Alliums, *A. oreophilum* (*A. ostrowskianum*) which has narrow grey-green leaves and smaller umbels of deep pinkish-purple flowers on 10–15 cm stems. The common Mediterranean *A. neapolitanum* is also worth growing for its pure white flowers on slender stems 20–30 cm in height, a rather delicate-looking species with fairly loose umbels. Quite different from the usual run of starry-shaped Allium flowers is *A. triquetrum* which has pendent bell-like blooms in white with a green stripe down each segment, and they are sweetly scented. The stems, which may reach 15–20 cm in height, are distinctive in being three-cornered, hence the name.

CULTIVATION The species mentioned can all be obtained and planted in the autumn about 4–5 cm deep. *A. karataviense*, *A. oreophilum* and *A. neapolitanum* all require an open, sunny situation in well-drained soil, but *A. triquetrum* needs semi-shade and, since it is capable of increasing rapidly, is best regarded as a bulb for naturalising, for it can become a garden weed in mild districts; it should not, for instance, be planted in a rock garden. *A. karataviense* is a striking plant which stands out rather well if a small group is planted in a space in a paved area, and it is also suitable for the front of a sunny border. *A. ostrowskianum* is best in a sunny pocket on the rock garden or at the front of a border among greyish-leaved plants such as Sage, while *A. neapolitanum*, with its slender, graceful appearance, can be planted with great effect in groups between low-growing, contrasting broad-leaved subjects such as Bergenias and Pulmonarias which

will be coming to the end of their flowering display when the Allium is in bloom.

Propagation of these Alliums is really simply a matter of lifting clumps of bulbs in late summer and dividing them. They are also likely to produce seeds, and self-sown seedlings will almost certainly crop up, so there is little need to collect the seeds and grow them on separately.

ANEMONE

There are many species of Anemone distributed in Europe, Asia and America, but only a few are tuberous rooted and fall within the scope of this book. Among these few, however, there are some very important garden plants, such as the 'De Caen' and 'St. Brigid' strains of *A. coronaria*. Some Anemones which have elongated rhizomes rather than tubers are also included here, since they are usually obtainable through bulb nurseries in their dormant state, although they should not at any time be dried out completely. The Wood Anemone (*A. nemorosa*) is an example of this type. Most of the species included here are compact and can be used in the rock garden, for naturalising among shrubs or, in the case of *A. coronaria* and *A. pavonina*, planting at the front of sunny borders.

CULTIVATION The Anemones described below are so varied in their cultural requirements that these are given under the individual species. For propagation purposes, it will be found that most of them increase naturally into patches and to increase them is simply a matter of division. Seeds take much longer to produce flowering plants, but in the case of *A. coronaria* it does produce strong young flowering tubers in about 18 months and some growers prefer to raise their plants in this way. The planting depth for the following species is about 5 cm except for *A. nemorosa* and *A. ranunculoides*; the rhizomes of these should be covered with soil to a depth of only 2–3 cm.

A. apennina. This easy and lovely species is from the mountains of southern Europe. It grows to about 10–15 cm in height, with ferny leaves overtopped by many-petalled bright blue flowers which open out flat in the sun in March or April. The best position is in leafmould-rich soil in semi-shade between shrubs, where it can be left undisturbed to increase into solid patches over the years. A white form, 'Alba', is sometimes available. The clumps can be divided and moved successfully in spring after flowering.

A. blanda. A well known early Anemone which is very hardy despite its origins in Greece and southern Turkey. It is about 5–10 cm in height, with attractive dissected leaves and 3.5–4.5 cm diameter flowers, each with 10–20 petals. There are several named varieties in blue, white, pink and red, including 'Atrocaerulea' (dark blue), 'Charmer' and 'Pink Star' (pink), 'Radar' (bright reddish magenta) and 'White Splendour'. A. blanda will grow in full sun or dappled shade and should be left undisturbed to increase naturally, when seedlings may appear as well. In some years it will bloom in late winter so is also included in the Winter Section on page 37.

A. coronaria. The much-loved 'Poppy Anemone' from central and eastern Mediterranean regions, which has been selected over a long period, resulting in the popular florists' Anemones 'St. Brigid' and 'De Caen'. Although naturally spring-flowering from an autumn planting, it is possible to buy the tubers for spring planting as well, for flowering in summer, and further details of these will be found in the Summer Section. The soil for A. coronaria should be well-drained and rich, with plenty of old compost added, and protection from frosts is necessary during the winter months to encourage well-formed flowers. A sheltered site in full sun is ideal and, by covering with a cloche, a succession of flowers can be obtained during any mild spell through the winter and early spring. A. coronaria

varieties grow to about 15–25 cm in height with parsley-like leaves and large flat flowers in a great range of colours, white, blue, red and violet. The 'De Caen' strain has single flowers and the 'St. Brigid' semi-double, both with a dark mass of stamens in the centre, often surrounded by a zone of cream or yellow.

A. fulgens. This red-flowered Anemone is so similar in its requirements to A. coronaria (above) that the comments made under that species will apply equally well. It is about the same size but has less finely-dissected leaves, especially the three small ones carried on the stem below the flower, which are only toothed. The flowers are brilliant scarlet, either with a few broad petals or, in the variety 'Multipetala', with many narrow ones; they are produced in March or April. This bright red Anemone can be grown with great effect in a group amid grey-leaved plants such as Lavender and Santolina chamaecyparissus.

A. nemorosa. The spring Wood Anemone. Being a British native woodlander this is very easily cultivated in cool, shaded places beneath shrubs, in soil which has been enriched with leafmould. The wild white form is attractive but may be too vigorous for small gardens, for its creeping, stick-like rhizomes soon form large patches, but it is fine for naturalising and flowers at the same time as Narcissus 'February Gold' in my garden, making a lovely combination under deciduous shrubs. There are several beautiful varieties, especially the soft bluish-lavender ones such as 'Robinsoniana', 'Allenii' and 'Blue Bonnet', and some interesting double and semi-double ones, for example 'Alba Plena'. They all grow to between 10–20 cm in height, with ferny leaves in early spring, overtopped by solitary flowers which, in the case of the large blue varieties, are up to 3–4 cm in diameter. The rhizomes, although usually offered by bulb nurseries in their autumn 'dry bulb' catalogues, should never be dried out completely and, if obtained in the dry state, must be planted immediately. It is better, when dividing or transplanting A.

nemorosa, to do this after flowering, in late spring. The more refined varieties are excellent rock garden or peat garden plants, for cool, semi-shaded situations.

A. pavonina. The Peacock Anemone from Greece is very similar to *A. coronaria* in its looks and requirements, although it does seem to be slightly more tolerant of our northern weather conditions and is more likely to settle down and make a long-lasting colony. Like *A. fulgens*, it can be distinguished from *A. coronaria* by its less-divided leaves. *A. pavonina* comes in a great range of flower colour, often in rather attractive pastel shades, and it is usually offered in catalogues as the famous 'St. Bavo' strain which contains a good mixture. The varieties of *A. pavonina* are as good for cutting as the 'St. Brigid' and 'De Caen' strains and are excellent for the front of a warm sunny border which has protection from cold winds. Grey foliage plants such as *Cistus* and Rosemary are ideal natural companions.

A. ranunculoides. This should be cultivated in the same way as *A. nemorosa* varieties and, indeed, is very similar in overall appearance except that it has bright buttercup-yellow flowers. These are about 1.5–2 cm in diameter, produced in March or April over the bronzy-green, ferny foliage and, apart from the 'ordinary' form, are to be found in a large single form known as 'Superba Major' and a double, 'Flore Plena'. Like *A. nemorosa*, the long rhizomes should not be dried out. It makes an excellent companion for other shade-loving plants such as *Hepatica* (*Anemone hepatica*), Hellebores and *Trillium* and is ideal in a cool part of a rock garden or on a peat bed.

ARISARUM

For those who enjoy plants for amusement as well as display, it is fun to grow the extraordinary *A. proboscideum*. The small tubers produce fairly ordinary green Arum type leaves on short stalks, so that they make a ground cover only about 5–8 cm high, and amid these in mid to late spring arise small, curiously shaped, deep brownish purple spathes with a white base, extended at the apex into a whip-like appendage up to 15 cm long, so that the whole plant has been likened to a group of mice diving down into a mat of foliage! It is not at all showy and one may have to search for the flowers amid the leaves, but it can be used as a carpeting plant of a most unusual kind.

CULTIVATION Although southern European, *A. proboscideum* is quite hardy and enjoys semi-shade in soil enriched with peat or leafmould, so it can be planted beneath deciduous shrubs as a ground cover. It increases naturally into a mat of tubers and can be divided easily for propagation purposes in autumn while semi-dormant, or in spring while in growth. Like many other hardy members of the Arum family the tubers prefer deep planting, at about 10 cm or more.

ARUM

The common British Lords and Ladies, or Cuckoo Pint, is an attractive part of our wild spring flora, but is scarcely of interest in the garden since it can usually be seen in hedgerows and woods nearby. There are, however, other species which either have more showy spathes than our greenish native one, or they have attractive foliage and are valuable as a foil for other plants or for flower arrangers. Three species are usually offered by bulb nurseries and these are really the best of the bunch, although for enthusiasts there are several others well worth growing and usually to be located in one or two of the specialist catalogues. *A. creticum* from Crete is the most showy species for its brightly coloured spathes which are carried on stems about 20–30 cm in height, overtopping the plain green leaves. The best form has yellow spathes, but there are creamy-white ones in cultivation as well. Unlike most Arums, the spathe of *A. creticum* curls back, leaving the yellow pencil-like spadix sticking up prominently. *A. dioscoridis* from Greece and Turkey is more like the Cuckoo Pint in having large, upright spathes carried amid plain green leaves, but in this case they are heavily and strikingly blotched with blackish-purple on a paler purple ground colour, or in var. *smithii*, on a pale green ground. Whereas *A. creticum* has a sweet scent, *A. dioscoridis* usually has a terrible smell, although this is only noticeable in a confined space, not in the open garden. The third species I have chosen, *A. italicum*, is not especially showy with its pale green spathes produced in spring, but is a superb foliage plant with beautifully creamy-veined arrow-shaped leaves produced in autumn and held all winter until late spring or summer, when they may be accompanied by spikes of bright red berries. The leaves, which are on stalks about 10–15 cm long, last well in water and therefore make ideal winter subjects for flower arrangers, but out in the garden they are also invaluable, being ideal for planting with Snowdrops and Hellebores in a semi-shaded situation. The variety 'Pictum' has the best foliage and is the form usually offered by nurseries. Since it is such a good winter foliage plant I have included it also in the Winter Section on page 38.

CULTIVATION Arum tubers are usually obtained in autumn, sometimes in spring, and should be planted deeply, at least 10 cm, in reasonably well-drained soil. *A. italicum* 'Pictum' does best in partial shade, in soil which retains moisture, rather than becoming hot and dry, so if there is a tendency to dry out it is best to add plenty of humus before planting. *A. creticum* and *A. dioscoridis*, however, prefer full sun, and a warm sheltered border is the best situation to choose. Once planted, they should be left undisturbed, unless it is wished to propagate them. With its yellow spathes *A. creticum* is rather striking against some dark foliage such as *Ceanothus* growing on a wall,

or can be attractive in front of the wall itself if it is a mellow brick colour. They all produce offsets and built up into clumps of tubers which can be lifted in early autumn for division, before growth commences, or, more easily, in spring. Do not forget, however, that they are deep in the soil and may well have pulled themselves down much deeper than the original planting, so that a spade rather than a trowel is usually necessary.

BULBOCODIUM

Although this name might be confused with *Narcissus bulbocodium*, there is certainly no question of muddling the plants, for this little bulb from the mountains of Europe is closely related to, and resembles, a Colchicum. *B. vernum* is the only species, producing its stemless, reddish-violet, funnel-shaped flowers in March or April, followed shortly after by two or three lanceolate leaves which elongate rapidly then die away for the summer months. Although not a striking plant, it is as attractive as any of the spring-flowering Colchicum species and certainly has a place in the bulb enthusiast's garden.

CULTIVATION *B. vernum* is a hardy plant and may be grown outside in a very well-drained, sunny position. The corms, which are shaped like a small Colchicum corm, are available in autumn and should be planted about 5 cm deep in sandy or gritty soil. Being a rather small species, only about 3 cm high when in flower, it is probably best placed in a raised bed or on a rock garden where it can be appreciated closer at hand and can be grown among other small alpines which will not swamp it later on. Propagation is not easy, for the corms do not divide up, so it is best to pollinate the flowers by hand in the hope of getting some capsules. If seeds are produced, they are best sown as soon as ripe and kept watered for the summer; germination should take place in winter or early spring and, at this stage, it is advisable to place them in a cold frame or greenhouse away from any hard frosts. The seedlings take four or five years to reach flowering size.

CALOCHORTUS

It is unfortunate that these gorgeous North American bulbous plants, which belong to the Lily family, are quite unsuitable for outdoor cultivation in most areas. In their native California, and in some of the adjacent States, they receive a good dry, warm summer rest period, and this seems to be one of the reasons for their failure to survive outdoors in countries with a damper climate. In pots in an alpine house or frame, where the watering can be controlled, they seem to be reasonably easy to grow. It is probable that long, wet winters with low light intensity are another reason for failure and, here again, protection from the elements undoubtedly helps.

I have successfully grown one of the easier species outdoors for a while, one of the Globe Lilies, *C. albus*, and this might be worth trying although it is seldom that any of the species are offered by even the specialist nurseries and it may not be easy to find. This flowers in late spring and is about 20 cm high, with several pendent white globe-like flowers which have the inner segments fringed and lined with hairs, quite unlike the much more showy Mariposa Tulips which have much larger, upward-facing flowers in gaudy colours. These appear to be even less amenable to outdoor cultivation, but the lovely yellow *C. luteus* is not too difficult to please.

CULTIVATION   Calochortus bulbs should be planted in autumn, about 6 cm deep in full sun in sandy, well-drained soil. The small group of *C. albus* which succeeded outdoors in my Surrey garden for several years was growing between some winter-flowering Heathers which must have provided considerable frost protection for the bulbs until they pushed through in spring. Seeds are normally produced fairly readily and they are not difficult to germinate, although it may be a wait of three or four years before flowers are seen.

CHIONODOXA

Commonly called Glory of the Snow, these small Scilla-like Turkish bulbs are among the first to appear in March or April. They all have bluish or lilac flowers, usually with a white eye in the centre, and differ from Scillas in having their stamens held together in a white cone; those of Scillas spread out away from each other on slender filaments. The flowers arise in a short raceme from between a pair of narrow leaves. It is unfortunate that in gardens the names of the various species have become interchanged and confused over the years, but I shall indicate the names under which they are most likely to be found in catalogues. In all, there are about six species, but three of these, from Cyprus and Crete, are rare in cultivation and not as showy as the Turkish ones.

The plant sold as '*C. luciliae*' is the species most readily available and is often seen in gardens, pushing up racemes of several flowers to about 10 cm in height, the flowers arranged more or less all on one side of the stem, especially in the bud stage. The usual colour is a bluish-lilac with a large white centre, but there are also pink and white forms which have been selected. The correct name of this is *C. forbesii*, but it is doubtful if this name has been generally adopted in nursery catalogues yet. Very similar to this, and really only differing in being stronger growing, with more flowers on the raceme, is a form offered as *C. siehei*. Likewise, one can find in literature and catalogues another slight variation under the name *C. tmoli* or *tmolusi*, referring to a mountain near Izmir in western Turkey. *C. sardensis*, however, is quite distinct from all these in having much clearer bright blue flowers with a small white eye, lacking the pinkish tinge which gives *C. forbesii* ('*C. luciliae*') its lilac-blue colour. *C. sardensis* also has several flowers on the raceme. The third species from Turkey is quite different in usually having only one or two flowers on each stem; these are larger than in either of the above species and are flattish and facing upwards, in pale lilac blue with a small white centre. This is known in gardens and nurseries as *C. gigantea* but its correct name, most unfortunately, is *C. luciliae*! This, too, has a pure white form which is most attractive.

CULTIVATION Chionodoxas are very easily cultivated in sun or partial shade, providing the soil is not too hot and dry in summer. The small bulbs are planted in autumn, about 3–5 cm deep in any reasonably well-drained soil which is best broken up with leafmould and sand if it is rather heavy. They are good rock garden plants and will also naturalise in slight shade under deciduous shrubs or at the front of borders which lack disturbance, in the sort of place where one would grow perennials such as Hellebores. Once settled in they are likely to seed themselves, so there is really no need to collect the seed and sow it separately; if this is done it can be sown straight away or kept until autumn. The bulbs also divide up to a certain extent, so that propagation can be by division of clumps in early autumn.

From time to time, one might come across a similar plant known as *Chionoscilla allenii*. This is a hybrid between *Chionodoxa forbesii* and *Scilla bifolia* and is somewhat intermediate between its parents, although more like the latter, with several smallish, deep violet-blue starry flowers in a raceme. Its cultivation needs are similar to those of Chionodoxa.

COLCHICUM

Most of the showy garden species of *Colchicum* belong to the autumn-flowering groups and they are to be found on page 24 in the chapter on the Bulb Garden in Autumn, but there are also some spring-flowering species which have much smaller Crocus-like flowers produced together with their leaves. Although goblet-shaped, roughly like those of a Crocus, it is easy to tell the difference by counting the number of stamens, three in *Crocus* and six in *Colchicum*.

Very few of the spring species are available in cultivation, and on the whole they are not robust plants suitable for outdoors, in contrast to the vigorous autumnal ones which form such an important part of the autumn garden display. The small *C. szovitsii* (*C. bifolium*, *C. nivale*) is occasionally encountered in the more specialist catalogues. This is a native of Turkey and the Caucasus, growing in meadows near the melting snows, and has pinkish flowers between a pair of leaves. Surprisingly, the most frequently available species is the oddity in the genus, the western Himalayan *C. luteum*, which has bright yellow flowers, the only species showing this coloration. Both of these are small plants, less than 10 cm in height at flowering time.

CULTIVATION These small spring Colchicums are best grown in an alpine house or cold frame where they have a little protection and can be dried off in the summer months, but if you have a raised bed for specialities such as these, or a rock garden, it is worth giving them a try. The corms should be planted in autumn about 6–8 cm deep, in a gritty soil to which some moss peat has been added, in a sunny position, ideally with a little protection from a dwarf evergreen, such as a Conifer, on the north side of the bulbs; this will break the cold winds of early spring.

Propagation is not easy, for their corms do not divide up very readily like those of the autumn species. Hand pollination might result in seed being produced and, if so, this can be grown on in pots for planting out after a year or two; it may, however, be three to five years before flowering corms are achieved.

CORYDALIS

There are a number of excellent tuberous-rooted species of these fascinating plants, which are actually related to the Poppies although their long-spurred flowers look more like those of a small Larkspur. It is a large group containing annuals, biennials and herbaceous perennials distributed all over the northern hemisphere, but the horticulturally most important are the tuberous species, mainly from Europe and western Asia, with a few in the Himalaya and Japan. Unfortunately, at present there are few in general cultivation, although they are becoming more popular and an increasing number of species is being offered by the more specialised nurseries. The underground part consists of a corky tuber, usually yellowish-brown in colour, and this produces attractively dissected leaves, frequently coloured bluish-green or grey, and these are overtopped in March or April by short, dense racemes of the long-spurred flowers. The European *C. solida* is the most easily obtained species and this is usually about 10–15 cm in height, with graceful tufts of leaves and, in the commonest form, flowers of a dull purplish-pink. Much better colour forms are around in cultivation and, hopefully, these will soon become more available for they range from a lovely delicate shade of pink to a deep brick red in the cultivar 'George Baker' ('*C. transsilvanica*'). There are also white forms of *C. solida*, but there are much better white-flowered Corydalis than this, notably *C. caucasica* 'Alba' which is a superb little plant with pure white blooms with an expanded lower lip, giving a much larger individual flower than *C. solida*. This is usually more dwarf than *C. solida*, at about 10 cm.

C. bulbosa (*C. cava*) is like a robust version of *C. solida*, reaching 20 cm in height, and this, too, has both purple and white forms; in this species, which is also European, the tuber is large and misshapen, whereas in *C. solida* it is about the size of a hazel nut and rounded.

Occasionally it is possible to acquire the Himalayan *C. diphylla* which is similar in size to *C. solida* but rather distinct in having more finely dissected, narrower leaves and looser racemes of whitish flowers which are tipped with purple on both the upper and lower lips.

Japan and eastern Asia give us the glorious blue *C. ambigua* which has only recently made its way into cultivation and is still very rare, but it is a tuberous-rooted species and much easier to grow than the intense blue Himalayan *C. cashmeriana* which prefers cool growing conditions and is not at all happy in the drier parts of the country but is prolific, for example, in Scotland; this latter species has a curious scaly rootstock, somewhat bulb-like, but it must never be dried out, whereas the tuberous-rooted ones can be treated in this way, although even they must not have a prolonged warm, dry period.

CULTIVATION Corydalis are obtained in the autumn and should be planted without delay about 4–5 cm deep in humus-rich soil. If peat is used it should preferably be of the moss type, not the black sedge peat. The humus should take care of any drainage problems, but if necessary some coarse, gritty sand can be worked in as well. The above-mentioned species are not plants for hot, sunny conditions and do best in partial shade where there is little disturbance, in association with other small perennials that will not swamp them. They are also ideal for a cool situation on a rock garden, especially the more unusual ones like *C. solida* 'George Baker', *C. caucasica*, *C. diphylla* and *C. ambigua* which will probably, because of expense, be obtained as a single tuber requiring close attention to make sure it does not get lost among other plants. The commoner, and therefore cheaper, species can be planted in larger quantities and these can be tried as an underplanting to various spring shrubs; for example, the purplish *C. solida* beneath yellow *Forsythia* or white *Magnolia stellata*, together with Hellebores, Pulmonarias, Primroses and other early Primulas such as 'Wanda'. I have also found that *C. solida* does quite well in rough grass, flowering at about the same time as *Narcissus* 'February Gold'.

The tubers of Corydalis divide up naturally so that established clumps can be lifted in late summer and split up. An alternative time is in late spring after flowering and, at this time, there is the advantage that you can still see the foliage and it is easy to find exactly where the tubers are. Seeds are also produced fairly readily and these will produce flowering tubers in only two or three years. They will normally give rise to self-sown seedlings, but if it is decided to collect them for separate sowing it is necessary to keep a daily watch on the capsules, for they suddenly split open and the seeds are lost. These must be sown immediately if a good germination is to be expected, and the pots kept watered for the summer.

CROCUS

This popular group of dwarf bulbs of the Iris family contains such a range of variety that they have the distinction of falling into the Spring, Autumn and Winter Sections of this book, for there are different species in flower from September through to April. Many of the ninety wild species are not, unfortunately, in general cultivation, but nevertheless there is still a wealth of different Crocuses, especially in the spring, the season with which their cheerful, goblet-shaped flowers are most associated. Unlike most of the autumn-flowering ones which often flower without their leaves, these lie in a state of semi-dormancy below ground through winter, waiting for suitable spring weather; the flowers and leaves then emerge together and the whole cycle of aerial growth is completed, through to the seeding stage, in only three months at the most.

Everyone knows the Large Dutch purple, white and striped varieties which are selections of the European *Crocus vernus* and whose large corms are sold in millions every year for forcing on the windowsill, for windowboxes or for an early splash of colour in the garden. There are many named varieties, but one can pick out a few exceptional ones, such as the intense deep shiny purple 'Paulus Potter', the paler pure whites like 'Kathleen Parlow' and 'Jeanne d'Arc', the silvery bluish-lilac 'Queen of the Blues' and conspicuously striped 'Pickwick' and 'Striped Beauty'.

Another very valuable, very popular, variety is the large yellow spring Crocus offered variously as 'Large Yellow', 'Golden Yellow' or 'Yellow Giant', which is a hybrid of the Balkan *C. flavus* (*C. aureus*), a species known in gardens since the time of Clusius in the sixteenth century. The hybrid is a sterile plant but increases at a tremendous rate by division of its corms, so the loss of its ability to seed is no drawback, and this is a superb garden plant with its large deep golden goblets in very early spring; in fact it is often so early that I have taken the precaution of mentioning it in the Winter Section as well!

These Large Dutch Crocuses are the product of a long process of selection, and another more recent group which is now achieving great popularity is that involving the Balkan and Turkish *C. chrysanthus* and its close relative *C. biflorus*. The former usually has yellow flowers and the latter blue, white or striped, but in cultivation the varieties of these and hybrids between them are usually grouped under the name *C. chrysanthus*, regardless of colour. They are delightful Crocuses, smaller and perhaps more graceful than the Large Dutch and flowering slightly earlier, as soon as the winter shows signs of letting up, usually in March in the open garden. There is a great range of variety now available, including mixed seedlings which can be great fun, since almost any combination can turn up. Good named varieties include 'E. A. Bowles' (yellow), 'Cream Beauty' (pale creamy-yellow with deep orange stigma), 'Gipsy Girl' (golden yellow striped brown), 'Snow Bunting' (pure white), 'Ladykiller' (white inside, strongly stained purple outside), 'Zwanenburg Bronze' (yellow inside, bronze outside), 'Blue Pearl' (delicate soft blue) and 'Bluebird' (white inside, blue outside).

Apart from these, there are forms of *C. biflorus* to be found in catalogues, including 'Parkinsonii' which has white flowers striped with purple on the outside and *C. biflorus* subsp. *weldenii* 'Fairy' which is white with a greyish exterior. The specialist nurseries may well offer quite a number of other varieties of *C. chrysanthus* and *C. biflorus*, as well as their wild forms which are in general rather smaller and less vigorous than the selected garden forms.

Mention has been made in the Winter Section of the earliest of the new year Crocuses, *C. tommasinianus*, since this prolific, lilac-flowered species normally accompanies the Snowdrops and Winter Aconites. The Greek *C. sieberi* will be found there as well, although this, and *C. ancyrensis* 'Golden Bunch', are really 'overlap-plants' which in some years will start to flower in winter but in cold seasons may be delayed until March.

Russia has provided us with two excellent yellow spring Crocuses, *C. korolkowii* from Central Asia and *C. angustifolius* (*C. susianus*) from the Crimea. The former has a brownish-bronze speckling on the outside of the yellow flowers and its corms are said to have the useful characteristic of being mouse-resistant, although I cannot comment on the reliability of this. *C. angustifolius*, the 'Cloth of Gold' Crocus, has flowers of a brilliant golden yellow, also bronze on the exterior, which turn themselves almost inside-out in the sunshine, the segments rolling right back past the horizontal. Sometimes also available is the Turkish *C. olivieri* which is an unmarked deep orange-yellow, with rather broad, deep green leaves.

A particular favourite of mine, although not a large-flowered, showy plant, is *C. fleischeri*, a species from western Turkey which has most interesting corm tunics, worth inspecting at close quarters with a magnifying glass, for they consist of intricately woven fibres. This has white flowers with a purplish stain near the base on the outside, a yellow throat inside and a bright orange-red stigma divided into many slender branches, so it really is quite a colourful Crocus, although diminutive.

Much larger-flowered is the Italian *C. imperati* which is usually sold as the garden selection 'De Jager'. This has biscuit-coloured buds, striped lengthways with purple-brown, but as they begin to open the bright violet of the inside is revealed, enhanced by a yellow throat and yellow stamens. Similar, in that it has bicoloured flowers which are violet on the inside and striped on the outside, is *C. corsicus* which is, however, smaller and is a paler, more lilac shade. This has the distinction of being one of the latest of the Crocuses to flower, usually in April, the other being its close relative *C. minimus* which also comes from Corsica. This is even smaller than *C. corsicus*, but the size does not detract from its beauty, for it is a very attractive bright lilac, with conspicuous markings on the outside, and the flowers are pleasingly proportioned.

Of the commonly available spring Crocuses I must not forget *C. etruscus* which is usually seen in its garden variety 'Zwanenburg'. This is a very vigorous, floriferous Crocus with lilac flowers shaded with a slightly paler greyish colour on the outside, perhaps not as colourful as some of the others described above, but nevertheless a first-rate garden plant.

CULTIVATION All of the Crocuses mentioned are easily cultivated in the open garden without protection and are obtained and planted in the autumn. The corms should be placed about 5–6 cm deep in a sunny, well-drained position for most species, although *C. vernus* varieties and *C. flavus* will tolerate a little shade. If the soil is very heavy it is best broken up by adding gritty sand and moss peat and, if very acid, it may be improved for Crocuses by adding garden lime, but not of course near any lime-hating plants such as Rhododendrons.

The more robust varieties of *C. vernus* ('Dutch Crocus') and *C. flavus* ('Large Yellow') are large and vigorous enough to be grown in mixed borders to give an early display before the herbaceous plants of summer begin to grow, but to me they are at their most attractive when planted informally in grass, perhaps dotting the ground beneath an early variety of Prunus (Almond or Flowering Cherry) or on a grassy bank where the mowing can be left until their leaves have died down in late May. *C. flavus* is also ideal for mass-planting beneath deciduous shrubs where, if the birds leave them alone, they will make a golden carpet in the spring sunshine before the shrubs come into leaf and provide shade for the area in the summer. There is, I'm afraid, little answer to bird damage, and the attacks seem to be quite haphazard and for no purpose. One can drape black cotton everywhere over the Crocuses, but that tends to spoil the effect anyway, and so on the whole it seems better to take a chance. After several years of losing all the flowers, I find that the last few seasons have been completely free of damage, as if the offenders have moved away or the new generation is not interested in Crocuses!

The *C. chrysanthus* and *C. biflorus* varieties are best in a sunny, well-drained spot where there is not so much competition and, being early flowering, are ideal for planting in a border near the house, where their very cheerful colours will brighten the first spring days. These like a position where the soil becomes fairly warm and dry in summer to ripen the corms. Most of the varieties are fairly cheap to buy, so it is worth experimenting with them in different places, sometimes with unexpected and pleasing results—such as the successful colony of 'Cream Beauty' which has built up in my garden in rough grass at the foot of a shrub.

The other species mentioned above are best grown in a rock garden or sunny border where they can be left undisturbed as long as they are doing well. They are certainly not bulbs for growing in areas which are frequently cultivated, such as a herbaceous border. Heavy soils should be broken up by adding coarse, gritty sand, for most bulbs and especially these spring Crocuses will not tolerate any stagnant waterlogging. They look at their best when growing among alpines or rock plants, which require similar cultural conditions, and by choosing suitable companions their effectiveness can be improved. The lilac and violet species associate well with greyish-leaved plants like some of the dwarf species of *Artemisia*, Lavender, *Anthemis* and *Achillea*, while the yellow and white ones show up best if growing near dark-leaved subjects such as deep green dwarf Conifers or small evergreen shrubs like *Daphne retusa*, but these paler Crocus colours also blend well with grey foliage so there is plenty of scope for experimental planting.

Most Crocuses, particularly the ones mentioned, will increase naturally by division, so that propagation is just a simple matter of lifting established clumps of corms in the early autumn and dividing them up. The speed at which increase takes place varies a lot from species to species, the *C. vernus* and *C. flavus* varieties being particularly vigorous in this respect. You can always tell whether the clumps have increased enough to make it a worthwhile operation, for each shoot which appears in spring represents a new corm for the autumn.

CYCLAMEN

Although the hardy Cyclamen species really come into their own in the autumn and winter with the superb *C. hederifolium* (*neapolitanum*) and *C. coum*, there are several attractive spring-flowering ones as well. The main drawback in the case of these is a general lack of hardiness, and the only one I have succeeded with for any length of time without the protection of a frame or greenhouse is *C. repandum*. This is a lovely plant, with rich reddish-carmine flowers stained darker towards the 'nose' of the flower, and with a delicious fragrance. These are produced in late April or May, together with the rather dark green heart-shaped leaves which have a certain amount of silvery zoning. In addition to a pure white form there are two geographical variants of this, the variety *rhodense* from Rhodes which has almost white flowers with a carmine 'nose', and 'Pelops' from the Peloponnese, which is a slightly darker pink. Both have leaves which are curiously splashed with silver, not in distinct zones like those of ordinary *C. repandum*. These are interesting variations for the specialist, but I find them less hardy and they are probably best reserved for a frame or greenhouse. Similarly rather tender are the small white *C. balearicum* and *C. creticum* which are very alike, often with very silvery leaves, and well worth trying in very sheltered southern gardens. *C. pseudibericum* from southern Turkey is a beautiful species, having large deep carmine flowers with an almost blackish-purple stain around the nose and attractively marked leaves which are toothed at the margin. *C. libanoticum*, a rare species from the Lebanese mountains, must also be mentioned for it is perhaps one of the loveliest of all the Cyclamen species, having large, soft-pink flowers with a ring of reddish marks like the letter 'm' around the 'nose'; this, too, has silvery-green zones on the leaves which are purple on the undersides.

CULTIVATION   *C. repandum* is the hardiest of the spring Cyclamen, apart, that is, from *C. coum* which will be found grouped with the winter-flowering bulbs on page 41. The ordinary form of *C. repandum*, which comes from Italy and Yugoslavia, is best grown in a partially-shaded spot in well-drained soil rich in leafmould. The tubers are normally obtained and planted in autumn, with about 3 cm of soil covering them. Each succeeding year in autumn it is beneficial to apply a dressing of loose leafmould or old compost, to keep the tubers well covered during the winter as an added precaution against severe frosts and to supply nutrients; no further feeding should be necessary, but if at any time they do appear to be weakening, some bonemeal in the early spring before growth commences should restore vigour.

C. repandum is also ideal for a rock garden in a slightly shaded pocket where there is a little protection from rocks on the north side of the plants to break any cold winds, for the spring foliage can be damaged by frost. It is an ideal subject for planting under a deciduous shrub such as one of the dwarf spreading, dissected-leaf forms of *Acer* (Maple) which will just be getting its fresh new leaves when the Cyclamen is in flower.

The varieties of *C. repandum*, and the other species mentioned above, are rather more tender and are likely to be damaged by hard frosts. They are really only suitable for outdoor cultivation in the milder districts, and a sheltered position should be chosen where there is protection from cold north and east winds by a dense evergreen shrub such as a compact Conifer.

Cyclamen species normally produce plenty of seeds and the capsules containing these will be found in summer at ground level where they have been pulled down by the coiling of the flower stems. In ideal growing conditions self-sown seedlings will appear, but it may be more desirable to collect the seeds and raise new tubers for planting elsewhere, so they should be gathered as soon as ripe and sown immediately. In a cold frame, and watered through the rest of the summer, these are likely to germinate during the next winter or spring and may flower in about three years. If there are quite a number to deal with, the young seedlings can be moved in their first season into trays of leafmould-rich soil and kept growing for as long as possible in a cold frame; when they do lose their leaves watering can be reduced, but at no time should they be dried out completely, for at this stage they can shrivel and die. Another alternative is to make a seedling bed in the open ground and prick them out directly into this for growing on to flowering size.

ERANTHIS

The Winter Aconite, although a harbinger of spring, is seldom in flower later than February in most parts of the country, and I have accordingly described it and its cultivation under the Winter Section on page 42. However, this does not mean that the plants should be ignored in spring, since this is the best time to lift and divide the clumps of tubers, while the foliage is still green and visible. They can be moved in the autumn but should not be left out of the ground for too long so that they dry out. Dried imported tubers bought in the autumn are usually cheap but have a low survival rate, so if possible it is best to obtain growing plants from one of the bulb nurseries which understand the importance of moving them in spring, as with Snowdrops.

ERYTHRONIUM

The Dog's Tooth Violets, which are mainly American although the commonest species is European, are among the loveliest of all spring flowers with their gracefully reflexed petals in a range of bright colours, and often attractively marble-patterned leaves. The common name derives from the strange elongated, pointed, whitish tubers which look rather like a dog's teeth. These first produce a pair of rather broad leaves at ground level and shortly afterwards leafless stems, to between 15 and 25 cm in height depending upon the species,

which carry one to five or sometimes more flowers. The leaves may be plain bright green, but in most of the cultivated species and varieties they are mottled with light and dark green or sometimes purplish-brown or silvery patterns. The flowers vary a lot in colour and there are species with white, pink, lilac and yellow flowers, often with well-defined zones of brown or yellow in the centre and the stamens differ in colour too, this in some cases being the feature which distinguishes between the species.

E. dens-canis is the only European species and the most commonly cultivated one; it is also the most variable in flower colour, ranging from white to lilac and pink or carmine with a conspicuous zone of brown or purple markings around the centre which itself may be yellow or brownish. The leaves are beautifully mottled and blotched with brown and bluish-green, probably the most attractive of all the species in this respect. Named varieties such as 'White Splendour', 'Rose Beauty' and 'Lilac Wonder' are available from some bulb nurseries, but the species is more often offered as a mixed collection.

Of the American Erythroniums, one of the best from the garden point of view is *E.* 'White Beauty' which is sometimes referred to as a variety of the widespread *E. revolutum*. 'White Beauty' has large white flowers with a ring of brown markings around the centre and bold brownish-green, mottled leaves. *E. revolutum* has similar foliage but the flowers are deep rosy-pink with yellow centres. 'Pink Beauty', 'Rose Beauty' and var. *johnsonii* are all good pink forms of this, of equal garden value. From time to time other white-flowered species, for example *E. oregonum* and *E. californicum*, become available and are interesting and beautiful although somewhat similar to 'White Beauty'. Quite different, however, is the Californian tongue-twister *E. tuolumnense* which has several bright buttercup-yellow flowers per stem, held over plain green, rather glossy leaves. This has been

61

62

63

64

65

66

61 *Fritillaria meleagris*, the Snakeshead Lily, is good in grass. **62** *Fritillaria pallidiflora*, a lovely species from Central Asia.
63 *Fritillaria persica* needs low-growing companions to accentuate its stature. **64** *Galanthus caucasicus* 'Hiemale', a truly
winter-blooming Snowdrop. **65** *Galanthus elwesii* has bold grey leaves and large flowers. **66** *Galanthus ikariae (latifolius)*,
unusual with its glossy green leaves.

67

68

69

70

71

72

67 *Galanthus nivalis* with Hellebores and Crocus. **68** *Galanthus nivalis* and Crocus in grass. **69** *Galanthus nivalis* 'Atkinsii', probably the best variety of Snowdrop. **70** *Galtonia candicans*, a tall stately Cape bulb for the summer border. **71** *Gladiolus byzantinus* with tall bearded Iris. A hardy species. **72** *Hyacinthus orientalis* with greyish Rosemary. One of the 'Multiflora' varieties.

crossed with one of the mottled-leaved species to give a vigorous hybrid, 'Pagoda', which has inherited the mottling but has paler, more sulphur-yellow flowers than *E. tuolumnense*. Another beautiful species is *E. hendersonii* which comes from California and Oregon. This is sadly rather rare in cultivation because it does not increase quite so freely as some of the others. The leaves are a dark green with bands of pale green across them, and the flowers are a lovely shade of lilac with a dark, rich purple centre, the only American species to have this sort of colouring.

CULTIVATION All the above-mentioned Erythroniums are woodland plants and enjoy semi-shaded situations with a good leafmould or compost content in the soil. This should ensure a cool, moist soil with free drainage, but if there is a tendency for the soil to be waterlogged it must be improved by digging in coarse gritty sand and raising the level above the surrounding land, for they will not tolerate stagnant conditions. On the other hand, they must not be grown in a site which will become hot and dry in summer. They are perfect plants for a cool, humus-rich pocket of the rock garden, or for a peat garden among other woodlanders such as *Anemone nemorosa*, *A. apennina*, dwarf Rhododendrons, Trilliums, Hellebores and Hepaticas. A choice of companion plants makes a great deal of difference to their appearance, and it is worth planning in advance of planting what the association will be, for the Dog's Tooth Violets are best left undisturbed once planted. For example a clump of *E.* 'White Beauty' is a marvellous sight among a drift of the ferny blue *Anemone apennina* or *A. nemorosa* 'Allenii', while *E. tuolumnense* shows up very well against dark evergreen foliage or the blackish peat of a peat garden. *E. dens-canis* will also grow in a rough lawn provided it is made up of the finer grasses and is not too strong-growing, in which case it will probably swamp the Erythroniums by the time they come into flower.

The tubers are obtained in autumn and should not be dried out too much at any stage. It is best to plant them straight away on arrival, about 10–15 cm deep to the top of the tuber, which is placed vertically in the soil; the old root scar should be visible to give an idea of which is the bottom. Once planted they are best left undisturbed to increase into clumps, which most species will do although *E. hendersonii* is an exception. Propagation is thus a matter of digging up clumps in autumn and dividing them, or by seed which is often produced fairly readily in long, upright capsules; the hybrids may not set seed but they usually clump up quite rapidly anyway. The seeds are best sown at once in pots and kept watered for the summer, in which case germination usually takes place in the following winter–spring. I prefer to sow thinly and keep the young tubers in the pots for one year, then plant out the whole ball of compost, thus avoiding handling them at this minute size. At no time after germination should they be dried out excessively, even when dormant, for they can easily shrivel and die. One tip, if you do decide to sort out the seedlings and handle them individually in the autumn, is that they are best looked for at the bottom of the pot. Erythronium tubers prefer to grow deeply and the young ones will rapidly pull themselves down, usually ending up among the crocks in the bottom.

FRITILLARIA

This large group of fascinating plants is distributed almost throughout the northern hemisphere and has a wide variety of types, from tiny species with flattish, upright flowers, to the more normal pendent bells and the large, showy Crown Imperials; some have solitary flowers while others have racemes of many flowers, and the colour range is wide, from yellow to red and green to chocolate brown or almost black, sometimes attractively chequered, sometimes striped.

Unfortunately, many of the species are rare in cultivation but the majority are, in any case, best grown in the protection of a cold frame or glasshouse where they can be given individual treatment and their flowers seen to better advantage. A few, however, do make excellent garden plants and, although mostly fairly expensive, are well worth obtaining for their charm and interest. The best is undoubtedly *F. meleagris*, the British native Snakeshead Lily which adorns several water meadows in the south of England. This grows to about 20–35 cm in height, with slender stems bearing narrow grey leaves and topped by a single large nodding bell in pinkish-purple, tessellated darker. There are several varieties differing in depth of colour and a pure white, 'Alba', which is perhaps the most beautiful. These varieties can be purchased under their separate names, such as 'Artemis', 'Charon' and 'Saturnus', but it is more usual to be offered a mixed collection at a cheaper rate and this is perfectly satisfactory for most purposes.

The most well-known Fritillary, popular for at least 400 years, is the Crown Imperial, perhaps one of the most stately and dramatic of all hardy garden plants. Its stout stems rise to a height of 60–90 cm and carry whorls of glossy green leaves in the lower half. The upper leafless portion of the stem, which is often purplish, is crowned in April by several large pendent bells which are in turn over-topped by a cluster of glossy leaf-like bracts, an arrangement which gives the Crown Imperial a unique appearance. In its native Iran, *F. imperialis* normally has flowers of a brick-orange colour, and this is the most usual form in gardens, but there are several named varieties such as 'Aurora', a coppery red, 'Rubra', bronze red, 'Rubra Major', red with dark veins, and 'Lutea Maxima', a bright yellow variety with paler green leaves. Looking inside the flowers one can see a large glistening drop of nectar at the base of each petal but this is normally hidden from view inside the nodding bells. If there are any points against the Crown Imperial they must be for its disagreeable smell, not unlike that of a fox, especially noticeable when the plant has just appeared through the ground in spring. However, this is a small criticism of an otherwise superlative plant.

Quite different from either of the above is *F. persica*, another native of the Middle East. This is also a tall-growing species, to about a metre when growing well, with the stems clothed in narrow, grey-green leaves and bearing a raceme of small pendent, deep-purple bells overlaid with a greyish waxy 'bloom' on the outside. The best form in cultivation carries the name 'Adiyaman', after a town in southern Turkey.

From farther east, in Central Russia, comes a splendid species which is as yet a little expensive, *F. pallidiflora*. It is very hardy and easy to grow, so the extra expense is perhaps justified for this beautiful plant. The stems reach about 30 cm at most and bear broad grey leaves and large, squarish, nodding bells of pale yellow flecked with brown.

The majority of Fritillaria species have flowers of green or brown, or a mixture of the two, and there are several in this colour range which are generally available. The Pyrenean *F. pyrenaica* is one of the best of these, with one or two purple-brown bells on 30–35 cm stems, their tips gracefully curled back to show the greenish-yellow interior. *F. acmopetala* from Turkey is of similar size and shape, but here the three outer petals are pale green, alternating with the three brown inner ones to give a markedly bicoloured effect. *F. pontica*, also Turkish in origin, has pale green bells with only a hint of brown and the petals are scarcely recurved at their tips; the most noticeable feature, however, is the whorl of three greyish leaves overtopping the flowers.

Rather smaller than these but nevertheless attractive is *F. uva-vulpis* (*F. assyriaca* of some nurseries) which is usually only 15–25 cm tall, with glossy green leaves and narrow purple bells tipped with yellow. *F. camtschatcensis*, from the Far East and Alaska, is an unusual species with whorls of glossy leaves and almost black bells on 20–30 cm stems, perhaps more a curiosity than a beauty but not difficult to grow and of definite interest value in the plantsman's garden.

CULTIVATION   Fritillaria bulbs are sold in the dried state in the autumn and should be planted more or less straight away, without further drying out. The bulbs of *F. meleagris* are often over-dried before they reach the customer and are damaged to the extent that they give poor results. Thus with this species it is best, if possible, to obtain fresh bulbs which have been cultivated and lifted just prior to selling, although few nurseries follow this practice. The soil for all the Fritillaries mentioned should be well-drained, and may be alkaline or acid, although the former is preferable. If it is inclined to be heavy and poorly drained, some sharp sand mixed in thoroughly will improve the conditions. For the smaller kinds the bulbs need be only 5 cm deep, but for Crown Imperials a depth of 15 cm of soil over the bulb is necessary.

Most of the species described above are best in full sun or perhaps dappled shade which dries out in summer. *F. pontica* is a woodland plant in the wild so will tolerate more shade than the others, and *F. camtschatcensis* needs cool, humid growing conditions, so is better suited to the woodland or peat garden. *F. uva-vulpis*, on the other hand, is ideal for the rock garden in view of its smaller size and should be planted in a sunny position with good drainage. Crown Imperials can be rather temperamental plants, flowering well and increasing for some people but dwindling away for others. There seems to be little reason behind this as far as I can ascertain, and it is probably largely a matter of local soil conditions and the climate of a particular garden. A position which dries out in summer seems to be essential, for if the bulbs lie dormant in cold, wet soil they will certainly not thrive. I have also noticed that they flower better with me when planted at least 15–20 cm deep. Almost certainly they prefer neutral or alkaline soils rather than acid, and I apply lime to my heavy soil before planting the bulbs. It is beneficial to apply fertiliser in the early spring before the new shoots emerge, and a potash-rich one is best, certainly not one with a high nitrogen content. Proprietary brands such as those produced for tomato crops are suitable.

F. meleagris is an ideal plant for growing in grass or in a perennial border containing other plants that enjoy cool growing conditions, such as Hellebores, Hepaticas, Snowdrops and Erythroniums. The white variety looks particularly fine if planted in a clump, with a few Forget-me-Nots allowed to seed around it. The green and brown Fritillaries can easily be lost among other plants and care must be taken that adjacent subjects do not compete. They are perhaps best planted in small groups on a rock garden where their sombre flowers will stand out. Nothing, however, can detract from the showy blooms of *F. imperialis*, and these look fine whether growing in a mixed border or on their own in a group surrounded by paving on a terrace. The yellow variety stands out particularly well against dark green shrubs and the orange-red colours are also enhanced by dark backgrounds, so it is worth choosing the site with care. A surprisingly effective planting I once saw was a group of orange Crown Imperials backed by a bush of purplish-leaved *Berberis thunbergii* 'Atropurpurea'.

Propagation of Fritillaries by seed is fairly simple in the case of the smaller species, but is very slow for *F. imperialis* and *F. persica* which may take many years to flower. They do, when growing well, divide up slowly, so that established clumps can be lifted and divided from time to time. When growing from seed it is best to sow in pots and keep the young bulbs in the pots for two growing seasons after germination, planting them out in the autumn at the start of the third season. Flowering will usually be in three to five years for the quickest ones, and up to seven for the slowest.

GALANTHUS

Depending upon the season and mildness of the district, the Snowdrops are either winter or very early spring flowering, apart from the oddity *G. reginae-olgae* which blooms in the autumn. I have therefore written about them in detail in the Winter Section on page 43, for even in the bad winter of 1985 they were past their best in March, having pushed up as the snow melted, and had finished their display even before the Squills, Chionodoxas and Grape Hyacinths had appeared. Nevertheless, Snowdrops are of course an essential part of the early spring garden, lifting the meagre display of mid-winter bulbs and carrying it through to the time when there are a host of others to take over.

As I have mentioned in the main entry to Galanthus, the best time to divide and replant them is in spring, just after flowering—'in the green' as the Snowdrop enthusiasts say—so spring is a time of activity if you want to spread them around the garden and create new plantings.

HERMODACTYLUS

This is the correct name for *Iris tuberosa* which is, to all but a botanist, quite obviously an Iris, albeit a rather curious one. The underground parts consist of odd-shaped elongated tubers which creep along and divide, eventually forming patches. These tubers give rise to long leaves which have a square cross-section like those of *Iris reticulata* and, in April or May, flower stems about 15–25 cm in height which carry typically Iris-shaped flowers about 5 cm across from the tip of one of the falls to another. The colour is perhaps the oddest thing about this Iris, for it is a greenish-yellow shade, almost translucent, and at the tips of the falls this changes to a dark brown or nearly

blackish-purple, these sombre colours having led to the common name of Widow Iris. Although not showy, it is a most unusual plant with delicately fragrant flowers and is occasionally seen as a cut flower in florists' shops.

CULTIVATION Being a native of warm Mediterranean hillsides, it is not surprising that *H. tuberosus* needs to be provided with a hot, sunny situation in the garden. It enjoys the same sort of conditions as *Iris unguicularis*, and a bed at the foot of a south wall is ideal for both these plants, where they can receive a long, warm rest period in summer. The creeping nature of the tubers means that it will tend not to stay in one place, so it is not a plant to be grown in a bed where there is to be frequent disturbance of the soil. It is not especially fussy about the type of soil so long as it is not waterlogged and dries out well in summer, but is especially good on chalky soils. The tubers should be planted in early autumn, about 6 cm deep, and old clumps may be lifted and divided at this time of year for propagation purposes.

The darkish colours mean that it stands out best against a light background, and I well remember seeing a magnificent colony in Yugoslavia, set off beautifully by a whitish limestone rock background. Thus a creamy or white wall would suit a planting of this Iris, or some grey foliage plants.

HYACINTHUS

The Hyacinth needs no introduction, for everybody knows the large-flowered forms of the deliciously fragrant *H. orientalis* which adorn almost every home in the country at any time from Christmas onwards, in a great range of colours. Apart from their immense value for forcing indoors, they are good garden plants and are ideal for formal bedding with their brilliantly coloured symmetrical spikes. In such displays the bulbs are normally replaced each year by new vigorous ones which will give the maximum effect, but this does not mean that Hyacinths only perform well for one year. They are excellent garden plants for growing informally among other subjects and, if conditions are reasonable, will go on for many years flowering reliably and sometimes increasing into clumps.

The wild *H. orientalis*, a Turkish native, has loose spikes of small flowers in mid blue, or occasionally pink or white, and this is a graceful plant, lacking the very heavy appearance of the large-flowered varieties. Unfortunately it is rarely obtainable and the nearest one can get in appearance are the varieties known as Roman Hyacinths, or the Multi-Flowered Hyacinths, which produce more than one stem per bulb. For those who object to the very formal almost artificial stiffness of the large-flowered ones, these are a much better choice, although not available in such a wide range of colours.

Quite different from this is the Pyrenean *H. amethystinus* which is also known as *Brimeura amethystina*. This is a small, slender plant, only 15–20 cm in height, with narrow leaves and a loose raceme of funnel-shaped bright blue or white ('Albus') flowers, each about 1 cm long and held in a somewhat one-sided spike, giving it the appearance of a miniature Bluebell.

CULTIVATION Hyacinth bulbs are obtained during the autumn and, for outdoor use, the 'prepared' bulbs should be avoided since these are the most expensive and are intended for forcing in pots indoors. They should be planted during the autumn, about 10 cm deep, in well-drained ordinary garden soil, acid or alkaline, with no special preparation necessary. They prefer a site that receives a fair amount of sun, but will take dappled shade and can be used with great effect in front of deciduous spring-flowering shrubs such as Forsythia. Both white and blue varieties of Hyacinth look splendid near one of these brilliant yellow shrubs and one can experiment with other combinations, such as pink Hyacinths next to white *Magnolia stellata* or *Spiraea thunbergii*, both of which flower in March or April, depending upon the weather. A chance success in my garden was an established clump of pink Hyacinths adjacent to an upright greyish Rosemary bush, a delightful combination which lasted for over five years until the Rosemary died of old age. Used in this way, informally around the garden, I regard Hyacinths as one of the most valuable of bulbs for creating splashes of colour here and there in mid-spring.

H. amethystinus is a much more refined little plant and needs placing at the front of a border or on a rock garden where it can be seen more easily. It is, however, not at all difficult to cultivate and, if growing well, will sometimes seed itself to form a colourful patch. The smallish bulbs should be planted about 5 cm deep.

The propagation of Hyacinths for the nursery trade is a specialised business which is, on the whole, best left to the nurseryman, and it is hardly worth the effort on a small scale since new bulbs are so easily obtained from any garden shop or nursery. Planted out in the garden, the varieties of *H. orientalis* often increase naturally and can be lifted and divided from time to time in the autumn. *H. amethystinus* usually produces seeds readily and these can be sown separately in pots for growing on to flowering-sized bulbs in about three years.

IPHEION

This is one of the few hardy spring-flowering bulbs from South America which have had any impact on our gardens, most of the lovely bulbs from the region being tender. *I. uniflorum* (*Milla uniflora*) is an excellent exception, producing its large, starry blue flowers, 3–4 cm in diameter, in April on stems not more than 15 cm long, over tufts of narrow, pale green leaves. Although, as its name suggests, only one flower is produced on each stem, more than one stem may be produced by each bulb, so that a clump can be very floriferous. This little plant, which comes from Argentina and Uruguay, is probably related to the Alliums and the small white bulbs do have a slight smell of Onions, but this is not noticeable unless they are bruised and even then is not strong enough to be disagreeable.

Apart from the 'ordinary' mid-blue form there is an excellent large-flowered white one, 'Alba', and several deeper blue-flowered ones of which 'Wisley Blue' is the most readily obtainable.

CULTIVATION The bulbs of *Ipheion* are best obtained and planted in autumn, for they start to grow and produce leaves early, and should be planted about 4 or 5 cm deep in well-drained soil which has been lightened with sand and leafmould if necessary. I find that it will not grow satisfactorily in the naturally cold, damp, heavy soil of my garden but is very prolific, for example, at Kew and Wisley, in semi-shaded leafmould-rich soil. When growing well the bulbs divide rapidly to form large patches which can be lifted and split up in early autumn or in late spring after flowering, so that propagation is very simple and it is not necessary to bother with seeds which seem to be produced rarely in any case.

IRIS

Although the word 'Iris' is most likely to conjure up thoughts of the colourful tall, bearded rhizomatous Irises of May and June, there are some earlier flowering bulbous types which are less well-known but very valuable garden plants in a less dramatic way.

The earliest and most popular are the dwarf 'Reticulata' Irises which are only about 10 cm in height at flowering time. These have a distinctive bottle-shaped or egg-shaped bulb, covered with a latticed tunic, and remarkable narrow greyish-green leaves which are almost square in their cross-section, except in one species, *I. bakeriana*, which has cylindrical leaves. All the Reticulatas flower very early, usually in February, so I have dealt with them in full in the Winter Section where their descriptions and method of cultivation are to be found.

Slightly later, in March or April, we have the 'Junos', a large group of fascinating Irises, barely known in gardens, although a few of them are very easily cultivated and are stocked by several of the specialist bulb nurseries. The dwarf species, such as *I. persica*, are on the whole difficult to keep and really require the protection of a bulb frame or alpine house, but the taller, more robust ones from Central Asiatic Russia, are good garden plants. The aptly named *I. magnifica* is one of the best, producing leafy stems up to about 60 cm in height and, in April, in the upper leaf axils, soft lavender flowers with an orange-yellow blotch in the centre of each of the falls. A characteristic feature of these Junos is that the leaves are not flat, like those of the bearded Irises, but are channelled and, since they are produced in one plane, not in a rosette, they look rather like a Leek plant in the early stages; but as the stem elongates they become spaced out alternately along its length. The flowers, too, have a point of distinction in that, instead of the standards being large and erect as in most Irises, in Junos they are small and reflexed, protruding at the base of the flower.

Quite a different colour from *I. magnifica*, but also from Central Asia, is *I. bucharica* which is slightly smaller at about 30–45 cm in height when in flower. This has either creamy flowers with a yellow blade to the falls, or wholly yellow ones in the form which appears in catalogues as '*I. orchioides*'. There are several species in various shades of blue, and one of the best known is *I. graeberiana*, another Russian species, which is rather shorter than *I. magnifica* at about 30 cm, with mid bluish-mauve flowers marked with pale yellow and brownish veining in the centre of the falls. The more western *I. aucheri* (*I. sindjarensis*), from Iraq, Turkey, Iran and Syria, is about the same in size but, in its best form, a rather better shade of pale blue than *I. graeberiana*. A hybrid of this, known as *I. × warlsind* (*I. warleyensis × I. aucheri*), is pale bluish-lilac with a large yellow area on the falls which are tipped with darker blue at the apex. Its other parent, *I. warleyensis*, is a beautiful species, apparently not difficult to grow but sadly very rare in cultivation at present. This has flowers of a delicate pale blue with a very intense violet blotch at the tips of the falls. Doubtless as more people become interested in this fascinating group of Irises, more will be propagated and made available through at least the specialist nurseries and, hopefully, some of the larger bulb houses as well.

CULTIVATION The species mentioned above are all easily cultivated, especially *I. magnifica* and *I. bucharica*, providing they have good drainage and an open, sunny position. The bulbs, which have thick, fleshy roots attached at the base, are obtained in autumn and should be planted at any time during August, September or early October. If the soil is at all heavy or lumpy, it must be lightened with coarse, gritty sand and broken to a fine tilth so that it can easily be poured around the bulb and its roots. A large hole must be taken out, deep enough to accommodate the bulb and its long roots, with about 10 cm of soil above the neck of the bulb. In soils which are not sharply drained it is an advantage to place some of the coarse sand around the bulb and its roots before filling in with soil. I find that in 'lumpy' soils which leave large air spaces when disturbed, slugs can get easy access to the bulbs and cause a lot of damage, so the sand also assists in the prevention of this problem. Juno Irises are probably better on alkaline soils than on acid ones, and do extremely well on the well-drained chalk of the Downs and the limestone of the Cotswolds, but they grow quite satisfac-

torily in my own garden in Surrey, which has a heavy acid soil.

Once planted, they should be left undisturbed so long as they are growing well, for in time they will build up into good-sized clumps. However, when replanting is necessary, perhaps when they are becoming too crowded or the soil is in need of improvement, the clumps can be dug up in late summer and, with great care, so as not to break the brittle fleshy roots, the bulbs separated out and replanted. Propagation is also possible by seed which, in the case of *I. magnifica* and *I. bucharica*, is often produced in great quantity. It is best to sow these in the autumn, thinly in pots, and place them in a cold frame for the winter. After germination the seedlings can be grown on for a year or two before planting them out into permanent positions.

Obviously, with unusual plants such as these, they are not going to be purchased in any quantity, and new plantings will usually be restricted to at most a few bulbs and, more likely, only one. A site must therefore be chosen where they will stand out from the surrounding companion plants which should thus be fairly dwarf so as not to overtop and spoil the effect of the Irises. Care must also be taken that the surrounding plants do not grow over the Juno bulbs when they are dormant, for they need to receive all possible warmth from the sun to ripen and produce flower buds for the coming year. The pale silvery-lilac blooms of *I. magnifica* show up well against a dark background; any deep green evergreen such as a conifer will be ideal, and will give some protection from cold winds if it is situated on the north side of the bulbs. The cream and yellow *I. bucharica* is enhanced by blue flowers, so a planting of Grape Hyacinths in front of a small group of the Iris makes a pleasing combination.

Although more expensive than the other bulbous Irises, these delightful plants are well worth trying, for they add a touch of the unusual to the garden and, when treated properly, can be very long-lived and provide years of pleasure.

IXIOLIRION

This small genus, possibly consisting of only one variable species, comes from western and central Asia. *I. tataricum* (*I. montanum*, *I. pallasii*) grows on sunny, rocky hillsides or in fields, producing from its small tough-coated bulbs wiry stems with narrow leaves to about 30–35 cm in height and bearing several large blue funnel-shaped flowers in late spring. It is little-known in cultivation, in spite of being relatively inexpensive and easy to obtain.

CULTIVATION   The bulbs should be obtained in autumn and planted about 7–8 cm deep in a sunny, well-drained site which is sheltered from cold winds, for example against a south or south-west wall. In the wild, *Ixiolirion* often grows with grey-leaved plants and this association is worth trying in cultivation, using such silvery foliage plants as *Artemisia*, Lavender and *Nepeta*. The bulbs increase naturally by division so that propagation is by lifting established clumps of bulbs.

LEUCOJUM

The Snowflakes are relatives of *Galanthus* but are easily distinguished by their nodding bells which have six equal segments, not with three large outer ones and three small inner ones like the Snowdrops. There are about eight species, of which several are very rare in cultivation and others are autumn-flowering and have been mentioned in the Autumn Section on page 32. Of the spring-flowering ones, the Spring Snowflake *L. vernum* and the Summer Snowflake *L. aestivum*, both European plants, are the best known, but a third species, *L. nicaeense* (*L. hiemale*), is a delightful tiny plant also well worth growing.

   L. vernum produces, from its Daffodil-like bulbs, strap-shaped, bright green leaves to-gether with the 15–20 cm flower stems which bear usually one but sometimes two large, white pendent bells, the segments tipped with green or occasionally yellow (in var. *carpathicum*). These usually appear in March but are occasionally in flower a little earlier, with the Snowdrops in February. Later, in April or May, the so-called Summer Snowflake, *L. aestivum*, comes into bloom. This is a more robust plant with Daffodil-like leaves and taller flower stems, about 30 to 45 cm in height, bearing several flowers which are individually very like those of *L. vernum*. The variety 'Gravetye Giant' is large-flowered and more robust and is a worthwhile variant to look out for.

   At the other end of the size scale, *L. nicaeense* is a delicate little plant only 10 cm or less in height, with thread-like leaves and, in March or April, one or occasionally two small flowers per stem in pure white, without any green markings on the tips of the segments. It is a native of southern France and Monaco but is surprisingly hardy in more northern climates.

CULTIVATION   *Leucojum* bulbs are normally on sale in the autumn bulb catalogues although, like Snowdrops, they are probably best moved while still in green leaf in the spring. *L. aestivum* and *L. vernum* prefer moist soils which will not become hot and dry in summer but at the same time will not thrive in deep shade. In light soils which tend to dry out, it is best to dig in plenty of compost or leafmould which will help to retain moisture, and to plant the bulbs in semi-shade, although in heavier, moisture-retentive soils they will take full sun. *L. vernum* is small enough to grow in a cool, damp part of the rock garden or among Hellebores at the front of a perennial border. *L. aestivum*, being taller, can be placed farther back to overtop some of the early perennials, such as blue *Pulmonaria angustifolia* and greeny-yellow *Euphorbia polychroma* (*E. epithymoides*). It also does well in damp, rough grassland and is rather elegant planted alongside a garden pool where the dangling flowers are reflected in the water.

L. nicaeense requires rather different treatment and is best grown in well-drained soil on a raised bed or rock garden in full sun, where its bulbs will receive a period of dry, warm rest in summer, planted among a collection of small alpines that will not smother it.

L. aestivum and *L. vernum* can be propagated simply by lifting the clumps, which build up quite rapidly, and dividing them up into single bulbs. This can be done in late summer or early autumn, or in spring after flowering. Seeds are produced, but in the case of these species it is not necessary to go to the trouble of raising new bulbs in this way. *L. nicaeense*, on the other hand, is best increased by seeds which are freely produced and which give flowering bulbs in only two to four years. It can be sown in pots at any time between its collection in spring and the autumn and, certainly for the first year after germination, the young bulbs should be given the protection of a cold frame and not dried out too much in the summer months. The bulbs of this species are small compared with the Daffodil-like ones of the other two, so as soon as they are large enough to handle easily, at a few millimetres in diameter, they can be planted out into their permanent position.

MUSCARI

The Grape Hyacinths, with their dense spikes of tiny, almost spherical blue flowers, are familiar bulbs of mid-spring, often seen as continuous strips of edging along paths, so prolific are they in their method of propagation. The species most commonly seen, and the most rapid increasers, are *M. neglectum* (*M. racemosum*) and *M. armeniacum* which are both about 10–15 cm in height, the first with fragrant dark navy-blue flowers with a white rim and the latter a paler, almost sky-blue, also with a whitish mouth. A selection of *M. armeniacum* called 'Blue Spike' has double

flowers of mid-blue in enormous heads and, although individually not attractive, a group of these make a good splash of colour. 'Cantab' is a paler Cambridge blue. Both of these species are common European and Turkish plants.

M. botryoides is a shorter plant with very dense spikes of bright blue flowers, and this has a white form 'Album' which is a pleasing variation. This species, from southern European mountains, does not increase so rapidly as the other two, so can be planted in more choice sites without fear of it taking over.

M. tubergenianum, too, is a rather refined species, keeping in its place, and is one of the most attractive. The stocky spikes, about 15 cm in height, have intense blue lower flowers and paler upper ones, giving it the nickname of Oxford and Cambridge Grape Hyacinth. *M. latifolium* has similarly bicoloured spikes, although the lower flowers are of a darker blue, and it differs from all other species, which have two or more narrow basal leaves, in having only one broad greyish-green leaf from each bulb. The charming bright blue *M. azureum* and its white form 'Album' differ from most other Grape Hyacinths in having spikes of small bell-like flowers, not constricted at the mouth.

Quite different from the above Grape Hyacinths, which all have dense racemes, is the Mediterranean *M. comosum* (Leopoldia), the Tassel Hyacinth, which flowers a little later, in May. This is taller, up to 30 cm in height, with the brownish flowers spread out on the stem which is crowned by a tuft of bright blue, sterile flowers, hence the allusion to a tassel. There is a form of this, a curiosity in which all the flowers are violet-blue and sterile, known as 'Plumosum' or 'Monstrosum', which has larger spikes of a feathery appearance, and it is sometimes called the Feathered Hyacinth.

For its scent alone it is worth trying *M. moschatum*, a plant of hot, rocky situations in Turkey and the Greek islands. This has spikes of small, egg-shaped purplish flowers which change to a yellowish colour as they age—

perhaps not very spectacular but with a most delicious fragrance, so it needs to be grown in a position where this can be appreciated.

CULTIVATION The bulbs of the above Grape Hyacinths are obtainable in the autumn and should be planted straight away since they mostly start to grow fairly early, some of them even producing leaves before the winter. Depending upon the size of the bulbs, they should be planted 5–6 cm deep, and about 8–10 cm in the case of those with larger bulbs such as *M. comosum* and *M. moschatum*. They are easy to grow in any reasonably well-drained soil, acid or alkaline, and are best in a sunny situation, although the tolerant *M. neglectum* and *M. armeniacum* will take partial shade without a reduction in flowering. In deeper shade, however, they will not flower well and become drawn up and out of character. *M. comosum* and *M. moschatum* require hot, sunny situations and, once planted, are best left undisturbed for as long as they continue to flower well. A position at the foot of a south wall is best, where other sun-loving bulbs such as *Iris unguicularis*, *Nerine bowdenii* and *Zephyranthes candida* thrive. The more prolific blue Grape Hyacinths can be successfully used to make a good splash of colour in association with some yellow Primroses, Polyanthus or Violas, *M. armeniacum* 'Blue Spike' being particularly effective in this respect. For those who like a formal display, *M. neglectum* and *M. armeniacum* are ideal for providing a blue edging to a path in April, although the leaves are rather untidy for a while until they die down in summer. They will also grow well in rough grass and flower at just the same time as Daffodils, the contrasting colours and sizes of the two making a splendid combination. *M. botryoides* and its white form are less vigorous and are attractive on a rock garden.

All the Grape Hyacinths mentioned above need little encouragement to propagate themselves and to increase them is simply a matter of lifting and dividing the clumps periodically in late summer. There is certainly no need to collect seeds, and it may be preferable to pinch off the old flower stems to prevent seeding in places where they are to be kept in bounds. *M. moschatum*, however, does not increase rapidly by bulb division, and in this case it is best to try to get seeds and raise a few extra bulbs in pots for planting out after a year of growth.

NARCISSUS

Few plants arouse thoughts of spring more than the Daffodils which, thanks to the patience and skill of the plant breeders, are now with us in flower for a good three months in a great range of form and size, and even longer if you count the one or two oddities which flower in the depths of winter. To be complete I should also mention the autumn-flowering ones, but these are not outdoor plants and give a rather fleeting, unspectacular display with their very small flowers. It is really the spring-flowering *Narcissus* species and their hybrids which make this such a justifiably well-known and popular group, but of all the sixty or so wild species, only a handful have contributed to the large number of hybrids which are available to us today. Thus one can usually make a safe guess at the original parentage of a particular hybrid, although it may be the result of a long line of separate crosses. For example, the large trumpet Daffodils are derived from *N. pseudonarcissus* and its many variations; those with very late flowers with small, reddish cups from *N. poeticus*; those with medium-size cups and several flowers to a head from *N. tazetta*; and hybrids between these show intermediate, but still distinguishable, characteristics. The Royal Horticultural Society has produced a classification of Narcissus in order to bring some order to the many hybrids which now exist, the eleven groupings being based on the size and proportions of the trumpet or cup and on the species from which the hybrids are derived; for example, Division 1 contains Trumpet Daffodils with the trumpet as long as or longer than the petals, while Division 6 embraces those hybrids derived from *N. cyclamineus* and therefore showing the swept-back petals characteristic of that species. Apart from the hybrid groups, there is one Division, no. 10, for the wild species, only a few of which are in general cultivation, although most are obtainable from the specialist nurseries. These are fascinating, often very small plants, some of which are really only suitable for growing in the safety of a bulb frame or alpine house; but a number of them are perfectly at home in the open garden and are described below under the appropriate Division.

Division 1.
Large Trumpet Daffodils
These are of course, to most people, the essence of what a Daffodil should be like and are by far the commonest types to be seen in gardens, especially in the wholly deep yellow form known as 'King Alfred'. There are many varieties, some completely white, such as 'Cantatrice' and the superb 'Mount Hood', others bicoloured with yellow trumpets and white petals, like 'Queen of Bicolors' and 'Trousseau'. Other good varieties which are entirely golden-yellow are 'Unsurpassable', 'Rowallane' and 'Golden Harvest'. An unusual variety is 'Spellbinder' which is at first a rather lemon-yellow throughout, but as it ages the trumpet turns off-white with a yellow rim.

Division 2.
The large-cupped Narcissi
Here the corona is large but more cup-shaped and flaring than in the trumpet varieties. The cup is more than one third the length of the petals and there is only one flower per stem. Again the colour range is large, with wholly yellow ones like the famous 'Carlton', white ones with an orange-red cup such as the dramatic 'Kilworth' and the most attractive 'Ice Follies' which has white petals and a widely expanded cup, opening pale lemon-yellow and changing to white with age. 'Green Island' has a lovely rounded white flower with broad overlapping petals and a frilly cup which is almost white, margined with yellow and with a greenish-yellow eye in the centre. For those who like the pinkish-cupped varieties, 'Passionale' is a good one, with white petals and a frilled, flaring cup of soft pink.

Division 3.
The small-cupped Narcissi
These have one flower per stem, the flowers with a small cup, one third or less than a third as long as the petals. With their very small cups, several of these charming Narcissus varieties resemble the Pheasant's Eye, *N. poeticus*, which has certainly contributed to their pedigree. 'Barrett Browning' is a fine one in this group, with a flat, white flower with a wide shallow cup of orange-red, crinkled at the margin. 'Birma' is a striking one with a similar ruffled, orange-scarlet cup but with sulphur-yellow petals. 'Verger' is less gaudy, delicate in colour with white petals and a lemon cup which is edged with orange. Pure white varieties, with white cups as well as petals, are not to be found so easily in catalogues as the bicolors, but 'Polar Ice' is worth searching for.

Division 4.
Double-Flowered Varieties
This group includes all the double Narcissi and Daffodils, some of which are cluster-headed and are derived from *N. tazetta*, so have the marvellous scent of that species. I must confess that on the whole I do not like the doubles as much as the single versions, for they do tend to fall over in wet, windy weather and their flowers lack the clean-cut lines of a single flower. However, I must admit that some of them are beautiful plants and their flowers last well when picked. Among the very popular varieties, 'Cheerfulness', with its heads of creamy flowers, and its wholly yellow counterpart, 'Yellow Cheerfulness', are known to all who enjoy buying early cut flowers. These also do well in the garden, not just for forcing

indoors. 'Irene Copeland' has a very nicely shaped flower for a double, with regular white and yellow petals mixed, while 'White Marvel' has wholly white flowers with large outer petals and a tightly double centre, several carried on each stem. The old double yellow Daffodil, very robust and easy to naturalise, is 'Telamonius Plenus' or 'Van Sion', as it is also known. Another of these old double varieties, known for at least a hundred years, is 'Rip Van Winkle', a stocky little plant about 15–20 cm in height, with completely double yellow flowers in which both the petals and trumpet are split into many narrow segments.

Division 5.

Varieties derived from N. triandrus

These delightful plants are mostly rather short, between 20 and 35 cm in height, and often carry more than one flower per stem. The cup is usually rather funnel-shaped and the petals in some varieties are swept back a little, characters inherited from the dwarf Spanish species, *N. triandrus*, the Angel's Tears Narcissus, which has pendent flowers with reflexed petals. 'Thalia' and 'Tresamble' are both beautiful white-flowered varieties, while 'Liberty Bells' has wholly lemon-yellow flowers, nodding slightly and several per stem. 'April Tears' is an excellent dwarf variety, with several pendent deep-yellow flowers on each 15–20 cm stem.

Division 6.

Varieties derived from N. cyclamineus

These are rather distinctive Narcissi, with rather long trumpets and reflexed petals inherited from *N. cyclamineus*, a dwarf species from Spain and Portugal. The leaves are bright green, not at all greyish, and this shows in several of the hybrids as well. They are mostly between 15 and 35 cm in height.

Perhaps the most popular in this group, and one of the best modern Daffodils of all, is 'February Gold' which, although never actually making February in my garden in Surrey, is always the first of the taller Narcissus to bloom, usually in early March. This has

elegant deep golden-yellow flowers with swept back petals. Another favourite is 'Dove Wings' with recurved white petals and a shorter, primrose-yellow trumpet. 'Charity May' is similar in shape, but has wholly soft yellow flowers, while 'Jenny' is entirely creamy white. One of the smallest, but robust in constitution, is 'Tête-a-Tête' which has one or two deep-yellow flowers on each 15 cm stem. There are quite a number of other varieties in this group, all attractive garden plants and rather elegant and early flowering.

Division 7.

Varieties derived from N. jonquilla

These varieties are between 15 and 45 cm in height and bear several smallish, sweetly-scented flowers on each stem, wholly yellow with a small cup in the wild species but variously coloured hybrids and varieties have been raised. The petals are sometimes slightly reflexed. *N. jonquilla* itself has cylindrical deep-green leaves, but the hybrids usually have flat leaves. 'Trevithian' is a tallish one, with two or three delicate pale lemon-yellow flowers on each 35–40 cm stem, while at the other end of the scale, at about 15 cm, is 'Sundial' which also has two or three flowers in a deep lemon-yellow colour, tinged with green on the cup. 'Suzy' is a colourful variety with up to four flowers, the petals bright yellow and the cup a strong orange. The popular 'Lintie' is similarly bicoloured and is an excellent dwarf variety with very wide shallow orange cups.

Division 8.

The selections of N. tazetta and hybrids with N. poeticus (Poetaz varieties)

N. tazetta is the lovely cluster-headed, sweetly-scented species which is very popular in the Mediterranean region and frequently sold as a cut flower in winter, notably the varieties 'Soleil d'Or' and 'Paper White'. These, however, are not good garden plants in most of the country and are best grown in pots for a winter display indoors. The double 'Cheerfulness' is mentioned above under Division 4 with the other double varieties, but some nursery catalogues place it here, for it is surely derived from *N. tazetta*. The crosses with the Pheasant's Eye Narcissus, *N. poeticus*, are much better in the open garden than the true Tazettas and they are colourful, hardy plants, often with several flowers per stem. 'Geranium' is probably one of the best, about 40 cm tall with up to five large, flat white flowers with wide, shallow orange cups. 'Minnow' is a particular favourite of mine, only 15–20 cm tall with two to four small flowers, the petals lemon and the cup slightly darker yellow.

Division 9.

N. poeticus varieties
This small group is reserved for the Pheasant's Eye Narcissus and its forms, characterised by the solitary flattish, white, very strongly-scented flowers with a very small deep orange-red cup. It is usually one of the last of all Narcissi to flower. The most well-known variety, apart from the old original Pheasant's Eye, is 'Actaea' which has flowers nearly 10 cm across, the shallow cup yellow, rimmed with red. Especially good also is 'Cantabile' with perfectly formed broad overlapping petals and a greenish cup edged with red. These are excellent garden plants, and perfect for cutting since they have a delicious scent.

Division 10.

The Wild Species—see below.

Division 11.

Miscellaneous Daffodils, including the new Split Corona, 'Collar' or 'Orchid Flowering' Daffodils
This is a fairly modern development of the Daffodil in which the trumpet or cup (corona) is split and the sections of it are flattened out and pressed back against the petals. They have one flower per stem and are in the height range of 40–45 cm.

'Cassata' has white petals with a yellow corona which is split into about six segments, each segment nearly as long as the adjacent petal and spread out so that it is flattened against it. 'Orangery' also has white petals, but the collar is smaller and orange and its segments are interleaved between the petals,

giving a semi-double bicoloured appearance. 'Baccarat' is a stronger-coloured variety with yellow petals and a flattened orange collar covering about two thirds of the flower.

These are unusual plants, not to everyone's liking, but an extraordinary development, and one wonders what other trends may be followed in the future.

The Narcissus species (Division 10)

Most of the species of Narcissus are fairly dwarf plants, suitable for a rock garden or for naturalising in short grass. They are enormously variable in size, shape and form and for this reason are a fascinating group of plants in which, fortunately, a number of nurserymen have taken an interest, so that they are readily available at a reasonable price. Nearly all the species come from Spain, Portugal and North Africa.

One of the earliest to flower is the Hoop Petticoat, *N. bulbocodium*—in fact so early in the case of one of its variations, var. *romieuxii*, that I have mentioned it in the Winter Section. It is normally offered in its variety *conspicuus* which is a 12–15 cm high plant with thin, rush-like leaves and golden-yellow flowers. These, typical of all the *N. bulbocodium* group, have a wide, funnel-shaped corona, in fact like an old-fashioned hooped petticoat held out horizontally, and very narrow petals which are almost insignificant in size compared with the corona. Sometimes var. *obesus* is to be found in catalogues, this being a particularly large-flowered form, and var. *tenuifolius*, which has very narrow leaves and is even more dwarf, at about 8–10 cm. There are white variations also, known as *N. cantabricus* (*N. clusii*) but these are rare and expensive and really best grown in the protection of a cold glasshouse since they are so early-flowering. Interestingly, the Hoop Petticoats do not hybridise readily with other species, whereas most Narcissus will cross quite freely and have given us the enormous range of varied Daffodils and Narcissus described above.

The species with Daffodil-type trumpets

are excellent garden plants, mostly very easy to grow and delightful miniatures of the garden Daffodils. The smallest, and earliest, is *N. asturiensis* (*N. minimus*) which is only about 5 cm high at flowering time, with perfect tiny golden-yellow trumpets with frilled margins. *N. nanus* is rather larger, at about 10–12 cm, and this has bicoloured flowers with yellow trumpets and paler creamy-yellow petals. The true wild Daffodil which comes from western Europe, mostly Spain and the Pyrenees but also some English woodlands, is *N. pseudonarcissus*. This is enormously variable and many forms of it have been given names, some of which are offered in the nursery trade and are first rate dwarf Daffodils. The 'ordinary' *N. pseudonarcissus* or Lent Lily is about 15 cm tall with yellow trumpets and paler yellow petals. Subspecies *obvallaris*, the Tenby Daffodil, is similar in size with deep yellow flowers, while subsp. *alpestris* (*moschatus*) from the Pyrenees is a delightful favourite of mine, with pendent creamy-white flowers, unfortunately not always easy to obtain. Halfway between these is subsp. *pallidiflorus* with pale straw-yellow trumpets, a rather delicate colour. Subsp. *abscissus* is another one which I like for its straight yellow trumpets cut cleanly across at the mouth. *N. lobularis* is frequently seen in catalogues and this, too, is well worth having since it is an early dwarf Daffodil, usually March-flowering, with soft primrose-yellow flowers.

Also a trumpet Daffodil, but very distinct, is *N. cyclamineus* whose main feature is the sharply reflexed perianth, the petals swept right back in Cyclamen fashion leaving the long, narrow trumpet projecting downwards. The flowers are a deep golden-yellow on 10–15 cm stems and accompanied by deep green leaves, with no hint of grey like so many of the *N. pseudonarcissus* forms. In recent years this has been difficult to obtain, although it is an easy enough Narcissus to grow, and if you like the turned back 'ears' appearance of this species you may have to resort to buying one

of the Cyclamineus hybrids of Division 6 above.

Also with reflexed petals is *N. triandrus*, another dwarf at about 10–18 cm, which has more than one flower per stem. These are pendent with bell-shaped cups rather than trumpets, and have the stamens protruding beyond the edge of the cups. It is fancifully called the Angel's Tears Daffodil. The most commonly seen form, 'Albus', has delicate creamy-white flowers, but sometimes var. *concolor*, with wholly yellow flowers, is offered. This species has given rise to a range of lovely smallish Daffodil hybrids which have inherited some of its more attractive characteristics. These are described above in Division 5.

The Pheasant's Eye, *N. poeticus*, needs little introduction, for its deliciously fragrant flattish white flowers, with a small orange-red crown-like cup, are loved by all. The wild species grows to about 40–45 cm in height, flowers very late—usually in May—and has the petals slightly recurved and not as widely overlapping as in the garden forms. This is sometimes offered as 'Recurvus'.

The remainder of the species likely to be encountered in catalogues are all small-cupped types and are dwarf plants with narrow foliage, so best suited to a rock garden or some other choice spot where they will not be overgrown by other plants. *N. canaliculatus* is like a small Tazetta Narcissus with 3–4 sweetly-scented flowers on 15–24 cm stems, white with an orange cup. It is unfortunately shy-flowering unless planted deeply in a very hot, sunny situation.

The lovely Jonquil, *N. jonquilla*, is well known for its strongly-scented, deep-yellow flowers, up to six on each 22–25 cm stem. Related to this is the tiny *N. juncifolius*, only 10–15 cm tall with one to three yellow flowers amid rush-like leaves, and the even smaller *N. rupicola* which reaches at most 10 cm in height and bears solitary flowers in bright yellow. These miniatures are certainly best on a rock garden where a close eye can be kept on them, or at the front of a border near the house.

CULTIVATION With many of the 'ordinary' Daffodil varieties, cultivation is just a matter of obtaining them in autumn, planting them so that there is about 10–15 cm of soil above the tops of the bulbs and leaving them alone to build up into clumps. A sunny or slightly shaded position is best, in soil which is reasonably well-drained but not too light and sandy so that it dries out excessively. Alkaline and neutral soils are particularly successful but perfectly good results are obtained on acid soils as well, provided they are not too poor and sour. Most of the varieties in Divisions 1, 2, 3, 4, 6, 9 and 11 are easy garden plants and can be planted in mixed borders, shrub borders or in grass, although the more expensive varieties should perhaps be given choice positions until they have increased sufficiently. The Triandrus hybrids of Division 5 seem to prefer slightly warmer, more well-drained conditions, and I prefer to plant these in sunny places near the front of a border. Similarly, the Jonquils of Division 7 like a sheltered, sunny spot, although not one which is too dry. In Division 8, the Tazetta types, such as 'Soleil d'Or' and 'Paper White', are really of little use outdoors in most parts of the country and will only flower if they are growing in a site which is sheltered in winter and sunbaked in summer. However, the hybrids between the Tazettas and *N. poeticus*, the 'Poetaz' varieties, are good garden plants and the popular 'Geranium' will grow and flower freely between shrubs and does well with me in a patch of rough grass.

This leaves the Narcissus species of Division 10 which vary considerably in their requirements and call for individual comment. Few people are lucky enough to achieve a display of *N. bulbocodium*, the Hoop Petticoat, such as can be seen on the alpine meadow at the Royal Horticultural Society's garden at Wisley. Growing there in thousands, one might assume that it was the easiest plant in the world to grow, but it seldom settles in so readily to cultivation in turf, and one assumes that at Wisley there happens to be an ideal site where there is the unusual combination of a grassy slope which has water seeping through it, hence a constant supply of moisture which is never stagnant. If one has such a position in the garden then it is well worth trying *N. bulbocodium*, but failing that, it can be quite successful in a rock garden or sunny peat garden. *N. triandrus*, too, will sometimes take to cultivation in grass, if it is not too coarse, but I find it best in a raised part of the peat bed.

The small species of trumpet Daffodil are on the whole rather easier to grow, especially the variants of *N. pseudonarcissus* which are good for naturalising in borders or in grass. The smallest ones, such as *N. asturiensis*, are, however, best kept in the rock garden where their size and form can be appreciated at close quarters. *N. cyclamineus* is a moisture-loving plant for the peat garden or the damp margins of a pond or stream, and most of its hybrids in Division 6 show a tendency to thrive in damp soils.

The latest species to flower, *N. poeticus*, is a native of moist alpine meadows and this, in my garden, certainly does best in damp spots, flowering long after all the other species are finished.

Of the Jonquil group, *N. jonquilla* itself is an easy plant to grow, flowering best in a sheltered, sunny border but its small relatives, *N. juncifolius* and *N. rupicola*, are too diminutive and should be grown in a raised part of the rock garden.

N. canaliculatus deserves special comment, for it is a delightful little Tazetta-like plant and is easy to obtain, but after the first season is reluctant to flower. The reason is that it prefers a hot sunny situation with the bulbs planted deeply, about 10 cm at least, to encourage flowering. The secret in getting it to flower every year lies in the proper ripening of the bulbs during the summer dormancy, a feature common to all the Narcissus belonging to this Tazetta group.

The feeding of Narcissus and Daffodil bulbs should be restricted to low nitrogen fertilizers containing higher proportions of potash (K) and phosphate (P). Proprietary brands can be used, or sulphate of potash and hoof and horn, which are recommended by some growers. Light dressings in autumn and early spring will encourage healthy growth and a good size of bulb for the following season. Once established, the bulbs are best left undisturbed until they become crowded, and then they must be lifted in June or July and divided, and replanted either straight away or some time before September.

Propagation is simply by means of division of established clumps, and in the case of named cultivars this is the only method of keeping them true to name. Seeds are produced, but the hybrids will not breed true and it takes a very long time to grow flowering-sized bulbs in this way. However, it can be fun if one wishes to try for new varieties. The species can be raised quite easily from seed, especially the small ones like *N. bulbocodium*, *N. triandrus* and *N. juncifolius* and in general these remain true unless one deliberately tries to hybridise them.

There are, of course, many ways in which Daffodils and Narcissus can be used around the garden and I personally prefer to see them in grass as much as anywhere, especially some of the daintier varieties such as the Cyclamineus hybrids like 'February Gold', the small wild trumpet Daffodils, *N. pseudonarcissus*, and the Pheasant's Eye, *N. poeticus*. Some of the smaller pale yellow and white ones, such as 'Dove Wings' and 'Thalia', look fine when planted to offset the gaudy colours of the early *Tulipa greigii* varieties, or combined with a drift of blue *Muscari* 'Blue Spike'. The pinks and reds of winter flowering Heathers (*Erica carnea*) make an ideal foil for groups of the smaller white-flowering Narcissus varieties,

but the vigorous, robust trumpet Daffodils look best to me when seen in sizeable clumps in large borders or in grass, where the scale is better.

ORNITHOGALUM

Of the large number of species of 'Star of Bethlehem', only a few are offered in the nursery trade, perhaps because many of them are so similar and repetitive. It does seem to be a case of 'if you've seen one you have seen them all', but the position is not quite as bad as that, for there are a few which are distinct enough to make them worthwhile growing, and their brilliant-white, starry flowers are a cheerful sight in mid to late spring. A characteristic which most of them share is a green stripe on the outside of the petals so that in bud the flower is green and insignificant and it is only on a good sunny day that they spread widely, showing the glistening white interior. Most of the spring-flowering species are also similar in having a type of raceme in which the lower flower stalks are longer than the upper, so that the flowers are held roughly at the same level, giving a flat-topped appearance to the inflorescence.

The European *O. umbellatum* is probably the best-known species, which grows to about 15 cm in height when in flower, producing its many relatively large, shining-white, upward-facing stars in May. Earlier than this—usually March or April—is the more compact Turkish *O. balansae* which has rather broad, glossy green leaves and wide-petalled flowers which push up just as the leaves are emerging. Rather different from either of these is the most attractive European woodlander, *O. nutans*, which has its flowers closely packed on short stalks, thus almost forming a spike rather than a flat-topped raceme. This is a taller species at about 20–25 cm and flowers in May. A most attractive feature of *O. nutans* is that the flowers have elegantly recurved petals coloured silvery-green on the outside showing

73

74

75

76

77

78

73 *Ipheion uniflorum* in a woodland in spring. **74** *Iris* (English) *latifolia (xiphioides)*, a good summer border plant. **75** *Iris* (Spanish) *xiphium* var. *lusitanica* is just one of many varieties. **76** *Iris* (Dutch) 'Golden Harvest' with variegated Ivy. **77** *Iris* (Dutch) 'White Excelsior' with grey foliage and Quaking Grass. **78** *Iris* (Juno) *bucharica*, an unusual bulbous Iris.

79

80

81

82

83

84

79 *Iris* (Juno) *graeberiana* for the connoisseur's garden. **80** *Iris* (Juno) *magnifica* looks best with a dark background. **81** *Iris* (Reticulata) *danfordiae* with grey Dianthus leaves. **82** *Iris* (Reticulata) *histrioides* in grass. Also good for the Rock Garden. **83** *Iris* (Reticulata) *reticulata* with the grey conifer, *Abies koreana*. **84** *Leucojum aestivum* (Summer Snowflake) in grass, enjoys damp places.

through to the inside, giving the whole flower a soft grey-green appearance. Apart from these spring species there are a few later-flowering ones occasionally on offer, such as the green *O. pyrenaicum*, 'Bath Asparagus', and two tall ones with long spikes of white flowers, *O. narbonense* and *O. pyramidale*. These are June-to-July flowering and somewhat lost in the summer garden, but the South African *O. thyrsoides* is very attractive and will be found in the Summer Section.

CULTIVATION *O. umbellatum* is a very easily grown species, suitable for almost any type of soil in partial shade, where sun will catch the flowers for at least part of the day or they will not open fully. It is ideal for naturalising beneath deciduous shrubs, flowering at the same time as Forget-me-Nots and making a charming association. *O. nutans* is similarly easy and will take more shade, and is also successful when planted in grass. *O. balansae*, on the other hand, is better in sun and is a fine spring bulb for the rock garden or for the front of a sunny border.

Propagation is simply a matter of lifting established clumps and dividing the bulbs in the autumn, for they produce offsets quite freely. Ornithogalums also produce a lot of seed, but there is little point in collecting this to sow separately, for the self-sown seedlings usually appear in quantity; in fact it may be necessary to pick off the old flowers to stop them seeding in places where they are to be kept in bounds, but for naturalising this is a welcome characteristic.

Ornithogalum bulbs are available in the autumn and should be planted soon after arrival, at a depth of about 5–6 cm.

PUSCHKINIA

This small Scilla-like bulb is perhaps not quite as showy as some of the rich blue Squills or its other relative, *Chionodoxa*, but nevertheless it is well worth growing for its 10–15 cm long racemes of pale blue flowers which appear in March or April. *P. scilloides* (*P. libanotica*) is a native of the western Asiatic mountains, notably the Caucasus, eastern Turkey and Iran, spreading south to Lebanon. It occurs naturally at quite high altitudes and is unquestionably hardy in cultivation. The individual flowers are attractive and worthy of closer inspection, since each perianth segment has a dark blue line along its centre and in the middle of the flower is a small white cup, which is the feature distinguishing it from both Chionodoxas and Scillas. Like these two, *Puschkinia* has a pair of basal leaves that appear at flowering time.

In addition to the pale blue form there is a pure white, with no central blue stripe on the segments, known as 'Alba'.

CULTIVATION The bulbs are planted in autumn, about 3–5 cm deep in a well-drained, sunny position with sand and moss peat added to the soil if it tends to be on the heavy side. It is ideal for a rock garden or the front of a border and associates well with the deep blue *Pulmonaria angustifolia* and yellow dwarf *Doronicum cordatum*, both of which flower at about the same time, but care must be taken that these two vigorous plants do not increase too much and swamp the *Puschkinia* bulbs. The white form needs a spot where its flowers can be seen against a dark background, such as a dwarf deep-green Conifer.

Propagation is, in my experience, rather slow by natural bulb division, and seeds are not produced very readily either. Fortunately it is a relatively inexpensive plant to buy, so that home propagation is not quite so important.

ROMULEA

These close relatives of the Crocus are little-known in gardens and are mostly not showy, although the tender South African species have amazing colours. The hardy ones, which are mainly from the Mediterranean region, are easily cultivated and do perhaps have some appeal for the bulb enthusiast, but for garden display they lack the size and rich colours of the Crocuses. Romuleas grow from a tiny corm, not unlike a small Colchicum in that it is lop-sided, which produces almost thread-like but wiry leaves in the spring, followed shortly afterwards by funnel-shaped flowers which will open out flat in strong sunshine; although somewhat Crocus-shaped, they do not have a long, slender tube to the flower, so are quite different in this respect. The best and most easily obtained of the hardy species is *R. bulbocodium* which has relatively large flowers in pale bluish-lavender with a yellow throat; *R. ramiflora* is smaller and paler but very easy to grow.

CULTIVATION The hardy Romuleas are obtained and planted in autumn in as sunny a position as possible, about 4–5 cm deep in well-drained sandy or gritty soil; acid or alkaline conditions are equally satisfactory. Because of their size, a site on a rock garden is ideal, but the front of a sunny border will do, providing it is a situation where they can be left undisturbed. A sunny wall bed is ideal for them, planted in a group in front of some other sun-loving subject such as *Iris unguicularis* which is a natural Mediterranean companion. I have, by chance, found that they also do well in grass, a small patch of *R. ramiflora* having built up in my garden from corms left in some old potting compost which was used to fill hollows in the turf. Romuleas mostly flower in March or April and by the time the Daffodils and other bulbs in the grass are ready for cutting down, the Romuleas, too, have completed their growth.

Propagation is rather easy, for the corms increase naturally to some extent and seeds are produced without fail every year. These can be sown in pots where they will produce flowering corms in only two to three years.

SCILLA

The Squills, with their predominantly blue flowers, are one of the highlights of the early spring display and are on the whole inexpensive, so that drifts of bulbs can be planted with great effect. Some, such as our native Bluebell, are perfect for naturalising. The best and hardiest species are from the European and western Asiatic mountains, *S. bifolia* being the most widespread in both continents. This has a pair of basal leaves and, in February to April, a loose raceme of several small, starry flowers in a deep violet-blue, or pink in the variety 'Rosea' and white in the variety 'Alba'. The best form, if you can obtain it, is 'Praecox', a very robust, many-flowered version, much more striking than the usual one. Also very early is the pale blue Iranian *S. tubergeniana* which has larger flowers, slightly cup-shaped but opening out to nearly flat in the sun. The broad, shiny pale-green leaves are very short as the first flowers push through the soil, and at this stage the whole plant is only 4 or 5 cm in height; but as it develops, flowering continues until it may be up to 10 or 15 cm, with one or more loose racemes to each bulb. Closely related and similar in appearance is *S. siberica* which comes from Russia and Turkey, but this has intense rich blue flowers, individually more bell-shaped and nodding. The most striking form of this is 'Spring Beauty', richly coloured and robust, and there is also a white form, 'Alba'.

The Turkish *S. bithynica* comes slightly later than these, usually in April, and is very different in appearance, for it has several strap-shaped leaves per bulb and racemes of many small starry flowers on stems up to 20 cm in height in an attractive mid-powdery-blue shade. *S. amoena* is not unlike this and of similar garden value. Also in late spring comes an unusual species from the Pyrenees, *S. liliohyacinthus*, which is perhaps more interesting than showy. The large bulb is yellowish and made up of loose scales, thus looking very like that of a Lily. This produces a rosette of bold, rather wide glossy-green leaves and a densely-flowered raceme, up to 25 cm tall, of pale blue flowers, or white in the albino version 'Alba'.

The western European Bluebells scarcely require a description, especially the native English one whose rather one-sided nodding racemes of tubular blue flowers are such a spectacular feature of our woodlands in April or May. This may be found in literature and catalogues in a bewildering array of names, including *S. nutans*, *S. non-scripta*, *Endymion nutans* and *Hyacinthoides non-scripta*, so you have been warned! There are blue, pink and white forms of this, as there are of the related Spanish Bluebell, *S. campanulata* (*S. hispanica*). This differs in several respects, being firstly an altogether more robust plant up to 40 cm in height; the leaves are wider, the flowers are a more open bell-shape and they are produced all round the stem, not on one side as in the English Bluebell. Another point of distinction is that the raceme of *S. hispanica* does not bend over at the apex into a nodding position, which is the feature noted by the name *S. nutans*. The two may hybridise in gardens and the resulting hybrids will not have such clear-cut differences as the wild species. There are named varieties of the Spanish Bluebell, but it is more usual to be offered collections of mixed colours in the catalogues.

CULTIVATION   The English and Spanish Bluebells are very easily cultivated in all but hot, dry situations, and are ideal for naturalising beneath shrubs, although one must consider the matter carefully before introducing them into the garden at all, for they can seed about and become quite a weed in favourable situations. With plenty of room, however, they are superb plants for the semi-wild garden, and will also do well in rough grass.

The other species mentioned above are all smaller and less invasive and are suitable for semi-shaded situations under deciduous shrubs or on a cool part of the rock garden. The blue colours associate rather well with grey-leaved plants, as I found with a pleasing chance association in my garden, when a self-sown plant of the grey, bushy *Euphorbia characias* appeared behind a planting of pale blue *Scilla tubergeniana*. *S. bithynica* seeds itself freely and is a delightful plant for naturalising beneath shrubs and, with me, has also seeded into the edge of the gravel drive, but it need not become a nuisance for it is easy to pull off the dead flowers before the capsules ripen. The very early *S. bifolia*, too, needs a place where it can be left undisturbed and, being rather small, is ideal for the front of a border where perennials such as Hellebores are growing. Contrasting colours are effective, for example blue Scillas in front of white *Helleborus orientalis*.

The bulbs of Scillas are sold in the autumn and should be planted straight away, about 6–7 cm deep in well-drained soil which has had leafmould or garden compost forked in beforehand. This helps to retain moisture, for the spring Scillas do not like a dry, dusty soil.

Propagation is simply a matter of lifting and dividing clumps of established bulbs, since they mostly increase readily by themselves. It is usually not necessary to gather seeds and sow them, for they will often spread naturally by this method.

TECOPHILAEA

Although only a very few hardy bulbs have come to us from the Andes Mountains of South America, the Chilean Blue Crocus, *T. cyanocrocus*, is perhaps one of the most dramatic of all spring bulbs, with its enormous funnel-shaped, intense gentian-blue flowers in March or April. The whole plant is less than 10 cm in height, with one or two narrow basal leaves, such a dwarf stature accentuating the size of the flowers which are about 3 cm in diameter and facing upwards. It is not related to Crocus although it does have a corm covered with a net-like coat and the flower is vaguely reminiscent of a Crocus, but there the similarity ends and it in fact belongs, with a few other genera, to its own family, the Tecophilaeaceae.

Apart from the 'ordinary' form, and even that is rather rare and expensive, there is a slightly paler blue one with a larger white zone in the throat, known as 'Leichtlinii', and a deep purplish-blue one, 'Violacea', which to me is not as interesting since the whole attraction of Tecophilaea is its intense blue colour.

CULTIVATION   This beautiful bulb provides us with an example of where our gardens can provide a haven for plants, for *Tecophilaea* is thought to be extinct in the wild and only survives because it is propagated and distributed by a few specialist nurseries and bulb enthusiasts. It is true that its extinction is partly due to the collection of its wild bulbs in the past but we can now help to make amends by ensuring its survival in cultivation.

It is mostly grown in the protection of an alpine house or cold frame, largely because of the expense of obtaining the corms, but it is hardy and does not require a very hot, dry summer rest period, which may in fact be detrimental if overdone. In times past it appears to have been successfully cultivated in open, sunny borders with well-drained, sandy soil. Obviously, because of its size it must be placed in a position where it will not be swamped by other plants. The lovely blue flowers would undoubtedly be enhanced by some dwarf silvery-foliage plants nearby and there is a wide range of small rock plants which would be suitable companions for *Tecophilaea*.

The corms are available in the autumn catalogues of a few specialist nurseries and should be planted about 4 or 5 cm deep; the surface can be covered with some coarse shingle for extra protection, and this is of benefit to the associated rock plants as well.

Having spent rather a lot of money on a corm or two it is highly likely that propagation will be of prime interest, and I would recommend hand pollination of the flowers with a small soft brush, in case insects do not do the job; in this way capsules are often produced, each containing several seeds. These can be sown in pots as soon as ripe in early summer, and kept watered through the summer and autumn. After germination it is best to keep the seedlings in their pot in a cold frame or greenhouse until they are large enough to plant out in two or three years. Although they die down in summer, they should never be dried out to the same extent as most Mediterranean bulbs, especially the young small corms which are easily desiccated.

Tecophilaea corms also produce a few offsets and these can, of course, be removed at repotting or replanting time.

TRILLIUM

Although these lovely plants are not bulbous and should never be dried out, a number of the bulb nurseries are now stocking them, usually in their spring lists. The short rhizomes are not damaged so long as they are kept in moist peat during transportation and are planted straight away on arrival.

The prefix of the name, *Tri*, indicates the most obvious feature of these North American and eastern Asiatic woodlanders, and that is that the flower parts and leaves are in threes. At the top of the stem is a whorl of three broad leaves, often attractively mottled, and in the centre of these arises the flower which has three green sepals and three larger, differently coloured petals. There are quite a number of species but only a selection of these are commonly available, probably the best of which is *T. grandiflorum*, the Wake Robin of the eastern United States. This has large, broad-petalled, snowy-white flowers set amid plain green leaves on stems up to 30 cm tall; the flowers are held on short stalks and face outwards. *T. grandiflorum* 'Flore Plena' has gorgeous tightly double flowers.

In *T. sessile* the flowers have no stalk and are erect, arising directly from the centre of the whorl of leaves, which are beautifully splashed with dark green on a paler ground. The flowers are large but narrow-petalled and, in the form usually offered, 'Rubrum', they are a deep, rich red. This is about 20 cm in height, as is the very similar *T. chloropetalum*, which differs mainly in the whitish flowers, which are set off beautifully by the mottled leaves.

T. erectum is curiously named since its stalked flowers are held facing outwards, not upright as in *T. sessile*. There are various colour forms of this, the most commonly available ones being a deep maroon, the white 'Album' and yellowish-green 'Luteum'. The flowers are not as large as those of *T. grandiflorum* and have rather narrow, pointed petals, but nevertheless it is an attractive and graceful species; its leaves are not mottled. The variety 'Luteum' is not to be confused with the species *T. luteum* which has mottled leaves and erect, pale yellowish-green fragrant flowers, in fact rather similar to *T. sessile* and sometimes treated as a variety of it.

CULTIVATION The Trilliums are on the whole very easy to grow, so long as they are given cool, moist growing conditions. The tubers can be planted in autumn or very early spring or, if pot-grown from a nursery, at any time of the year. The larger species mentioned above should be placed 8–10 cm deep in soil which has plenty of humus in the form of leafmould, moss peat or old compost. The drainage should be reasonably good, and in poorly drained sites it is best to dig in some coarse, gritty sand together with the humus. Dappled shade is best, although the plants will not scorch in full sun if they are supplied with plenty of moisture. A peat garden setting is ideal and they associate very well with other woodland plants which enjoy the same cool conditions. For example, a clump of white

Trilliums is charming when surrounded by pale blue *Anemone nemorosa* 'Allenii' and, conversely, the dull red flowers and mottled foliage of *T. sessile* are brought to life by the contrasting white flowers of a planting of *A. apennina* 'Alba'. There are lots of possibilities for attractive associations, using such plants as the early yellow daisy-flowered *Doronicum cordatum*, blue-flowered Pulmonarias and silver-leaved forms of *Lamium maculatum*.

Propagation of Trilliums is by division of established clumps in autumn or early spring before growth commences, and most species will build up into sizeable clumps when growing well. Seeds are often produced and these should be sown straight away in pots without drying out and then kept moist through the summer. In winter they can be left out to receive frost, after which they may germinate, or possibly delay for another season. The seedling tubers can be separated out after one complete growing season and either planted out into a humus-rich nursery bed where a close eye can be kept on them, free of competition from other plants, until they are large enough to be put into permanent positions, or they can be potted separately and grown in a plunge bed for two or three years.

TULIPA

The Tulips, perhaps even more so than the Daffodils, provide an impressive splash of colour in the spring garden, lasting from early April through to late May in a great range of size, colour and form of flower, both single and double. Although I have a personal preference for the interesting small wild species there is no doubt that the many large-flowered hybrids are the best for achieving spectacular displays in the garden and, even if one does not like formal bedding schemes, they can be most attractive when planted in small groups in association with other plants.

Most of the Tulips, be they wild species or garden hybrids, have their origins in the

Orient, although there are a few from southern Europe as well. The home of the great majority is in the central Asiatic mountains of the U.S.S.R., whence some of them were almost certainly introduced and cultivated by the Ottoman Turks in the sixteenth century gardens of Constantinople. Even at this early date, many varieties had been selected in Turkey, judged by horticultural committees and painted for reference purposes, and these paintings are preserved in the libraries of Istanbul. From these illustrations it is clear that Tulips with elegant, pointed petals were the most popular form, not unlike the group we have today known as the Lily-Flowered Tulips, and the large bowl-shaped and double varieties of the present seem to have been little known to the Ottomans. In the mid-sixteenth century travellers to Turkey, and principally Ogier Ghislain de Busbecq, saw these Tulips and introduced some to Europe, so originating what was to become a huge bulb industry, notably, of course, in Holland. Other more recent introductions of wild species which have also been used for hybridisation have led to a greater range of types than ever before and new varieties are being added every year. Especially interesting are the stocky, early-flowering ones derived from the Russian *T. kauffmanniana* and *T. greigii*, now available in a wide variety of flower colours and including some with beautifully striped and mottled foliage. The vivid red *T. fosteriana* also has several colour variants and this has been crossed with the Darwin Tulips to give a range of splendid garden varieties known as the Darwin Hybrids.

As with several other groups of bulbous plants which have been much-hybridised and selected, there is an internationally accepted classification of Tulips, for convenience when exhibiting them or describing them in catalogues. There are fifteen such Divisions, based on flowering time, stature of the plant, shape of the flower, whether the flower is single or double and, in the case of some Divisions,

which particular species has given rise to that group of cultivars. Then, of course, there are a considerable number of species in their original wild forms which are good garden plants, often with a grace of form which is lacking in the larger, more colourful hybrids; some of these are dwarf plants suitable for the smallest rock garden. To list all the varieties presently available would be a long and difficult task, and of little use since the selection changes every year, but I have provided a personal selection based upon what is currently on offer in each of the major Divisions, and a selection of the more readily obtainable *Tulipa* species, although specialist bulb nurseries are at times likely to be able to offer other rare ones.

I have included only the main Divisions which the gardener is likely to encounter in catalogues.

Single Early Tulips
These begin to flower in early to mid-April, are mostly rather short and sturdy in stature and are therefore fairly weather-resistant. The flowers are deeply cup-shaped with a rounded base and mostly with rounded petals.

'Keizerskroon' is an old favourite, about 35–40 cm in height, with carmine-scarlet segments, broadly edged with bright yellow.

'Brilliant Star' is bright scarlet with a blackish centre, a very early variety about 30 cm tall.

'Bellona' is about 40 cm in height, with fragrant, wholly golden-yellow flowers.

'General de Wet' (or just 'De Wet') has large scented orange-and-gold flowers on 35–40 cm stems.

Early Double Tulips
These also flower in early or mid-April and have many-petalled flowers which have been likened to small Paeonies, although the 'Paeony-Flowered' Tulips offered in catalogues are later double ones, usually on taller

stems. The stems of these are mostly short and stout.

'Marechal Niel' has yellow flowers, flushed with orange, on stems about 30 cm tall.

'Peach Blossom' is a rosy-pink variety with sturdy 25–30 cm stems.

'Orange Nassau' has very showy deep-red flowers, flushed with a paler red towards the edges, about 30 cm in height.

'Scarlet Cardinal' is a very early variety in bright scarlet, about 25–30 cm in height.

'Schoonoord' ('Purity'), as its name suggests, has pure white flowers, on stems about 30 cm tall.

Mendel and Triumph Tulips

These are later than the Early Single and Double varieties, flowering in the second half of April, and are sometimes to be found in catalogues grouped under the name Mid-Season Tulips. They are stocky plants, seldom more than 40–50 cm in height, with somewhat angular or rounded flowers. The Mendel varieties are not listed very often but the following Triumph and Mid-Season ones can usually be found, along with a number of others in various colours.

'Dutch Princess' is a rich bright orange, tinged with gold, rather taller than most at about 60 cm.

'Garden Party' has pointed buds opening to a bright pinkish-carmine flower with a wide white zone from the base to the tip on the outside of the petals; it is about 40 cm in height.

'White Dream' is a good pure-white mid-season variety, about 40 cm tall.

Darwin Tulips

These constitute one of the most popular groups, especially for bedding schemes. They have large, rounded flowers about 10–12 cm across, on stems 60–75 cm in height, produced slightly later than the mid-season ones, in early May, and are sometimes grouped together with the Cottage Tulips in catalogues under the heading 'May-Flowering Tulips'.

'Clara Butt' is an old, very popular variety,

still readily obtainable. It has lovely salmon-pink flowers on stems about 60 cm tall.

'Queen of Bartigons' is a beautiful clear pink and is a very strong variety of good constitution, about 60 cm tall.

'La Tulipe Noire' is one of the darkest-coloured varieties in a velvet-like blackish purple; about 60 cm tall.

'Bleu Aimable' is an interesting shade of strong lavender-mauve, about 60 cm in height.

Cottage Tulips

These are very similar to the Darwins and are now sometimes grouped together with them in catalogues as 'May-Flowering Tulips'. The large oval or rounded flowers are carried on strong, stiff stems to about 85 cm.

'Halcro' has large brilliant-red flowers shading to orange-red towards the edges of the petals; 75 cm in height.

'Palaestrina' is a deep salmon and rose mixture, very large on sturdy stems about 45 cm tall.

'Mrs. John Scheepers' is about 65 cm in height with large, oval clear yellow flowers, so good as to be considered by some as the finest yellow Tulip ever produced.

Viridiflora Tulips

Perhaps these are more curious than beautiful with their broad green, lance-shaped marks on the outside of the petals, but they can make a fascinating group in the garden if used in combination with other plants. They are rather late-flowering, about mid-May.

'Artist' is a stocky variety only 25 cm in height, with rose-salmon flowers striped green on the outside, the petals rather wavy and pointed.

'Golden Artist' is similar in shape and size to 'Artist', but the rose colour is replaced by golden-yellow which is enhanced by the green stripe.

'Groenland' is a lovely shade of pink with a green patch on the outside, the petals being less pointed than those of 'Artist'; the height is about 60 cm.

Darwin Hybrid Tulips

These are crosses between the Darwin Tulips and the Central Asiatic species *T. fosteriana*. They are slightly earlier than the Darwins, in late April, and are very vigorous plants, about 60 cm in height. The flowers are large, egg-shaped in bud and come in a range of colours, although the earliest crosses were mostly in bright reds, the colour of *T. fosteriana*. The foliage is conspicuously greyish.

'Apeldoorn' is a bright scarlet-red, about 60 cm tall.

'Golden Apeldoorn' is golden-yellow flecked with red on the outside, also 60 cm tall.

'Gudoshnik' is slightly taller, at about 65 cm, and has a yellowish ground colour covered with flecks and streaks of rose-red.

'Elizabeth Arden' has large flowers of deep rose with a slightly darker stripe in the centre of each petal on the outside.

Lily-Flowered Tulips

These are very distinct and graceful Tulips with narrow-pointed petals often curving outwards at their tips. They are May-flowering varieties which have strong wiry stems, 45–60 cm tall.

'Westpoint' is to me one of the loveliest Tulip hybrids, with clear lemon-yellow flowers having elegant, very narrowly pointed petals; 50 cm tall.

'China Pink' is a lovely shade of deep rose-pink, the tips of the petals outward-curving.

'Queen of Sheba' has urn-shaped flowers in deep red, the petals narrowly margined with yellow; 45 cm tall.

'Maytime' has elegant, pointed outward-curved petals in purple, fading to white at the margins; 45 cm tall.

'Mariette' is about 60 cm tall with deep rose-pink flowers.

Multiflowered Tulips

As the name suggests, these have more than one flower per stem. They flower in May and are not more than 50 cm tall.

'Georgette' has three to four flowers of bright yellow, veined and margined red.

'Orange Bouquet' has three to six bright scarlet flowers with yellow centres.

Parrot and Fringed Tulips

These are not to everyone's taste with their enormous flowers up to 20 cm across, their petals fringed or lacerated and often gaudily streaked with different colours. They are late, usually flowering in mid-May, and have fairly short stems 45–60 cm tall, but even so the heads are often too heavy for them and in windy and rainy weather they are liable to topple over. For those with a liking for the bizarre these curious Tulips will no doubt prove an attraction.

'White Parrot' has wavy white petals, feathered along the edges; 50 cm tall.

'Black Parrot' is an almost blackish colour with strongly lacerated margins to the petals; 60 cm tall.

'Blue Heron' is more conventional in flower shape, rather like a Darwin Tulip, but the violet flowers have a delicate whitish fringe around the apex of the petals; 70 cm tall.

'Estella Rijnveld' is a must for those who like extravagant displays in the garden. The wavy petals with strongly lacerated margins are white, strongly stained and streaked with cherry-red; 60 cm tall.

Rembrandt Tulips

These are mid-May flowering and represent Darwin or Cottage Tulips which have 'broken' colours with streaks and splashes of one colour on another.

'San Marino' has a yellow ground-colour, overlaid with a feathered pattern of rich red; 60 cm tall.

'Sorbet' is white shading to pink, with rose-red markings; 70 cm tall.

Late Double 'Paeony-Flowered' Tulips

These have very large double flowers in late April or early May, somewhat resembling those of a Paeony. Like the Parrot Tulips, they do not stand up to rough weather very well and therefore need a sheltered site where they will not get battered by strong winds. In good weather conditions they last a relatively long time.

'Mount Tacoma' is an old favourite of good constitution in pure white, about 50 cm tall.

'Hermione' has delicate pink flowers on strong stems about 55 cm in height.

'Gold Medal' is slightly shorter at about 45 cm, and has wholly deep golden-yellow flowers.

Fosteriana Tulips

Although some hybrids between this bright-red Central Asiatic species and the Darwin Tulips have been mentioned above under the Darwin Hybrids, there are a number of selections which resemble more closely the wild plant and these are normally listed in catalogues as 'Fosteriana Hybrids'. They are stocky plants at about 25–40 cm in height, flowering in early to mid-April.

'Cantata' is scarlet-orange with a buff tinge on the outside.

'Madame Lefeber' is a brilliant fiery red, sometimes listed as 'Red Emperor'.

'Purissima' is a large white form, opening creamy and changing to a pure white.

'Orange Emperor' is a slightly taller one, about 35–40 cm in height, with beautiful clear orange flowers.

Greigii Tulips

The fascination of this dwarf race of Tulips, derived from the Central Asiatic *T. greigii*, lies partly in the brownish-purple striped foliage and partly in the early, very colourful flowers. They are only 15–35 cm in height and normally flower in March or early April.

'Red Riding Hood' has brilliant scarlet flowers with a blackish base.

'Oriental Splendour' is lemon-yellow inside with a blackish base, while the outside is carmine-red, margined yellow.

'Donnabella' is creamy-yellow with a blackish base.

'Corsage' has very showy flowers of a bright apricot-orange mixture over beautifully marked leaves.

Kauffmanniana Tulips

These are also derived from a Central Asiatic species, the Waterlily Tulip, *T. kauffmanniana*. This is a dwarf, early-flowering plant with broad grey leaves which in some varieties have purple stripes or dots on them, a character inherited from *T. greigii*. There is a wide range of colourful cultivars which are the earliest Tulips to flower, usually opening in March and, being only 12–25 cm in height, are very suitable for window boxes and rock gardens.

'Ancilla' has pointed flowers of ivory-white inside, with a ring of red near the centre, while the outside is carmine, edged with pale ivory-yellow.

'Shakespeare' is a curious but striking mixture of pale yellow suffused with red on the inside and salmon-orange on the outside.

'Stresa' is bright golden-yellow inside, marked near the base with red, and the outside of each petal is crimson with a yellow margin.

The wild Tulip species

Apart from all the above groups of hybrid Tulips, there are many wild species and their various forms, and at the present it is possible to find well over fifty of these offered in the specialist bulb catalogues. However, some of these are not easy to keep without the protection of a bulb frame and others, at several pounds per bulb, are too expensive to experiment with in the open garden, so I shall restrict my list to a few well-tried favourites which will give great pleasure to the keen gardener and which can be replaced if necessary at no great expense. They mostly flower in April or early May.

T. acuminata is a curiosity with long narrow

petals in yellow and red and is not a true wild species. It is 45–60 cm tall.

T. aucheriana is a lovely dwarf species from Iran, with pinkish lilac flowers with a yellow centre, only 8–10 cm tall.

T. batalinii from Central Asia is about 10 cm in height, with grey, wavy leaves flat on the soil and lovely soft yellow flowers. 'Bronze Charm' has a flush of orange on the outside.

T. clusiana is, to me, one of the loveliest of all Tulip species, with stems to 30 cm in height and slender white flowers stained crimson on the outside, with a purple centre inside. It comes from Iran and the western Himalaya. Its var. *chrysantha* (or *T. chrysantha*) is similar in size but has yellow flowers stained red on the outside. Var. *stellata* (*T. stellata*) is white with a red exterior, but differs from *T. clusiana* in having a yellow centre and narrower petals.

T. eichleri is a Central Asiatic species about 25–30 cm in height, with very large orange-red flowers up to 12 cm in diameter, with blackish blotches in the centres.

T. hageri and the very similar **T. orphanidea** and **T. whittallii** are Turkish and Greek plants which grow to about 30 cm in height and have curiously coloured flowers, in shades of dull orange-brown or reddish bronze, with yellow and green suffusion and a blackish centre. Although not spectacular, they are rather attractive.

T. linifolia is an excellent showy dwarf species from Central Asia, with narrow grey wavy leaves and bright scarlet flowers on 10–15 cm stems, opening out flat in the sun.

T. praestans has more than one flower per stem, so is unusual in this respect. It is a Central Asiatic species with broad leaves and stems up to 35 cm tall, carrying two to five intense scarlet flowers. 'Fusilier' is a striking pillar-box red variety.

T. pulchella is a dwarf Turkish species, very variable in its flower colour, so there are several named varieties. It grows only 10 cm in height, with narrow greyish leaves amid which nestle the flowers in various attractive shades of purple, lilac or violet, usually with a yellow centre, although there is a rare and expensive white form with a blue centre. 'Violacea', 'Humilis' (*T. humilis*), 'Violet Queen' and 'Magenta Queen' are all good varieties, flowering early, often in March.

T. saxatilis is an unusual species from Crete and Turkey with broad, glossy green leaves and bright pinkish-lilac flowers with yellow centres. It often has more than one flower on its 30–45 cm stems and is stoloniferous so that it eventually forms patches.

T. sprengeri has the distinction of being the latest Tulip to flower, usually not until June, and I have described it in the Summer Section.

T. sylvestris is a woodland species from Europe and western Asia which has yellow scented flowers on 20–30 cm stems. It is easy to grow but does not flower freely.

T. tarda is a delightful miniature species from Russia, about 10 cm tall with a rosette of leaves and several starry white flowers with large yellow centres.

T. turkestanica from Central Asia has small white yellow-centred flowers which are stained green on the outside, several to each stem which is about 20 cm tall.

T. urumiensis is a good dwarf species only 10–15 cm tall, with bright yellow flowers suffused with green and red on the outside. It originates from N.W. Iran.

CULTIVATION Tulips mostly grow wild on open rocky sunbaked hillsides, often in rather heavy alkaline soils, and the main lesson to be learnt from this is that they prefer plenty of light during their growing season and a fairly warm, dry rest period in summer while dormant; for this reason many people lift their Tulips once the foliage has turned yellow and store the bulbs in a dry place until the autumn. Also, of course, in the case of bedding schemes, they are lifted in order to clear the ground ready for a display of summer bedding. When planted in groups in mixed perennial borders for use in association with other plants, they can be left in place and are often extremely long-lived plants, requiring only that the site should not become too overgrown in summer. Some of the wild species Tulips are, however, less long-lived if left in the ground and it is on the whole better to lift them for the summer or they tend to dwindle away. The more expensive rarer species are certainly best taken care of in this way, but with the cheaper kinds it is probably easier just to replace the bulbs from time to time.

Exceptions are *T. saxatilis* which is best planted in a very hot, sunny situation against a south-facing wall or fence and left to build up into a colony, *T. sprengeri* which, although expensive, is a very easy, long-lived species which seeds itself freely, even in damp situations, *T. sylvestris* which is a woodland plant best left undisturbed in the dappled shade of deciduous shrubs and *T. clusiana* which seems to keep going for several years if planted in a sunny, well-drained position.

The dwarf species are best in a raised part of a rock garden or front of a sunny border and can be successfully combined with spring-flowering rock plants and alpines. It is worth trying out various associations; for example the dwarf yellow *T. tarda* is a superb companion for purple ferny-leaved *Pulsatilla vulgaris*, and the bright red *T. linifolia* is enhanced by grey-leaved subjects.

In sunny borders and bedding schemes there is even more scope for experiment with various combinations of colours, apart from the traditional mixture of Tulips with Forget-me-Nots and Wallflowers, which of course is most attractive and takes a lot of beating. The purple-flowered Honesty makes a good setting for a group of white Darwin, Lily-Flowered or Cottage Tulips and, alternatively, the white form of Honesty enhances golden or purplish Tulips. A favourite spring corner in my own garden is a clump of 'Golden Apeldoorn' near a greyish Rosemary bush which usually bears its soft blue flowers at the same time as the Tulips are in flower. Silvery pink Tulips also

go well with grey leaves and by chance I once found that a group of pale purple Cottage Tulips looked marvellous behind the broad grey leaves of tall bearded Irises, just beginning to elongate prior to flowering.

Tulip bulbs are purchased in the autumn and can be planted at any time through to November since they do not start rooting as early as many of the bulbous plants. They should be planted deeply, about 15 cm being a good average; on light sandy soils the varieties with large bulbs should be 20–25 cm deep, while the small bulbs of some of the species need only 10 cm of soil over the bulbs. The type of soil for the large Tulip cultivars is not too critical, especially if they are to be lifted for the summer months anyway. For any which are to be left in the ground it is best to ensure that the site is freely draining by mixing in some coarse, gritty sand, if the soil is inclined to be heavy; on acid soils it will help to apply some garden lime, worked in thoroughly well before planting.

After flowering, bedding Tulips can be dug up if the site is needed for other things, and the bulbs planted in an odd corner of the garden out of the way until their leaves turn yellow. They can then be lifted again for the summer and placed in boxes in a dry shed or garage where they will be warm but not in direct sunlight; when dry they should be cleaned of the old stems, roots and soil and kept for replanting in autumn. Obviously only the large flowering-size bulbs should be kept if a display is required the next season. Most people probably will not want to bother with growing on the young bulblets since this may take several years, but it can be done and is a way of increasing the stock without extra expense. These small bulbs can be planted in rows, between 5 and 10 cm deep depending upon their size, and left to reach flowering size, which will vary from one to three years.

The species Tulips, and any rare or expensive varieties, are best left in their flowering positions until the foliage has died down, and then the bulbs can be lifted and dried in boxes as described above.

With Tulips which are not bedded out but left in the ground as a permanent feature, the only care needed is to pull off the old leaves and stems once they have withered and to keep the site relatively clear of other vegetation during the summer to that the bulbs receive some warmth from the sun to ripen them. An annual dressing of a potash-rich fertiliser, or sulphate of potash, is beneficial to Tulips, as it is for most bulbous plants, and this is best applied in the late winter or early spring, before the young shoots appear.

Propagation of Tulips is by offset bulbs as mentioned above, or by seeds, although one has to be very patient to wait for them to reach flowering size, for it may take up to seven years. With the more unusual species, however, this may be the only way of acquiring more stock. It is best to sow the seeds thinly in pots and then plant out the young bulbs, after one season of growth, in the autumn into a bulb frame which can be covered in the summer to give them a 'proper' rest period. Grown in this way they can be left in the soil in the frame until they reach flowering size, but when you go to lift them for final planting out, remember that the mature bulbs might well have pulled themselves down to about 30 cm, so don't despair if at first you don't find them!

4

THE BULB GARDEN IN SUMMER
(June–August)

Whereas in spring bulbous plants formed the backbone of the garden display, by the time summer has arrived many shrubs and herbaceous plants are in bloom and will be the focus of our attentions. Bulbs flowering at this time of year are thus mostly used in combination with other plants in mixed borders or in some cases in a more formal way, as with Gladiolus in bedding schemes. Gone are the patches of rough grass which earlier were bright with naturalised Daffodils and Crocuses, for these areas must be mown during summer, continuously through until September when the first of the autumn bulbs appear. There are a few taller species, for example some Lilies, which do well in grass, but if utilised to extend the season in this way they automatically dictate that the area must be left uncut throughout the year, and few gardeners find this desirable, with its unkempt appearance and seeding weeds.

Interestingly, the summer-flowering bulbs are mostly tall plants, in contrast to the numerous dwarf spring species, where Daffodils represent the tallest end of the scale.

It is as well not to plant summer-flowering bulbs with or near spring-flowering ones, since their treatment is so radically different. Their growth cycles are completely opposed, so that in summer, when the autumn-winter-spring growers are dormant and requiring warm, dry conditions to ripen their bulbs, the summer growers are in need of much moisture to fulfil their period of maximum growth.

For a number of our summer bulbs we rely on the southern hemisphere and especially southern Africa which provides us with Gladiolus, Crinum, Eucomis, Galtonia, Moraea, Rhodohypoxis, etc. These all change their growing season by about six months when they are brought northwards, so that here in Britain they reach their peak in June, July or August. The only other major group of summer-flowering bulbs is Lilium and its relatives, many of the best of which come from parts of Asia which receive a monsoon type of rainfall in the months coinciding with our summer. Others occur in mountain areas which do not have a noticeably warm, dry season and so can make their growth through the summer and lie dormant in winter. Only a very few Lilies, such as *L. candidum*, occur in a Mediterranean-type climate and make their main growth between autumn and spring when plenty of moisture is available. Many Lilies are ideally suited to container cultivation and can be most effective when grown in tubs or large pots on a terrace or patio; in gardens where Lilies do not thrive in the open ground this is a good way to treat them, since they can be given careful individual attention.

Most of the tender bulbs, such as Gladiolus, Acidanthera and Tigridia are sold by nurserymen in the spring so that planting can take place soon after their purchase; there might be a slight delay in waiting for the soil to warm up, but usually only a week or two and, if this is the case, the bulbs can be left in their packets in a cool place out of direct sunlight.

Some, such as Lily bulbs, are usually on sale in the autumn and these should be planted straight away (see cultivation notes on page 111), for Lilies begin active root-growth early in the season. Often they can be bought in spring as well and, if purchased at this time of year, must be planted as quickly as possible, for they are usually looking a bit dried up by this time unless they have been stored with considerable care.

Bulbs which require winter storage out of the ground can present some problems, for they need to be away from frost but at the same time not too hot and dry, for they may become desiccated and die; if they are moist and warm they may begin to grow, or rot off. Those which are grown in containers do not present quite as much of a problem since they can be carried into the protection of a shed, garage or greenhouse and left to dry out. During very frosty weather some sacking or old clothing may be necessary to prevent the pots from freezing, but normally they will be safe enough and in their soil will not become too dry. No water should be given until after they are repotted into fresh compost in the spring.

Bulbs which are dug up from the open ground must be dried out to some extent and the loose soil removed, discarding at that time any which are obviously diseased or damaged since they may rot and affect the others. They can be stored in trays or boxes of moss peat (not the black sedge peat) which is not quite dust-dry, or in sand which is similarly almost dry but not quite. This should prevent desiccation but be dry enough to stop them from growing too early. A cool place must be chosen to store the boxes where they cannot be frozen during hard weather, and it pays to inspect them from time to time during such spells to make sure that all is well. A minimum temperature of roughly 45°F is about right for the majority of these bulbs. In some years, if I have rather a lot of bulbs to store and not much time available, I put them into polythene bags which are stood upright in deep card-board boxes with the necks of the bags left open. These, too, need to be kept in a cool place indoors, perhaps an unused, unheated room in the house, or in a slightly heated (frost-free) glasshouse. Stored in this way they do need checking fairly regularly to make sure that they are not too dry or too moist because they can desiccate or rot fairly quickly if conditions are not quite right.

Planting out of these stored bulbs is usually in late March or April depending upon the season, but certainly not before the ground has begun to warm up and the danger of serious ground frosts is over.

Obviously, those summer bulbs which are hardy do not require lifting and storing and can be left in the ground for as long as they are thriving. If container-grown, however, even the hardy ones are best moved to a place where they will not be frozen solid, for few bulbs will survive this treatment. Wooden tubs give reasonably good protection, but clay pots can freeze completely through and this, apart from damaging the bulbs, may also result in cracked pots.

The Summer-Flowering Bulbs

ACIDANTHERA

These Gladiolus-like plants from the mountains of East Africa can usually be found in catalogues under this name, although they are now botanically regarded as species of Gladiolus. They are cormous plants, with long, bold sword-shaped leaves overtopped in late summer or early autumn by the flower stems which reach between 60 cm and a metre in height and carry up to ten flowers. In the most commonly available species, *A. bicolor* (= *Gladiolus callianthus*) and its variants 'Murielae' and 'Zwanenburg', the flowers are pure white with a very dark, prominent eye formed by a deep purple blotch at the base of each segment, and the whole effect is made more graceful by the long curving perianth tube up to 12 cm in length. There is not much to choose between the ordinary *A. bicolor* and its cultivars and, from a decorative point of view, they are all equally attractive.

CULTIVATION Like Gladiolus, these are not hardy except in very favourable southern gardens and it is usual to obtain the corms in spring and plant them out in early to mid-May. The site should be sheltered and sunny, along a south wall or protected by evergreen shrubs behind so as to form a sun-trap, and the soil needs to be well-drained and fairly rich, for these are vigorous plants. Plenty of water is required in summer, so on poor, sandy soils or in stiff clay it is best to mix in thoroughly old rotted compost or manure which will retain moisture; the corms are best planted about 10–15 cm deep. They are slow to reach the flowering stage, so need a long growing season and it may be late autumn before there is any sign of dying down for the winter. At this stage they can be dug up and dried off for storage in a frost-free place; it will usually be found that cormlets have been formed, and these are more useful for propagation purposes than seeds which can take a very long time to produce flowering-size bulbs.

I normally buy new corms each spring and pot them up in a cool greenhouse in March for planting out in May; this gives them a good start and flowers are likely to be produced before there is a risk of autumn frosts. They are also very suitable for growing in tubs on a terrace where the scented flowers are delightful on late summer evenings. I recently found a pleasant association between a patch of about ten Acidantheras planted on the sunny side of a blue-grey Conifer, *Chamaecyparis pisifera* 'Plumosa'.

ALLIUM

Most of the bulbous ornamental species of 'Onion' are late spring or summer-flowering and range from small plants suitable for a rock garden to really tall ones up to a metre or more in height. Although the later ones mostly begin to make their root and leaf growth in winter and spring, they take a long time to reach their peak of flowering and it may be mid-summer before their dense heads of small flowers, known as umbels, expand. There are a great many species, in fact it is one of the largest groups of bulbous plants, but most are of little decorative value and can be ignored. The big summer-flowering ones are often popularly referred to as 'drumsticks', since they have long bare stems with a round umbel of flowers, and a few of these are excellent for cutting and drying for winter decoration. Of the taller species, the following are all good plants for open sunny borders.

A. albopilosum (*A. christophii*) from Central Asia is particularly good for drying, since its starry flowers become almost spiny after they have passed their peak. When fresh they are of a metallic purplish colour, produced in an umbel about 15–20 cm in diameter on 25–50 cm stems. *A. caeruleum* (*A. azureum*), also Asiatic, is unusual in the genus in having bright blue flowers in a very tight smallish umbel about 3–4 cm across in June or July.

One of the largest and most striking is *A. giganteum* which has broad grey-green leaves and a stout stem which can reach two metres in height. This has masses of pinkish-purple flowers in a very dense spherical head up to 15 cm in diameter, so it can be a very striking plant indeed. *A. elatum* is occasionally to be found in catalogues and this is very similar. Both of these are also from the mountains of Central Asia which is probably where *A.*

aflatunense originated, although its exact whereabouts are now obscure. This is an excellent drumstick type, about 75 cm tall with dense purple-flowered umbels 10 cm across, differing from *A. giganteum* in its narrower greyish leaves.

Another of these Asiatic ones which may be encountered in catalogues is *A. rosenbachianum* which is about the same height and also has a spherical umbel but is slightly less densely-flowered and usually darker purple. *A. stipitatum* is similar.

The shortest species in this Asiatic group, *A. karataviense*, is only about 15–20 cm in height but has large umbels resting between bold greyish, purplish-tinged leaves. This normally flowers earlier and is also mentioned in the chapter on the Bulb Garden in Spring.

Europe also has some interesting and attractive taller Alliums suitable for the border and, of the summer-flowering species, it is worth mentioning *A. sphaerocephalon* which has small, tightly globular heads of dark reddish-purple flowers, on stems about 30–50 cm tall. *A. pulchellum* grows to about 20–30 cm in height and is quite different in that the individual violet flowers dangle on pendulous stalks which turn upwards as the flowers go into seed; there is a white form of this, *A. pulchellum* 'Album'. *A. flavum* is very similar in shape, size and general appearance, but has attractive yellow flowers. *A. moly* is also a yellow-flowered early summer species, only 15–25 cm in height, with the individual flowers relatively large and enhanced by the greyish leaves; however, although a most attractive plant, it can sometimes become invasive when it finds an ideal site, since its bulbs produce many offsets.

For rock gardens there are few summer-flowering bulbous species which are dwarf enough, but the very special Asiatic *A. oreophilum* (*A. ostrowskianum*) is a plant not to be missed. It reaches only 15 cm at most and carries relatively large, showy umbels of carmine-pink flowers in early summer.

The curious *A. siculum* (*A. dioscoridis*), with its pendent greenish flowers, will be found under *Nectaroscordum*, its correct name.

CULTIVATION All of those mentioned above can be grown in open, sunny situations in well-drained soils. The bulbs are sold in autumn and should be planted straight away, as soon as they arrive, the most robust types about 10 cm deep and the smaller kinds 5 cm. Drainage must be good, especially for the Asiatic ones which are mostly natives of rocky hillsides, and if the soil is rather heavy it needs to be made more open with a coarse, gritty sand, well mixed in. All are hardy and should suffer no damage from frosts, except perhaps *A. giganteum* which seems to have tender foliage susceptible to spring frosts; this is best given a warm, sheltered position. The tall species make fine border plants, especially in sunny beds by a wall or fence, and look particularly attractive when surrounded by lower-growing greyish foliage plants such as *Santolina chamaecyparissus*, Sage (*Salvia officinalis*), Lavender, Dianthus and *Ballota pseudodictamnus*. If planted in the foreground, the foliage of these will help to hide the rather untidy leaves of the Alliums which are usually beginning to die back by flowering time.

A. moly can be naturalised in semi-shade since it is a plant of light woodlands in Spain, but even this will not tolerate stagnant soils with poor drainage. It is worth trying among shrubs which have already flowered in winter and spring, such as *Viburnum farreri* and Witch Hazel (*Hamamelis*), to add some interest to an otherwise dull part of the summer garden.

Most Alliums produce seed freely and this is easy to grow, although the larger ones may take three or four years to reach flowering size. It will be found that some increase naturally by bulb division, depending upon how well they are growing.

85

86

7

88

89

90

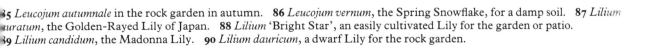

85 *Leucojum autumnale* in the rock garden in autumn.   86 *Leucojum vernum*, the Spring Snowflake, for a damp soil.   87 *Lilium auratum*, the Golden-Rayed Lily of Japan.   88 *Lilium* 'Bright Star', an easily cultivated Lily for the garden or patio.   89 *Lilium candidum*, the Madonna Lily.   90 *Lilium dauricum*, a dwarf Lily for the rock garden.

91

92

93

94

95

96

91 *Lilium* 'Fire King' in front of purplish-leaved *Rosa rubrifolia*.   **92** *Lilium* 'Golden Splendour', a superb Trumpet Lily hybrid.   **93** *Lilium henryi* can reach three metres when growing well.   **94** *Lilium martagon*, a good deep pink form of the Martagon Lily.   **95** *Lilium monadelphum*, an unusual species from the Caucasus.   **96** *Lilium pumilum (tenuifolium)*, a delicate but easily-grown Lily.

97

98

99

100

101

102

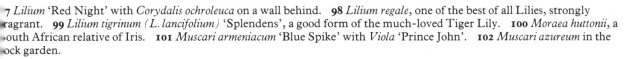

97 *Lilium* 'Red Night' with *Corydalis ochroleuca* on a wall behind. **98** *Lilium regale*, one of the best of all Lilies, strongly fragrant. **99** *Lilium tigrinum (L. lancifolium)* 'Splendens', a good form of the much-loved Tiger Lily. **100** *Moraea huttonii*, a South African relative of Iris. **101** *Muscari armeniacum* 'Blue Spike' with *Viola* 'Prince John'. **102** *Muscari azureum* in the rock garden.

103

104

105

106

107

108

103 *Muscari azureum* 'Album' shows the unconstricted flowers of this Grape Hyacinth.   **104** *Muscari comosum*, the Tassel Hyacinth with its crown of sterile flowers.   **105** *Muscari tubergeniana* is one of the best Grape Hyacinths.   **106** *Narcissus bulbocodium* in grass at Wisley Garden.   **107** *Narcissus* 'Dove Wings' with early Primulas and Tulips.   **108** *Narcissus* 'February Gold' with *Anemone nemorosa* in grass.

ANEMONE

Although the tuberous Anemones are mainly associated with spring flowering (see page 53) certain groups can be purchased at almost any time from autumn through to spring for a succession of flowers. The multi-coloured varieties of the Poppy Anemone, *A. coronaria*, flower about three months after planting so that if, for example, they are obtained and planted in April, they will flower in June or July. The 'De Caen' and 'St. Brigid' Anemones are some of the most well-known, much-loved for their cut flowers in winter and satisfactory garden plants if given a very warm, sunny position. The De Caen varieties are singles, the St. Brigids semi-doubles, and both come in a great range of red, blue, purple and violet shades, sometimes with paler zones around a black boss of stamens in the centre. It is usually only possible to obtain mixed collections, although there are named varieties in commerce.

CULTIVATION For summer flowering, Anemones of this type can be planted at any time from about March onwards, about 5 cm deep, in a sunny situation sheltered from cold winds, so a south-facing border alongside a wall would be ideal where the soil warms up rapidly. It should be well-drained, acid or alkaline, but rich, with a good humus content to retain moisture during dry weather. For the front of a border they can make showy patches of colour and look better if placed between clumps of low-growing, grey-leaved, sun-loving plants such as *Alyssum saxatile*, Lavender or Sage.

ANOMATHECA

Only one species of this small genus is at all hardy, *A. laxa*, or *Lapeirousia cruenta* (*A. cruenta*) as it is sometimes called in literature and catalogues. It comes from the summer rainfall regions of South Africa and its corms are in consequence dormant in winter, giving them a good chance of survival in frosty weather. It has fans of narrow leaves and, in June or July, 15–20 cm stems bearing a few upward-facing red flowers which are flattish but with a long tube; in the centre, at the base of the petals, are some darker red blotches. In addition to this, the most colourful form, there is a white version and one with pale lilac-blue flowers with a purplish blotch in the centre.

CULTIVATION *A. laxa* is a very easily cultivated little plant in a sunny, well-drained position. The small corms are planted in the spring about 3–4 cm deep and in reasonably mild areas may be left in the ground permanently; they have survived for many years in Surrey where I have recorded temperatures down to −15°C. In districts where the ground freezes hard to several centimetres deep it is best to lift the corms in autumn and store them for the winter. Being fairly dwarf, this is a plant for the front of a border or rock garden where it will associate quite well with small rock plants which are not vigorous enough to swamp it. I have one pleasing combination where the whitish ferny-leaved *Corydalis ochroleuca* has seeded next to a clump of the Anomatheca.

Seeds are produced freely, easily visible because they are bright red, and these should be sown in early spring in pots in a frame or greenhouse if available. They usually give rise to flowering-sized corms in only one or two years.

ARISAEMA

This is a fascinating large group of tuberous-rooted plants related to the Cuckoo Pint and Arum Lilies, but unfortunately only a few species are readily obtainable at present. They are mainly Asiatic, from the Himalaya and Japan, although a few occur in other continents as well, and the most garden-worthy one is from China. This is *A. candidissimum*, a very hardy species with whitish hood-like spathes about 10 cm in height, beautifully suffused with pink and green stripes. They unfurl in June and are soon overtopped by the large three-lobed leaves which are not unattractive but require plenty of space. *A. consanguineum* is much more sombre in its colours, the spathe being green with purplish brown stripes, but it is of impressive dimensions with a stout, dramatically spotted stem up to a metre in height, bearing an umbrella-like leaf with many narrow leaflets held just above the spathe. Later on, in late summer, this one usually produces a large head of scarlet seeds which is very striking, but *A. candidissimum* rarely produces good seeds.

CULTIVATION Both of these are hardy and can be grown in any good garden soil to which some humus has been added in the form of leafmould or old compost. Although stagnant, waterlogged conditions must be avoided, they do prefer a soil which has plenty of moisture available during the summer months to allow their robust leaves to develop properly, and very hot, dry situations are not suitable. *A. consanguineum* is best in semi-shade, but *A. candidissimum* seems to be tolerant of a wide range of conditions, from sunny wall beds to peat gardens in shade.

The rounded tubers are completely dormant in winter and are usually obtained in spring for planting in March or April at about 8–10 cm deep. They often take a very long time to emerge from the soil and there may be nothing visible before June, so it is best to avoid the temptation to scratch away the soil to investigate any earlier than this, for it is easy to damage the growing point.

Propagation is fairly easy, since the tubers often produce offsets which can be detached and grown on separately. The best time to do this is either in autumn, when the foliage has died down, or in early spring before growth commences. Seeds, if obtained, can be sown in pots in spring and the young tubers planted out in their permanent positions in spring a year after germination.

BRODIAEA

These North American bulbs, which are not unlike the Onions (*Allium*) in having umbels of flowers, are not widely known in gardens, although a few of them are most attractive for an early summer display. Although the species mentioned below are usually obtainable from nurseries under the name *Brodiaea*, they do in fact belong to the closely related *Triteleia* and may appear in literature under this name. The most likely one to be encountered is the Californian *T. laxa* (*Brodiaea laxa*) which has 25–45 cm stems bearing many-flowered umbels of funnel-shaped blue flowers, each 2.5–4 cm long. The variety listed as 'Queen Fabiola' may well be a selection of this species, or possibly a hybrid, and has flowers of a rich, deep blue. The leaves of these plants are barely noticeable at flowering time, being narrow and almost withered away by early summer. *T. × tubergenii* is a vigorous hybrid with bluish-lilac flowers, possibly a hybrid between *T. laxa* and *T. hyacinthina* (*Brodiaea lactea*). The latter is a common plant in the western United States and differs in having many whitish flowers in a dense umbel. *T. ixioides* may sometimes be seen in gardens and this, too, is very different, having yellow flowers with a purplish line along the centre of each petal. It is also a Californian native but seems to be reasonably frost-hardy.

CULTIVATION The Triteleias require sheltered sunny situations with good drainage. The bulbs are planted in autumn, about 6–8 cm deep, preferably in light soil which, if necessary, has had some gritty sand worked in to improve the drainage. A warm border at the foot of a south-facing wall is the best site, since the ground is unlikely to freeze to a great depth here, even in cold districts. Flowering as they do in early summer, they are useful for extending the bulb season in a bed where one would grow many of the autumn-flowering bulbs such as *Amaryllis* and *Nerine* which will be dormant at this time of year. As I have commented in the chapter on autumn bulbs, it is well worth planting a few grey-leaved, evergreen plants such as Sage and Lavender to provide interesting foliage which will enhance the otherwise rather bare appearance of the bulbs.

CAMASSIA

These large Scilla-like bulbous plants are almost entirely from North America where their bulbs were formerly eaten by the Indians, hence the name *C. esculenta* (edible) for one of the species. The correct name for this one is now *C. quamash*, derived from the Indian name for the plant. This flowers in early summer, in May or June, and has a tuft of long, linear greyish-green basal leaves followed by long racemes, up to 60 or 70 cm high, of starry blue flowers, each much larger than those of a Scilla, at about 3–5 cm across. Another species occasionally offered is *C. leichtlinii*, a vigorous one up to a metre or more in height with single blue, single white ('Alba') or double flowers ('Semiplena').

CULTIVATION Camassias are often native in moist grasslands, so in gardens it is consequently necessary to provide them with plenty of moisture in the growing season. The bulbs are obtained in autumn and planted about 6–7 cm deep in good garden soil which has a high humus content to assist in the retention of moisture. They can be grown in clumps in the border along with other perennials and are attractive alongside a garden pool where they enjoy the extra moisture in summer. I have also succeeded with them in some rough grass where other bulbs have been naturalised, but the drawback with this siting is that they prevent the cutting of the grass until mid to late summer.

A few bulbs of Camassias will, when growing happily, soon clump up and can be divided from time to time. Seeds are also produced and are easily raised to flowering-sized bulbs in about three to four years.

CARDIOCRINUM

This close relative of the Lilies is a bulbous plant of enormous proportions, the most well-known species, *C. giganteum*, being capable of reaching a height of 2–4 metres, with heart-shaped leaves up to 45 cm across! In July and August, at the apex of the stout stem, are borne between five and twenty pendulous fragrant trumpet-shaped flowers, white with reddish purple staining in the throat, up to 15 cm long. This lovely Himalayan plant has one great disadvantage in that its bulb dies after flowering, but at the same time it produces several offset bulbs around the exhausted parent and these can be grown on to flowering size in about three years. So, if you do intend to grow this plant year after year, it is worth buying a bulb or two—they are usually too expensive to buy many—each year for about three years, when there will be a succession of young ones coming on. However, they really are only for the gardener with a fair amount of space available, for bulbs should not be planted closer than about a metre to allow for the large leaf growth.

CULTIVATION Cardiocrinum is a woodland plant requiring a degree of protection from surrounding small shrubs which will keep off any hard frosts in the early spring. It also enjoys cool, moist growing conditions in summer so, again, it requires light shade for its roots. The soil should be rich, with plenty of old manure worked in to at least 60 cm deep and any available leafmould, peat or old compost which will provide the woodland-type soil so necessary for its well-being. The bulbs are obtainable in the autumn and should be planted while they are still damp and fresh, with the tip level with the surface, covering shallowly with a thin layer of loose leafmould. Flowering in late summer, a small group of these can be highly dramatic in a clearing with dappled sunlight, near dark green-leaved shrubs such as Rhododendrons, but for success you must not forget the need for water during hot, dry spells. After flowering in the autumn, the young bulblets are dug up and replanted in a newly prepared position where they are left until flowering size in a few years' time.

CRINUM

The only really hardy member of this lovely race of primarily tropical bulbs of the Amaryllis family is *C. × powellii*, a hybrid between two South African species. It has pink or white ('Album') funnel-shaped flowers in an umbel, on stout stems up to a metre in height, produced in late summer or early autumn.

A fuller description of this plant is given under the Autumn Section on page 26, together with cultivation and propagation details and recommendations as to where to place it in the garden.

CROCOSMIA (Montbretia)

Although the common orange Montbretia (*C. × crocosmiflora*) is somewhat scorned by keen gardeners because it is such a prodigious increaser, it is a fine, colourful late summer bulb which will grow in a variety of situations with the minimum of attention. In addition to the 'original' one there are other cultivars in various colours which are less rampant, very suitable for the herbaceous border, and one impressive tall, large-flowered species, *C. masonorum*, which can make a fine focal point in a border.

Crocosmias are South African plants, having corms which produce replacements every year, but the old ones do not die away as in Gladiolus, so there is a tendency for clumps of

corms to build up. They are winter-dormant summer growers and in spring push up fans of rather Iris-like leaves, but it is not until July or August that the flower stems appear. *C. × crocosmiflora* varieties grow to about 60–80 cm in height, with branched stems bearing trumpet-shaped flowers about 4 cm long. Many nurseries offer mixed collections in colours ranging from yellow to orange and red, but it is possible to obtain specific colours in named varieties such as 'Bressingham Orange', 'Emily McKenzie' (orange with brownish-red marks in the centre), 'Canary Bird' (bright yellow), 'Emberglow' (orange-red), 'Lucifer' (red), 'Jackanapes' (yellow and orange flowers mixed), 'His Majesty' (orange-scarlet with a yellow centre), 'Spitfire' (fiery orange), 'Star of the East' (rather wide open, pale orange flowers), and a particular favourite of mine with bronze foliage and yellow flowers, 'Solfatare'. The species *C. masonorum* is a taller plant, about 75 cm in height, with broader pleated sword-shaped leaves. The large orange flowers have widely spreading segments which leave the stamens and styles protruding prominently, and they are packed closely along the upper side of gracefully arching stems. The parents of the hybrid Montbretias, *C. pottsii* and *C. aurea*, are rarely cultivated.

CULTIVATION   In all but the very mildest parts of the country, the best situation for these plants is a sheltered, sunny border, for they can suffer in the winter in cold, damp soils. Drainage must be good in order to avoid these wet winter soils but, conversely, plenty of water is necessary in summer to maintain vigorous growth. Plant the corms in early spring about 5–8 cm deep, in groups of at least five to be effective, preferably in light soil so it may be necessary to add gritty sand in poorly drained situations. In cold districts where the ground regularly freezes in winter, it is best to lift the corms and store them in not-quite-dry sand in a frost-free shed until the following spring, but in milder areas they are better left in their permanent positions for clumps to build up. *C. masonorum* is certainly best if it can be left undisturbed, so choose a warm, sheltered spot and, in cold areas, cover the site with loose material such as bracken or dry leaves in winter.

The brightly coloured flowers of Crocosmias associate well with a range of other herbaceous plants, but look particularly effective against dark-leaved backgrounds such as *Cotinus coggygria* 'Royal Purple' or a Copper Beech hedge.

Propagation is simply a matter of dividing established clumps, although seeds are produced and can be sown in spring if one wishes to try to raise some mixed colours, for the named ones will probably not breed true.

CURTONUS

This large Montbretia-like plant grows wild in the Eastern Cape region of South Africa and is thus a summer grower, flowering in August or September. *C. paniculatus* (= *Antholyza*) is the only species, a bold plant reaching to over a metre in height, with broad, pleated sword-shaped leaves and a branched zig-zag flower stem which carries many tubular orange-red flowers 4–5 cm long. These have fairly small lobes, not widely spreading like those of the somewhat similar *Crocosmia masonorum*.

CULTIVATION Like the Montbretias, a well-drained, sunny position is best, but one which will not be dry and dusty in summer, for they require plenty of moisture to support the vigorous growth. The corms should be planted in spring, about 6–8 cm deep and, during planting, must not be allowed to dry out. If the soil is inclined to be heavy or poorly drained, mix in some coarse sand and leaf-mould or moss peat to help break it up. In most districts there should be no problem over hardiness if a sunny, sheltered site is chosen, but in cold areas it is advisable to cover the

resting corms with some loose litter such as bracken, leaves or rough peat.

Propagation is a matter of dividing established clumps in early spring or by seed sown in spring, although this is, of course, a much longer process.

Curtonus is a stately plant and can be most effective if it is not surrounded by other tall summer plants. The bright orange flowers are seen to the best advantage if something dark is placed in the background, such as a purple-leaved *Berberis*, *Cotinus* or deep blue-green Conifer. Low foreground plants in grey, like *Stachys lanata*, accentuate the stature of this striking plant.

CYPELLA

This curious South American plant is somewhat like an Iris in its overall shape of flower, in that there are three large, wavy outer segments (known as 'falls' in an Iris) and three smaller, inner ones, but in the case of Cypella the inner ones are curiously folded and inrolled and the plant is bulbous, more closely related to *Tigridia* than Iris. *C. herbertii* is the most likely species to be encountered in cultivation and is the hardiest.

Although *Cypella* has the same disadvantage as *Tigridia*, of the flowers each lasting less than a day, it makes up for this by producing several in succession and they are of such interest that it is well worth planting a small group. The stems of *C. herbertii* are about 30–50 cm in height with mostly basal leaves which are pleated lengthways, and these are overtopped by the branching flower stems in July. Each flower is about 5 cm in diameter, a deep mustard or golden yellow, spotted with purple in the centre.

CULTIVATION *C. herbertii* is hardy in the warmer parts of the country and, unless the ground regularly freezes hard in winter, it is well worth trying some bulbs in a sheltered, sunny position along a south wall or fence. If there is any doubt about their chances of survival, the bulbs can be lifted and stored like Tigridias when they become dormant in autumn. They are usually offered in spring bulb catalogues and should be planted as soon as the warmer weather arrives, in April or May, in light, well-drained soil about 4–5 cm deep. Alternatively, they can be potted and started into growth in a cold frame or greenhouse until late May and then planted out. In favoured spots, *Cypella herbertii* may well start seeding itself around, for seeds are normally produced in large quantities. In colder districts these can be gathered in autumn and sown in pots in the spring, planting the young bulbs out at the start of their second summer growing season after germination, when they should reach flowering size.

Cypella associates well with other sun-loving plants, but they should not be too brightly coloured and distracting. Lavender bushes or *Nepeta* (Catmint) make a good foil for the yellow flowers and provide some protection for the dormant bulbs during the winter months.

DIERAMA

The Wand Flower or Angel's Fishing Rod is one of the most graceful of all the members of the Iris family, but it is seldom seen in gardens. *D. pulcherrimum*, the most commonly offered one, is South African and comes from the summer rainfall region where it grows in rather damp places and never dries out completely. It has slender leaves and long, wiry stems reaching 1–1.5 metres in height, arching over at the apex so that the funnel-shaped flowers are held in a pendulous position, hence the fishing rod analogy. There are many colour variants from pale pink to deep purple, some of which have been given cultivar names such as 'Kingfisher' (pale pink), 'Skylark' (deep violet) and 'Windhover' (pink), but the most usual form seen has mid pinkish-

purple flowers. A shorter variety, about 45–60 cm in height, is known as 'Pumilum' and there is a beautiful white, 'Album', which unfortunately seems to have become rather difficult to obtain.

CULTIVATION Dieramas are best planted in spring, and if possible it is preferable to acquire pot-grown plants for they do not like disturbance and once established are best left alone. Being summer growers, they need plenty of moisture through the season, so hot, dry situations are not suitable. The best group I have ever seen were self-sown ones, from an original planting, which were seeding into all the cracks in paving around a sheltered garden pond. The corms pulled themselves naturally down to at least 10 cm in the soil, to give you an idea of the correct planting depth, and at that level seemed to be extremely hardy. In spite of having corms, Dieramas never really go dormant and, although they die back somewhat in winter, they are more or less evergreen plants. For this reason they are seldom offered by the nurseries which deal primarily in dried bulbs, but some of the more specialised smaller firms sometimes have them for sale in the growing state.

Propagation can be by division of established clumps, but since these plants are best when undisturbed it is really better to collect seeds and sow them thinly in pots in spring, planting the young seedlings out one year later into their permanent positions.

DRACUNCULUS

There are some plants which are worth growing for their curiosity value rather than beauty, adding a touch of interest that raises the whole garden above the ordinary. *Dracunculus vulgaris* is one such plant, a rather impressive Mediterranean member of the Arum family which has rounded tubers giving rise to stout, prominently blotched stems up to a metre in height. This is first topped by an elegantly divided leaf and then, in June, a huge maroon-purple spathe 30–45 cm in length, with an erect pencil-like shiny maroon spadix protruding from the centre. The main drawback to this impressive plant is the disgusting smell emitted by the spathe to attract flies which are its means of pollination, but unless it is planted very close to a door or window this will not cause much concern.

CULTIVATION In the wild, *D. vulgaris* grows in Mediterranean scrub at low altitudes, so it is a rather tender plant in cold parts of the country. A sheltered, sunny position suits it best, where its tall stems can push up between other plants while the dormant tubers gain some protection from them in winter. Cistus bushes are ideal and appropriate, for they are natural wild companions of *Dracunculus*. The tubers normally produce their own offsets, so propagation is simply a matter of lifting the clumps in late summer and dividing them before replanting. The planting depth should be about 15 cm.

EUCOMIS

The Pineapple Flower is an unusual member of the Lily family, so called because of the tuft of small leaves which overtop the flower spike, like those of a pineapple. There are several species from the summer rainfall part of South Africa, and in our northern gardens they lie dormant in winter and come into growth in summer. I have found them to be surprisingly hardy and have become more and more adventurous in trying several of them outside in permanent positions; so far none has been killed by winter conditions.

The large, rounded bulbs first produce a rosette of fleshy leaves, deep green or purplish-tinged, sometimes wavy at the margins, and then a stout central spike of star-shaped waxy flowers in late summer, topped by the tuft of smaller leaves. Depending upon the species, the flowers are white, green, or pinkish-

tinged, varying widely in the size of the spike from about 20 cm in the small white *E. zambesiaca* to a metre or more in *E. pole-evansii* which is an enormous plant rarely seen in this country. *E. undulata* (*E. autumnalis*), with greeny-white flowers and wavy-edged leaves, is less uncommon and the striking *E. comosa* (*E. punctata*) is also to be found in cultivation. This has its flowers often tinged pink and the ovary is purple, giving a dark eye to each flower, so it is one of the more colourful species. The most likely species to be encountered is *E. bicolor* which is usually on offer in the spring bulb catalogues and, although not a striking plant, has a quiet charm and is especially attractive for growing on a patio in a wooden tub or large clay pot. The bold, rich green leaves are overtopped in July and August by purple-spotted stems bearing 30 cm spikes of many green flowers, each petal of which is margined with violet. Although not strongly fragrant, *Eucomis* attract many insects when in flower, and they last in good condition for weeks since there are so many flowers to open in succession.

CULTIVATION If Eucomis are planted out in the garden, a sheltered, sunny position should be chosen, against a south or west wall or fence, and the bulbs planted in spring at least 10 cm deep. The soil needs to be well supplied with moisture in summer, so a liberal amount of well-decayed compost or manure should be dug in deeply before planting. In pots or tubs, one bulb will need a container about 20 cm in diameter and three bulbs, which will look much better, require one at least 30 cm across. They can be kept dryish in winter and housed away from frost, then started into growth in April, keeping well watered and fed with a liquid fertiliser every two weeks; a John Innes no. 2 potting compost is suitable, with some old manure at the bottom of the container. It is worth repotting them every year, when division can be carried out if the bulbs have split up naturally. Seed is usually produced and can be sown in early spring in pots in a greenhouse to begin with, potting on or planting out as they grow through the summer.

If planted in the garden, care must be taken not to place colourful plants alongside, for the quiet colours of the *Eucomis* will be completely lost among taller, brighter subjects or strong greens. It is worth trying some shorter companions such as the golden-leaved and purple-leaved varieties of Sage (*Salvia officinalis*).

FREESIA

Although these familiar tender South African bulbs are associated mainly with the winter cut-flower market and greenhouse cultivation, it is possible to obtain 'treated' corms in the spring for planting outside in April or May for flowering in late summer; they will, of course, not survive through the winter and it is probably better to buy in new ones, similarly treated, each year than to try to keep the old ones. They should be planted about 5–7 cm deep in a sheltered situation in reasonably rich, well-drained soil and kept well watered through their growing period. Their well-known funnel-shaped, curiously 'lop-sided' spikes of fragrant flowers come in a great range of colours; the bulbs are usually offered in mixed collections.

GALTONIA

Of the three or four known species of this attractive South African genus, only *G. candicans* is at all well known and is generally obtainable. However, it is the most showy of the group, the others being greenish-flowered, although also attractive in their own quiet way. Galtonias are natives of the eastern Cape, receiving summer rainfall, and are thus dormant in winter, and they behave in the same way in northern hemisphere gardens. The bulbs are obtained and planted in the spring,

make their growth through our summer and flower between July and September.

G. candicans is a stately plant with long, slightly greyish-green basal leaves and a stiff, straight flower stem reaching about 1 metre or more in height, which carries up to 30 pendulous, creamy-white scented bells. These are about 3 cm in length and well spaced out on the upper part of the stem and, since they open in succession, provide a display over quite a long period.

CULTIVATION Galtonias are hardy in most southern districts, but in areas where the ground freezes solid in the winter it is best to lift and store them in late autumn. Planting can take place between February and April, depending upon the district and season, but do not plant while there is still a chance of the ground freezing. The planting depth is about 10–15 cm. The soil should be reasonably fertile and well-drained and, if inclined to be sandy and dry in summer, it is best to dig in deeply some well-rotted compost which will help to retain moisture. Heavy, cold clays are not very suitable but can be improved enough to grow this lovely plant successfully by digging in gritty sand and humus. Plenty of moisture must be supplied during the growing season. Propagation is by seed, sown in the spring.

The best site is a sheltered but open sunny spot in a mixed herbaceous border or shrub border and this is a particularly good plant for brightening up an area where there is a dark background, perhaps of Rhododendrons which are so drab during their non-flowering season. Galtonias are unimpressive as individuals, so bulbs need to be grouped together, about ten in a group, to be really effective. In the herbaceous border they are only really striking if surrounded by low-growing companions which accentuate their stature. In a sunny bed by a wall they do well and look particularly attractive with silver and grey plants.

GLADIOLUS

This genus needs little description, for everyone knows the summer bedding types with their gaily coloured, one-sided spikes of flowers which are becoming, by breeding and selection, more varied and colourful by the year. As a whole the genus is an interesting and very widespread one in both the northern and southern hemispheres, and the species from different areas behave very differently in cultivation. Broadly speaking, there are three main groups to consider from the garden viewpoint:

(a) Those from Europe, the Mediterranean region and western Asia; these are hardy, small-flowered species which begin to grow in autumn or winter, are in leaf in early spring and then flower in early summer, dying down for a rest period during the heat of mid-late summer. They are mostly not very showy plants and very little, if any, selection has taken place, so that they are mainly available as 'straight' species from a few specialist bulb growers. In this category come *G. byzantinus*, *G. communis*, *G. imbricatus* and *G. italicus* (*G. segetum*), of which the first is the most showy and is a valuable hardy garden plant.

(b) Those from the south-western part of South Africa which, like the Mediterranean, has winter rainfall. The many Gladiolus species from this region are, in consequence, winter-growing, and in cultivation they continue to behave in this way, mostly flowering in late winter or early spring. Unfortunately nearly all of them are not frost-hardy and, even in the relatively mild southern counties, they will not survive outdoors. I have seen the attractive creamy *G. undulatus* thriving unprotected in a very sheltered position, and this is occasionally offered by nurserymen, but mainly the species in this group are cool greenhouse plants and do not concern us here.

(c) Those species from the eastern part of South Africa, extending northwards through Tropical Africa to Ethiopia. There are a lot of species in this category and, again, most of them are tender, but the big difference from group (b) is that they are summer-growing and consequently can be lifted and stored away from frost for the winter. Most of the species are little-known and are not available in the nursery trade, but the hybrids between a few of them constitute the enormous range of showy summer Gladioli which we have at our disposal for bedding or as cut flowers. A few of the species from the mountains of the eastern Cape are hardy and can be left in the ground through the year, and some of the smaller hybrids are hardy in mild areas, but most of the Gladioli in this group are tender. In addition to all the 'Large Flowered' Gladiolus hybrids, 'Butterfly' hybrids, 'Primulinus' hybrids, 'Miniature' hybrids, and the varieties listed under *G. nanus*, the species *G. papilio* (*G. purpureo-auratus*) and *G. saundersiae*, which also belong to this group, are sometimes available.

Ignoring the group (b) winter-growing greenhouse types, we are left with the hardy northern hemisphere species, which can be planted in autumn and left in the ground all the year, and the summer-flowering varieties and species which are planted out in spring for the growing season and usually lifted again for the winter, although, as mentioned above, in some milder districts a few of these types can be left in the ground, and *G. papilio* is very hardy.

Northern Hemisphere Hardy Species and their Cultivation

These require open situations in warm, sunny borders and look well when planted in clumps near silver and grey-leaved plants, for their flowers are mainly in the colour range of pinkish-carmine to reddish-purple, a colour which needs something neutral nearby for the best effect. A background of Rosemary or a Cistus bush is ideal. The Mediterranean *G. byzantinus* is a particularly vigorous and easy plant and is probably the best of the group, with the brightest flower colour, a deep reddish-purple, about 60–80 cm in height and increasing rapidly to form clumps of corms; there is a white variety of this which has unfortunately become rather rare. *G. communis* is similar, but a paler colour in rose-pink, with dark and light stripes on the lower segments. *G. imbricatus* is occasionally offered for sale and has reddish-purple flowers all facing in one direction on the spike, whereas the others mentioned have them roughly facing in two directions. The common European species, sometimes a weed in fields around the Mediterranean, is *G. italicus* (*G. segetum*) and this too has its pinkish-lilac flowers in two ranks on the stem.

All the species in this group do well on chalky soils and appear to need warm, well-drained soils in order to flower well, although there must be plenty of moisture available during their development period. The corms should be planted at a depth of about 8–10 cm.

Southern Hemisphere Gladioli and their Hybrids

There are quite a number of summer-growing species in Africa which are nearly hardy because they are dormant in winter. However, only *G. papilio* (*G. purpureo-auratus*) can be claimed as reliably hardy and this, unfortunately, is not very showy. It does, however, have a quiet charm and is worth growing for its unusual appearance. The stem will reach up to a metre in height and carry up to ten strongly hooded flowers, rather like curved bells, in muted colours of yellowish-green flushed with purple. This likes cool growing conditions in moist, humus-rich soil and will do particularly well in open patches in the shrub border, flowering in late summer. Very occasionally *G. saundersiae* is to be seen in cultivation and this is quite spectacular by comparison, for it has much larger, bright red flowers, with the segments flaring outwards, the lower ones with large white zones. This needs a warm, sheltered position to do really well, but must have plenty of moisture in

summer and is best protected by some loose bracken, peat or leaves in winter.

The most important Gladioli in this summer group are, of course, the hybrids which have a very complicated parentage and history dating back to the early nineteenth century when new species were being introduced from South Africa via Cape Town to England. Although the early crosses were made in Britain, the main work took place on the Continent in France, Belgium, Germany and Holland, and the breeding and selection still continues, notably in these countries, Australia and America. Corms are produced by the million and new varieties are constantly being introduced, so that it is very difficult for the non-specialist to keep up with the latest developments. The British Gladiolus Society has a classification of the hybrids for ease of reference and for showing, and this is mainly based on the diameter of the flower. There are, in nurserymen's catalogues, usually four groups to be found: the well-known 'Large-Flowered' Gladioli, the smaller 'Butterfly' and 'Primulinus' varieties and the early-flowering 'Nanus' varieties; sometimes there are 'Miniature' varieties on offer as well, which are also small-flowered and fairly short compared with the Large-Flowered types. As hybridisation continues, these groups are becoming less obvious to distinguish by all but the very experienced enthusiast. Gladiolus belonging to the above groups, except the 'Nanus' varieties, are for spring planting, and corms are normally on sale from the late winter onwards. The 'Nanus' types are rather different and they are normally obtained and planted in autumn, at a depth of about 8–10 cm.

Cultivation of the Southern Hemisphere Gladioli and their Hybrids

Gladiolus are perfect for formal bedding schemes since their very stiff, symmetrical spikes lend themselves ideally to this form of gardening. They also have a great value in the mixed border, planted in small groups between other herbaceous plants and shrubs, but care must be taken that they get plenty of sun. Planting should take place from mid-March onwards, depending upon the weather, since frosty conditions must be avoided, and the corms should be about 10–12 cm deep and the same apart. The soil needs to be well-drained and reasonably fertile and, if at all on the heavy side, it is best to mix in some sharp sand at planting time. The flowering time varies from July to September, and, soon after this, the leaves will begin to die back so that by about mid-October, and before any serious frosts, the corms can be dug up, dried and stored in a dry, cool but frost-free place for the winter. Before replanting in spring, they need to be sorted for quality, cleaned up by removing old, loose skins and the cormlets detached and saved, if desired, for propagation. These can be grown on separately in rows in rich, well-drained soil, for example in a part of the vegetable garden; in good conditions they will reach flowering size in two growing seasons.

If the right companions are chosen for these Gladiolus hybrids their use in the border can be very effective, with some thought given to colour schemes. Their spiky, upright growths contrast well with plants of diffuse habit and the large sprays of white flowers of *Gypsophila paniculata* make an ideal foil for any of the reddish-orange and salmon-coloured varieties. Paler orange, yellow and white Gladioli could be enhanced by planting with the feathery, purple-leaved variety of Fennel (*Foeniculum vulgare* 'Purpureum') or lemon-yellows and creams could be tried near silver-leaved blue *Echinops*. It is fun experimenting with various combinations of plants, and the range of modern Gladiolus varieties gives almost unlimited choice of colour.

Although the easiest way to choose varieties is to go through a nurseryman's catalogue, or look at the colour pictures on the packs in garden centres, I have picked out a few named ones in each group which are fine varieties currently available.

The Larger Flowered Hybrids

These are robust plants, reaching 1.2 metres and carrying dense spikes of large flowers, each between 6 and 15 cm in diameter and flowering between July and September, depending upon the variety.

'Aristocrat'—beautiful shade of deep reddish-purple

'Blue Conqueror'—deep violet blue with paler throat

'Carmen'—bright scarlet with white throat

'Day Dream'—salmon pink with a cream throat

'Flower Song'—deep yellow-gold with carmine marking

'Green Woodpecker'—medium sized greenish yellow flowers with red marks in throat

'Mabel Violet'—large violet flowers

'Peter Pears'—soft orange shading to yellow, with red blotches in throat

'Toulouse Lautrec'—apricot-salmon with yellow throat and brownish-red blotches

'Traderhorn'—bright scarlet-red, white in the throat

'White Friendship'—large white flowers.

Butterfly Hybrids

These are rather smaller than the above types, with dense spikes of flowers, each of which is 5–10 cm across and often strikingly blotched inside on the lower three segments. They flower in July and August.

'Antoinette'—yellow with red throat markings

'Camborne'—lilac stained darker violet

'Impromptu'—white with bright red blotches in throat

'Melodie'—salmon-pink with scarlet throat blotches

'Oberon'—red with clear yellow blotches

'Orchid Beauty'—pink with deep red blotches

'Sunset'—red with darker blotches.

Primulinus Hybrids

These hybrids take their name from the African *G. primulinus* and to some extent they retain the distinctive flower shape of this species, with a strongly hooded upper segment. The flowers are more loosely arranged on the spike and are about 5–8 cm in diameter, produced in July and August. They are, to me, much more attractive than the enormous Large-Flowered hybrids and are not usually quite so garish as the Butterfly group.

'Carioca'—salmon-orange

'Columbine'—carmine pink with a white blotch in the throat

'Essex'—purple with a white throat

'Robin'—dark reddish-purple

'White City'—pure white

'Yellow Special'—a fine yellow variety.

Gladiolus 'Nanus' Hybrids and their Cultivation
These are early-flowering varieties, originating from a cross between the Cape species *G. tristis* and *G. cardinalis*, and are to be found under the names *G. nanus* or *G. × colvillei*. They are delicate-looking, small-flowered plants, about 45–60 cm in height, and flower in June or July when grown outside in the open garden. The corms are usually on sale in the autumn, for they normally begin to form new roots at this time of year, and in mild districts should be planted around October in a sheltered sunny position in any good, well-drained garden soil. A narrow border at the foot of a south wall is an admirable site. In cold areas, however, it is better to pot them up, about five corms to a 15 cm diameter pot, and over-winter them in a cool greenhouse for planting out in spring; any warmth applied during this time will encourage them into early growth, so it is best to keep them just frost-free, unless it is intended to keep them in pots for early flowering. Corms can sometimes also be obtained in spring for planting at the end of March. In situations where frost does not regularly penetrate deeply into the soil, they can be left in the ground permanently, perhaps with some protection from a layer of loose leaves or bracken.

'Amanda Mahy'—salmon with violet spotting

'The Bride' (*colvillei* 'The Bride')—white starry flowers with a greenish blotch

'Good Luck'—salmon pink with a darker red throat

'Guernsey Glory'—pink with reddish markings

'Nymph'—pure white with pink markings

'Prince Claus'—white with red blotches in the throat

'Spitfire'—scarlet-red with purplish throat blotches.

IRIS

The only groups of bulbous Irises which flower in the summer season are the western Mediterranean Spanish Iris (*Iris xiphium*), the Pyrenean 'English' Iris (*I. xiphioides* or *I. latifolia*) and the Dutch Iris hybrids. These are very popular when forced for the cut-flower market during the winter months, but are also excellent garden plants for the summer border. They are all very similar in appearance, producing from their sizeable brown-jacketed bulbs narrow-channelled leaves, which are usually silvery-green on the upper side, and then tough, wind-resistant 30–75 cm stems bearing terminal flowers in a wide range of colours. They are often in rather clear shades, giving them a very clean-cut appearance, and there is normally a contrasting yellow blotch or stripe on the three large outer segments, or 'falls' as they are commonly known.

CULTIVATION   The bulbs are obtained in autumn and should be planted about 8–12 cm deep, as early as possible. The English Iris is very hardy and will grow well in an open position in ordinary, reasonably fertile garden soil which is well supplied with moisture and does not dry out too much in summer, but the Dutch and Spanish both require sunny, sheltered situations, especially in cold districts, in well-drained soil. All will do perfectly well on alkaline soils. Unlike the English Iris, whose leaves appear in spring, the Dutch and

Spanish types produce their foliage in the autumn and, since this can be damaged during hard winters, it is best, in sites which are likely to receive sharp frosts, to keep a cloche handy, or some bracken if available, to place over them during cold spells. The Dutch hybrids are usually the first to flower, in June, followed shortly after by *I. xiphium*, the Spanish Iris and its forms, and finally by the English Iris varieties in July.

Although these Irises are often sold as mixed collections, it is possible to obtain separate colours under named varieties and these are preferable if you wish to experiment with plant associations in the garden; the mixed varieties are fine for making a splash of colour, or for cutting. I buy a few of the Dutch hybrids each year, since they are fairly cheap, for planting in small groups adjacent to something which is likely to harmonise with them; although this sometimes does not work, and the effect may not continue year after year because the bulbs deteriorate, it is certainly fun trying out new combinations of plants, even if it is for one season only. The white and bluish varieties, for example, look very attractive on the sunny side of a greyish-green conifer, and the yellows and browns are effective when backed by a variegated ivy on a wall, or some other variegated-leaved shrub. English Irises can be left in the ground permanently for as long as they are continuing to perform well, but the Dutch and Spanish varieties, unless growing in a very warm situation, will require lifting after they have died down in summer, and the bulbs dried out in a warm (not sun-baked) place until replanting time in September; this ripens the bulbs properly and encourages them to flower the next year.

Propagation of these bulbous Irises is by bulb division at replanting time, since young bulblets are naturally formed fairly readily. The following varieties of each of the three groups are sometimes available.

English Iris *(I. latifolia* or *I. xiphioides)*
This species has been selected to give quite a range of colour variants in blue, violet, purple and white, but not yellow or bronze such as exist in the other groups. They all have a yellow mark in the centre of the falls and usually have larger flowers than the Dutch and Spanish, on stems 45–75 cm in height. They are usually only available in mixed collections but the following varieties have been named.

> 'Almona'—pale lavender-blue
> 'Blue Giant'—deep bluish-purple
> 'La Nuit'—reddish-purple
> 'Mont Blanc'—pure white.

Spanish Iris *(I. xiphium)*
This is a more slender plant than the English Iris, with smaller, earlier flowers in a wider range of colours. The range is from light to deep blue, yellow, bronze, white or sometimes bicoloured, with the falls and standards different. They are smallish plants, usually 30–45 cm in height, and flower in late June, the flowers being slightly smaller than those of the English and Dutch types. These, too, are usually only available in a mixed collection, but there are named varieties and occasionally the yellow var. *lusitanica* can be obtained.

> 'Blue Angel'—bright blue
> 'Cajanus'—yellow
> 'Queen Wilhelmina'—white
> 'Reconnaissance'—purple standards and brownish falls.

Dutch Iris
These are the most popular and most readily obtainable, in a wide range of named varieties. They are the earliest of the three groups to flower, usually in the first two weeks of June from an autumn planting; prepared bulbs are sometimes on sale in the spring and these will not flower until late summer. They are hybrids in which the Spanish *I. xiphium* and the North African *I. tingitana*, a tender species which is seldom cultivated, have both played a part; they are excellent, robust garden plants, slightly easier to grow than the 'straight'

Spanish Iris varieties. They are mostly be-tween 40 and 60 cm in height.

> 'Bronze Queen'—bronze standards and deep yellow falls
>
> 'Distinction'—cream standards and pale yellow falls
>
> 'Golden Harvest'—deep golden-yellow
>
> 'Imperator'—deep blue, yellow-striped on falls
>
> 'Professor Blaauw'—gentian-blue with prominent yellow stripe on falls
>
> 'White Excelsior'—pure white with yellow stripe on falls.

IXIA

The South African Corn Lilies are actually members of the Iris family and are not hardy in most areas since they normally grow through the winter months, which makes them susceptible to frost damage. However, it is possible to obtain the corms in spring for flowering in June and July, and these should be planted about 5–7 cm deep in sandy soil, in a warm sunny position, as soon as the danger from serious ground frosts is past. They mostly grow to about 30–45 cm in height, with wiry stems bearing starry flowers in dense spikes. Although there are many species, it is usual to find only mixed collections in a great range of colours, yellow, white, red, purple and pink, usually with a dark 'eye' in the centre. They will not overwinter satisfactorily, even in the milder southern districts, and it is best to replace them each year since they are relatively inexpensive.

LILIUM

The Lilies constitute the major group of hardy summer bulbs and, although the many differ-ent species occur over a vast area of the temperate northern hemisphere, they all be-have much the same way in our gardens, being winter-dormant and summer-flowering. Only one well-known species, the Madonna Lily

(*L. candidum*), behaves as a winter grower, since it is Mediterranean in origin; even so, although it produces leaves in autumn and winter, it is summer before the flowers unfold. Altogether there are some eighty or so known species, but only a small proportion of these are cultivated to any extent and the most commonly seen Lilies in gardens are members of complicated hybrid groups which are the result of crosses between several species, the offspring of which have been selected and reselected in a long and painstaking business, until they show vigour and colours which are often unknown in the parents. In spite of being a 'species man' myself, who enjoys the purity and simplicity of original wild plant species, I have to admit that these hybrid Lilies are superb; I have quite a number of them in my own garden and am adding a few different varieties each year. I have to confess that I do not find them as easy to grow as the Lily pundits would have us believe, and the success I have is mainly because I grow most of them in large pots and tubs on the terrace. However, in my case, the lack of success with the planted-out bulbs is largely due to the awful soil conditions and not to any fault in the constitution or condition of the Lily bulbs. The example of my garden serves to highlight the major factor in the satisfactory cultivation of Lilies, drainage. Good drainage to a consid-erable depth is essential, whereas my soil is terribly drained, saturated on the surface in wet weather and dust-like if allowed to dry out for a couple of weeks. This can be improved, however, and I shall go into further detail under the section below concerning cultivation of Lilies.

Firstly, let us consider the Lily plant in general, before going on to describe the different species and varieties and how to grow them. Lilies are bulbous plants with scaly bulbs, mostly rather large, with many separate scales attached to a basal plate. Some Lilies, however, have a curious bulb which is almost rhizome-like, slowly moving horizontally through the soil, sometimes dividing and producing more than one bulb from the parent, while others produce long, slender stolons from the parent which bear young bulbs along their length, so that the plant does not stay in one place. Most of the commonly cultivated Lilies have an ordinary, upright bulb which may divide up from time to time but does stay in the same place as planted, forming a clump if growing happily. The roots from Lily bulbs grow out from the basal plate, and they are often rather thick and fleshy. From the bulb arises an aerial stem in spring and this bears leaves over most of its length, varying enormously in number and width depending upon the species; some produce bulbils in the axils of the leaves and these may be detached when ripe, for propagation purposes. An important feature of the stem is whether or not there are extra feeding roots produced just above the bulb, those Lilies showing such roots being known as 'stem-rooters'. Again, most of the commonly cultivated Lilies do have such roots, but it is necessary to know this before planting, since this factor has a bearing on the depth of planting and the subsequent top-dressing of the Lilies in summer. Notable exceptions, which are not stem-rooters, are the Madonna Lily and the North American species and their hybrids such as the Bellingham hybrids.

Lilies mostly flower in mid to late summer. It is, of course, in the flower shape that the most obvious differences occur between the various species and hybrids, and it is possible to pick out four broad groupings. Many have petals which recurve sharply or roll right back on themselves, giving the pendent 'Turk's Cap' type of flower, and a lot of the others have large, outward-facing trumpet or funnel-shaped flowers. *L. auratum* is alone in having large, outward-facing shallow saucer-like blooms with its segments widely spreading. The fourth group, although not large in number of species, is important for the excellent hybrids which have been raised. The flowers are upward-facing and bowl or cup-shaped in the true species but, since the hybrids have mixed parentage, sometimes with species from other groups, the characters of the groupings become a little obscured.

The presence of so many hybrids now makes the grouping of Lilies rather complex and, in order to clarify the matter, a horticultural classification has been worked out containing nine major divisions and a number of subdivisions within these. Although this is important from the point of view of breeding and showing, it is not necessary for the non-specialist to know the groups to which his Lilies belong and I will not repeat the classification here. For the enthusiast who wants to delve more thoroughly into his subject there are several good specialist Lily books (see Further Reading, page 139), and the International Lily Register produced by the R.H.S. is a mine of basic information about the origins and groupings of the 3,500 named cultivars. In the descriptive list of Lilies below, I have deliberately chosen those species and varieties which are known to be readily available from nurseries and which are reasonably easy to grow, since my aim is to encourage the gardener to try out these gorgeous plants. After a few successes with easy Lilies, one is encouraged to try the more unusual ones, and I strongly urge anyone not to go for the rarest, most expensive ones first in the belief that they will get more interesting results; more likely there will be some failures and a vow never to bother with Lilies again!

CULTIVATION As I mentioned above, the key to the successful cultivation of Lilies is good drainage. Even the so-called swamp Lilies from North America do not enjoy stagnant conditions, although they do need plenty of water in summer; in fact all Lilies need an adequate supply of moisture while they are making their growth and flowering, but this should soak down through open, freely-draining soil, making frequent watering necessary if there is insufficient rain. Other factors do, of course, have a bearing on whether Lilies grow well, for example the siting of the plants, the acidity or alkalinity of the soil, humus-content, etc., and at the end of this section will be found lists giving suggestions as to the best Lilies for certain garden situations and conditions.

Buying and Planting. Lily bulbs can usually be obtained from about October through to spring, but the earlier time is generally considered to be the best for planting, although some of the vigorous hybrid Lilies do not seem to suffer if left until spring. Most important is that the bulb has been looked after properly while out of the ground and not dried out too much, for, unlike many bulbs and corms, Lilies have no outer protective coat. This means that the fleshy scales can be easily damaged and they shrivel if over-dried. A good bulb will have plump scales, without signs of physical damage, and some strong, thong-like roots should be attached to the basal plate; without these the bulbs take much longer to re-establish themselves in their new situation. Planting should be carried out as soon as the bulbs are obtained, usually in the autumn, but if they are purchased in late winter or early spring they will have to be put in on the first reasonable day when there is no frost in the ground. With late-purchased bulbs I usually pot them and keep them in a frame or cool (not heated) greenhouse until good weather arrives, by which time they may well have started root growth and can be planted out with the ball of potting compost intact, with little disturbance. The planting depth of flowering-sized bulbs largely depends upon the overall vigour of the Lily; species and varieties with small bulbs need only 6–8 cm of soil covering them, whereas the vigorous trumpet Lilies with large bulbs need at least 10–20 cm. As mentioned above, most of the commonly cultivated Lilies have stem roots above the bulb and the planting depths given above will be sufficient to allow them to

develop; as the season progresses, stem-rooters will require top-dressing to keep the roots covered and moist. Those Lilies without stem roots can be planted more shallowly, about 10 cm at most depending upon the bulb size, and *L. candidum* is an exception which needs the tips of its bulbs only just beneath the surface. In the descriptions given below mention will be made of stem roots, or lack of them.

Soils and Sites. As we have seen already, good drainage is essential if Lilies are to be cultivated satisfactorily, so if the soil is poorly drained some measures will have to be taken to correct this. Usually the digging-in, to about two spades' depth, of very coarse, gritty sand and a lot of crumbly humus (leaf-mould is best) will suffice. This should all be thoroughly worked in with a fork until the mixture is light and open. The humus will help to make the soil more porous and freely draining, but at the same time retain some of the moisture which is necessary for healthy growth. Poor, sandy soils should have no drainage problems but may be too dry in the summer, so they will also require humus to retain moisture. On really heavy, waterlogged sites one may well have to put in a system of land drains, but this is in extreme conditions and in these cases it will be difficult to grow anything properly, not just Lilies.

The question of lime-tolerance also crops up in relation to Lily cultivation, for some will not grow on alkaline soils. However, the majority of species and hybrids will do perfectly well on soils which are slightly acid, neutral or slightly alkaline. With chalky soils, even with lime-tolerant Lilies, it is best to add plenty of leafmould to the soil before planting and also top-dress with it later on in the season. Comments will be made below, under the individual descriptions, about lime-tolerance. In areas where the natural soil is too alkaline, species which are completely intolerant of lime can be grown in containers of acid potting compost.

109

110

111

112

113

114

109 *Narcissus* 'Minnow', a miniature Tazetta Narcissus.   110 *Narcissus pseudonarcissus* subsp. *abscissus* with its straight trumpets.   111 *Narcissus pseudonarcissus* subsp. *alpestris* with Pulsatilla. An unusual form of Daffodil.   112 *Narcissus* 'Tête-à-Tête', a delightful dwarf Cyclamineus hybrid.   113 *Narcissus* 'Thalia' is one of the best of the Triandrus hybrids.
114 *Narcissus triandrus* 'Albus' for a rock garden or peat bed.

115 *Nectaroscordum siculum (Allium siculum)* is good in winter for dried decoration. **116** *Nerine bowdenii* against a warm wall in autumn. **117** *Ornithogalum balansae*, a good dwarf species for the Rock Garden. **118** *Ornithogalum nutans* in grass. Also good under shrubs. **119** *Ornithogalum thyrsoides* with a greyish background. **120** *Ornithogalum umbellatum* ('Star of Bethlehem') and Forget-me-Nots.

121

122

123

124

125

126

121 *Puschkinia scilloides*, a Scilla-relative from Turkey. **122** *Rhodohypoxis baurii*, a dwarf hardy summer bulb from Natal.
123 *Romulea ramiflora* in grass. Also suitable for a Rock Garden. **124** *Scilla bithynica* in a Rock Garden; also good for
naturalising. **125** *Scilla campanulata (S. hispanica)*, the Spanish Bluebell. **126** *Scilla siberica* 'Spring Beauty', a superb Squill
from Russia.

127

128

129

130

131

132

127 *Scilla tubergeniana* pushes through at the first hint of spring.   **128** *Sternbergia lutea* is one of the few yellow autumn bulbs.
129 *Tecophilaea cyanocrocus*, the Chilean Blue Crocus, an expensive connoisseur's plant.   **130** *Tigridia pavonia*, the Mexican
Tiger Flower, a striking summer bulb.   **131** *Tigridia pavonia* 'Alba', the pure white form of the Tiger Flower.   **132** *Tigridia
pavonia* 'Lutea', a yellow form of the Tiger Flower without blotches.

The best site for most Lilies is one which has plenty of light and air, not necessarily in full sun, and quite a lot of Lilies are actually best in dappled sunlight or at least shaded for part of the day. *L. candidum* is, again, an exception, needing full sun in a rather hot position, and quite a lot of the vigorous hybrids are perfectly all right in full sun as well.

Expense may dictate that only one bulb is obtained, but in general it is best to have at least three to make a show, planted in a triangle. At planting time, mark the position of the bulbs with small sticks so that later on, when larger canes may be needed for support, you can put them in in place of the small ones and will thus not spear through the bulbs.

Lilies in the Mixed Border. Most people now tend to go in for mixed borders of perennials with a few shrubs, perhaps also with some annuals sown into the bare patches, rather than herbaceous borders in the strict sense. Lilies fit in well with such a mixture, for all these plants have similar requirements: plenty of light and air and good drainage but with an adequate supply of moisture in summer. With careful planning of colours, some patches of Lilies can enormously enhance an otherwise fairly ordinary border, or they can be planted in front of shrubs which have flowered at an earlier season and are drab and forgotten in summer. There are some exciting colour combinations worth experimenting with, such as orange or reddish Lilies adjacent to the purple foliage of *Cotinus* 'Royal Purple', or the purple-leaved version of the hazel nut, *Corylus* 'Purpurea'. White trumpet Lilies like *L. regale* look splendid with blue *Agapanthus* and silvery-leaved *Santolina*, *Euphorbia wulfenii* or *Senecio laxifolius*, in a sunny wall border near the house.

The yellow ones are ideal for brightening areas which have dark background foliage, for example in Rhododendron borders; these provide ideal conditions for the Lilies in the open gaps between the shrubs, since they enjoy similar cool growing conditions in summer, and Hostas will associate very well with both.

Once planted, the Lilies are best covered with a protective layer of loose bracken or coarse rough peat for the winter, this being removed in spring when the threat of hard frosts is past. If the soil is well prepared there should be no need for extra feeding, but if root competition from nearby shrubs is strong, then it is advisable to give a dressing of a general granulated fertiliser such as National Growmore, once or twice through the summer. The nutrients will wash in slowly with rain or when watering. As long as the clumps of Lilies continue to grow and flower satisfactorily there is no point in lifting them, but as soon as there is a sign of loss of vigour it is best to lift them and prepare the site again, dividing the bulbs if they have increased.

Lilies on the Terrace or Patio. Growing Lilies in containers to stand out on the terrace can be an excellent method of cultivation if there is somewhere to store them for the winter, for they cannot be left out in case they freeze solid; although the majority of Lilies are very hardy, their bulbs are normally down in the soil below frost level, whereas in a pot they are vulnerable from the sides as well. A frost-free shed or greenhouse (but not heated or you will force the Lilies into early growth) is ideal, but if this is not available the pots can be plunged up to the rim in a sheltered part of the garden and then covered with a deep layer (5–10 cm) of protective material such as loose peat, leafmould, bracken or sacking. This is removed in spring when the hard frosts are over, and the pots placed on the patio when they are about to come into bloom.

Any large containers are suitable, but of course earthenware pots look particularly attractive, as do wooden tubs. The most important feature if the Lilies are to be successful is the depth, to accommodate the strong roots, and this should not be less than 30 cm. Plastic containers are also suitable, but care must be taken that the compost is a well-drained one, since these pots will not dry out as rapidly as clay ones and in wet summers with a poorly drained mixture this could be a problem, with the containers lying wet and soggy for a long period.

One bulb can be planted in a pot or container 20 cm across and 25 cm deep; three bulbs will need extra room, so one at least 30 cm across and 30 cm deep will be necessary. A layer of crocks or gravel is placed over the drainage hole, followed by some coarse material such as leafmould or very old, crumbly manure which will provide some extra nourishment for the roots when they reach the bottom. The potting compost should be a properly balanced one; I prefer loam-based ones such as John Innes no. 2 or 3, and if it is at all fine in texture I add some coarse moss peat or coarse leafmould to make it more open, since Lilies cannot stand closely-grained soils with few air spaces. The bulbs are potted as soon as they are obtained from the nursery and should be placed about half-way down the pot and then covered by about 5 cm of compost, followed by a good watering to settle the soil around the bulbs. This should suffice until the spring, but if at any time the compost does look exceptionally dry it should be watered lightly. Once the spring is under way and the Lilies are pushing up, they need water frequently and should not be allowed to dry out completely; on the other hand, do not go to the other extreme and keep them permanently soggy. Once warm weather has arrived the containers can be moved to their flowering positions on the terrace or patio. Since the roots are restricted to a small amount of soil and will quickly use up the nutrients, it is wise to feed the Lilies either once a month with a granular fertiliser (e.g. National Growmore) scattered on the surface, or with a liquid feed once a fortnight. The percentages of Nitrogen, Phosphate and Potash (N:P:K) are given on proprietary packs, and it is best to choose a well-balanced one rather than one which is high in Nitrogen content. A cane for support may be necessary for tall varieties and, where there are three bulbs in a pot, it is easy to place this in the centre of the triangle of bulbs and later tie the stems loosely to this central support. There should be plenty of room, with the planting depth recommended above, to add further layers of compost through the growing season; this will supply extra nourishment and, in the case of 'stem-rooters', keep the stem roots covered up.

After flowering the dead flowers can be picked off if seeds are not required, but if it is intended to try out propagation by seed the capsules will have to be left to mature. Usually it is well into the autumn before the leaves and stems die back, but when this has happened the stems can be cut down and the pots placed back in the shed or greenhouse or plunged in a bed of sand or soil, and partially dried off for the winter; pots plunged in the open may require covering with a plastic sheet or cloche to dry them off. In a good, big pot they should not need repotting every year and normally every two years should suffice, but if they are repotted, October or early November is a good time to do this, following the same routine as for initial potting. Those not repotted will require top dressing with new compost in the early spring, after all the old soil has been scraped away down to the level of the bulb.

In containers, you do, of course, have complete control over the growing of bulbs so that, for example, lime-hating species such as *L. auratum* can be accommodated by choosing a lime-free 'ericaceous-mix' potting compost. They can also be moved around to a sunny or semi-shaded position, depending upon the type of weather, and can be positioned in front of windows for the best effect, or near a shrub or group of plants that will enhance their appearance.

The Lily Species and Hybrids
The species are described alphabetically, followed by the major hybrid groups, where I have given a personal selection of those that

are usually available; similarly, I have chosen only species which are to be found, at least sometimes, in nursery catalogues. Some of the specialist growers (see page 137) occasionally have small quantities of the more unusual Lilies which they do not list but which they are willing to part with if approached.

L. amabile. This Korean species is a smallish, delicate-looking Lily bearing many narrow leaves on its 45–90 cm stems and up to ten pendulous turkscap type flowers in deep red, spotted black in the centre. It is very hardy, needing good drainage in sun or partial shade, and is tolerant of an alkaline soil; it is a stem-rooting type. There is a yellow-flowered variant of it called var. *luteum* which is also well worthwhile.

L. auratum. This well-known late summer to early autumn-flowering species, the Golden-Rayed Lily of Japan, has gorgeous large, very fragrant, saucer-like outward-facing flowers up to 30 cm in diameter. The ground colour is white, with a yellow band along the centre of each segment in the wild form, but this may be red in the variety *rubrum* or absent altogether, giving a pure white flower. There are also a variable number of red or yellow dots on the segments, depending upon the variety. It was used as one of the parents of the Oriental hybrids, such as the famous 'Imperial Crimson' strain, and has given rise to some astonishingly large and colourful Lilies which are mentioned below in the section on hybrids. 'Crimson Beauty' is a particularly fine cultivar with a cherry-red band along the centre of each segment.

L. auratum is a stem-rooting Lily which will not tolerate lime in the soil, and it does best if planted in a very well-drained humus-rich soil in dappled shade. Unfortunately, it is very susceptible to virus and, if possible, it is best to obtain guaranteed virus-free stocks from specialist nurseries, although these will be more expensive and need careful treatment if they are to remain clean; aphides must be ruthlessly controlled, since these may bring in the virus from any nearby infected plants. It is a very variable Lily in height, some forms only reaching 90–120 cm; but well-grown, vigorous varieties may reach nearly two metres, with up to twenty flowers.

L. canadense. A most beautiful and graceful Lily from North America, which has an unusual creeping rhizome-like bulb of many scales. It prefers moist, peaty soils in semi-shade and is good for growing near Rhododendrons, or in a peat garden among plants which like cool, acid growing conditions, for it is not tolerant of lime. It is not stem-rooting and may reach 60–90 cm, with separate whorls of leaves and an umbel of usually not more than ten flowers in cultivation, although up to twenty are possible. The pendent flowers are bell-shaped with the segments flared outwards, not rolled back in true turkscap style, and are normally yellow, although orange and red forms are also known; there is usually blackish spotting on the inside, but not always.

L. candidum. The Madonna Lily is the exception to most of the rules of Lily growing. Its bulbs should be planted just beneath the surface in August or September, for this Mediterranean species begins to make new growth in the autumn. A basal tuft of new leaves will appear at this time and these overwinter, followed by the flower stem which reaches about 90–150 cm at flowering time in June or July. It is not a stem-rooter so does not require top-dressing when in growth. It will take a good deal of lime in the soil, although this is probably not essential for its well-being, but it does require a warm, sunny situation and very good drainage, so that a bed against a south wall of the house is ideal. The deliciously scented, pure white flowers, which are like wide-open trumpets, have captured the interest of artists for hundreds of years and its history of cultivation certainly dates back to Ancient Crete, for it is depicted on a Minoan fresco of about 1500 BC.

L. candidum is unfortunately not easy to get started in a garden and when a clump is established it should be left undisturbed for as long as possible. When doing really well it may have up to a dozen flowers per stem, but this is unusual. Often it becomes infected with virus which reduces its vigour, and *Botrytis* is also a nuisance with this species. However, a good sunny site should help to control the latter disease, and it is such a gorgeous species that it is well worth trying again and again to get a small group going near the house.

It has been hybridised long ago with the scarlet turkscap *L. chalcedonicum*, to produce a plant with apricot-coloured flowers known as *L. × testaceum*. This, too, should be planted in early autumn in a sunny situation which, however, receives plenty of moisture during the growing period; like its parents, it is lime-tolerant. The flower is more of a turkscap shape than trumpet and is heavily scented.

L. carniolicum. This is a European mountain species, mainly Balkan in its distribution, of the turkscap type, with a few pendulous red flowers on 30–60 cm stems; it is a stem-rooter which likes good drainage and a sunny position, but is unfortunately rather rare in cultivation. Occasionally its yellow variety, *albanicum*, is offered, but this, too, is uncommon and expensive. Both are lime-tolerant and have a slight or, to some, unpleasant scent.

L. cernuum. Although quite rare in cultivation, this Korean species can be found in catalogues from time to time and is an attractive, unusual little plant with very fragrant turkscap flowers in pale purplish-pink with darker spots. It is a stem-rooter, the stems usually only 30–60 cm in height, with narrow leaves and up to six flowers in June or July. It is lime-tolerant and likes a gritty, well-drained soil in an open situation so, with its small size, it is suitable for the rock garden.

L. chalcedonicum. The common name, Scarlet Martagon, gives a clear indication of the general appearance of the flowers of this lovely Lily, but the leaves are completely different, being rather short and silvery green, densely clothing the 90–120 cm stem and

pressed almost flat against it. In July there are up to six pendent flowers of a brilliant, glossy, waxy red and these are of typical turkscap shape, with the segments rolled right back.

Although this gorgeous Lily, which comes from Greece, was known in cultivation to Parkinson in 1629, it is still rarely seen in gardens, but can be found in bulb catalogues from time to time. Like *L. candidum*, it needs good drainage in a sunny situation with the bulbs planted only shallowly, about 8 cm at most, for it is not stem-rooting. It is a lime-tolerant species, in fact probably better on chalky soils than acid.

L. concolor. This distinctive little Lily, only 30–80 cm in height, is delicate-looking enough to be planted on a rock garden if a spot can be found where its base is in shade and its top in the sun, for in China it naturally grows among small shrubs. The soil needs to be well-drained, with plenty of humus and grit to give a cool root run, but it will tolerate an alkaline soil. It is a stem-rooter, but the smallish bulbs need be planted only 8–10 cm deep. In June or July there are up to ten flat, upward-facing flowers of bright scarlet, usually unspotted, although there are spotted forms and also yellow variants.

Although *L. concolor* has considerable garden value of its own, it is because of its virtues as a parent that we have reason to be grateful for its introduction, for it is one of the species which has gone into the breeding of the Asiatic Hybrids such as *L. × hollandicum*, which in turn gave us varieties like 'Fire King' and the Mid-Century group, notably 'Enchantment'.

L. croceum. The Orange Lily can often be found in catalogues under this name but is also known as *L. bulbiferum* var. *croceum*. Like *L. concolor* it is one of the parents of some of the Asiatic Hybrids and also went into the breeding of 'Fire King'. This European species, from light woods and bushy places in the mountains, is a variable plant up to 1.5 m in height, with an umbel of upright bowl-shaped orange flowers. It is stem-rooting and tolerant of lime, and rather easy to cultivate in sun or light shade in ordinary, well-drained garden soil.

L. dauricum. This is a stocky plant from Russia and the Far East and, in its true wild form, is suitable for growing on a sunny rock garden or at the front of a sunny border, for it is only 30–60 cm in height. The upright bowl-shaped flowers are produced in June and are normally scarlet and spotted within but are very variable in the wild, and other colour forms including yellow are known. It is a stem-rooting Lily, sometimes with the stem wandering underground before emerging, and is generally reckoned to be best in lime-free soils. Like *L. croceum* and *L. concolor* it is one of the parents of the Asiatic Hybrids such as *L.* × *hollandicum*, *L.* × *maculatum* and the 'Mid-Century' group.

L. davidii. This Eastern Asiatic species gave rise, through hybridisation with *L. dauricum* (above) in Canada, to the Preston Hybrids and later, in Oregon, the well known Fiesta Hybrids which include the Citronella strain often seen in nurseries. It is a tall Lily, with very many long, narrow leaves densely packed on the stem which carries between ten and twenty bright orange flowers in a pyramid. These are pendulous and of the turkscap type, but are larger than those of the true Martagon Lily and each stands out from the stem on a long stalk; they normally have some raised black spots towards the base of the segments, but there is a plain, unspotted, form known as var. *unicolor*. The most vigorous form, which is more floriferous, is known as var. *willmottiae*. *L. davidii* is a stem-rooter which is lime-tolerant and should be grown in a leafmould-rich soil in semi-shade where it will get plenty of moisture in the growing season. It flowers in July and may reach 1.5 metres in height when doing really well.

L. duchartrei. A few Lilies make stolons from their bulbs so that they tend to move away from their original planting position and eventually form patches. The Chinese *L.*

duchartrei, otherwise known as the 'Marbled Martagon' Lily, behaves in this way and, although not showy, is an excellent and interesting plant for a peat garden or leafy/peaty bed, with Rhododendrons and other Ericaceous plants. It has a small bulb and is a stem-rooting variety, sending up wiry stems to about 60–120 cm, carrying from one to ten small white turkscap flowers which are spotted purple inside. It will tolerate lime in the soil if there is a high humus content.

L. formosanum. This large white trumpet Lily from Taiwan is unfortunately tender and is really only suitable for a heated greenhouse where it will flower in less than a year from seed, but it can be effective if grown in tubs for placing outside on a terrace in summer. The stems will grow to about 1–1.5 m in height and bear three or four flowers which are each up to 15 cm in length and highly fragrant, and have a variable amount of purple staining on the outside of the tube. It has only small bulbs for the size of the plant, but these should be planted about 10–15 cm deep since it is stem-rooting. The seeds can be sown early in the new year, directly into the final container of John Innes compost, and should be sown thinly. After germination, which may be only a few weeks, thinning can take place at intervals with the aim of ending up with several plants about 10 cm apart in the tub or pot. Once spring and warmer weather has arrived, they can be placed outside and given a liquid feed once a fortnight to encourage strong growth, which may result in flower stems being formed in about August. The bulbs can be kept for several years, but new ones are so easily raised that it is scarcely necessary to retain them for more than two.

There is a much hardier, dwarf form of *L. formosanum*, from high altitudes on Taiwan, known as var. *pricei*. I have grown this successfully for several consecutive years, planted out on a peat garden in Surrey, but it, too, seems fairly short-lived and new stock should be raised at least every other year to avoid the risk of losing it altogether.

L. hansonii. This is one of the Martagon Lilies, with its leaves in whorls up the stem which bears a raceme of up to twelve deep golden-yellow, brown-spotted pendent turks-cap flowers in June or July. It is a stem-rooting type from Korea and is a very hardy, lime-tolerant species which is easy to grow in a situation providing dappled shade in humus-rich soil. If possible, a site should be chosen where the sun catches the yellow flowers, to show off the thick wax-like petals to the best advantage.

L. henryi. Asked to choose the easiest Lily species to grow, one would be hard-pressed to be categorical, but the Chinese *L. henryi* must surely be somewhere near the top of the list. It is vigorous, growing up to two metres or more, hardy, likes lime in the soil and usually increases rapidly by bulb division and by additional bulblets on the stem base. In August or September the large orange pendent turks-cap flowers are produced on long, horizontal stalks, sometimes two per stalk, and usually up to twenty per stem. A most attractive feature is the mass of protuberances ('papillae') in the centre of the flower. It is best in semi-shade in a leafmould-rich soil, but not peaty, for this encourages the acid conditions that this species does not seem to like. It is a stem-rooting species and has very large bulbs which need to be 15–20 cm deep.

L. longiflorum. The Easter Lily of florists' shops is really only suitable for cool greenhouse cultivation, being a very tender species. The familiar long white trumpets, about 15–20 cm long, are carried on stems up to a metre in height, usually between one and five depending upon vigour. Although not hardy, it is worth trying some in pots for the patio, as was recommended for *L. formosanum*. Growing from seed is even more rapid than that species, and six months is the usual time required from sowing to flowering. The normal flowering time is June or July, but in the warm

greenhouse it can be forced into bloom for the spring. It is stem-rooting and the pots may need top-dressing during the growth period—certainly liquid feeds are beneficial.

L. mackliniae. The discovery and introduction of this species from the India-Burma border in 1946, by Frank Kingdon Ward, makes fascinating reading, for he was engaged in searching for crashed American aircraft at the time and incidentally found some dried seed heads which were sent back to England. In 1948 the seedlings flowered and it was realised that they represented a beautiful unknown Lily which was subsequently named after the discoverer's wife, whose maiden name was Miss Jean Macklin. It is not a difficult plant in cultivation if given a cool leafy or peaty but well-drained soil in semi-shade, for it cannot tolerate drought and more especially a dry atmosphere. The best plants to be seen are in the more humid west or north, and in Scotland it reaches a much larger size than in the south. It is a stem-rooting species, reaching 20–80 cm in height, and carries one to five pendent white bells about 4–5 cm long, flushed pinkish-purple on the outside. Although usually expensive and not easy to find, it is well worth tracking down and giving a trial if one has a peat or woodland garden.

L. martagon. The Martagon Lily or Turk's Cap Lily is one of the best known of all species and certainly the most widespread in nature, from Portugal eastwards throughout Europe and northern Asia to Mongolia. Often it grows on limestone rock formations and it is tolerant of alkaline soils in the garden. It is a stem-rooting Lily, reaching up to about 1.5 metres and carrying whorls of dark green leaves and in June or July a raceme of many small pendent flowers, up to fifty in really vigorous specimens, but usually far less than this in gardens. These are very turban-shaped, with the segments rolled right back on themselves and the tips tucked in to the centre, and are normally a dull, pinkish-purple with darker spots, but it is a very variable species and there are several named varieties. The pure white var. *album* is much more attractive than the pink, as are var. *dalmaticum* and var. *cattaniae* which have very deep blackish-wine-coloured flowers.

L. martagon is a plant for semi-shade in a shrub border, or in open places between trees where a few bulbs should be grouped closely together if a reasonable effect is to be obtained; the white variety looks best against dark foliage and associates well with Rhododendrons.

L. maximowiczii. This may sometimes be found in catalogues listed as a variety of the seldom-cultivated *L. leichtlinii.* It is rather similar to *L. tigrinum*, with deep-orange pendent turkscap-type flowers, spotted black within. When growing well its slender stems may reach two metres and they bear many narrow leaves and up to twelve flowers. It is a stem-rooting type with a stoloniferous behaviour, the stem running underground for some distance before turning upwards; it bears bulblets along the subterranean part. The best position for it seems to be in semi-shade in a non-alkaline soil which is rich in leafmould.

L. monadelphum. There are several Lilies rather similar to this species, all of comparable garden value, but *L. monadelphum* and possibly *L. szovitsianum* are the only ones likely to be found in commerce, and then rather rarely. It is a beautiful Lily, sending up stout stems to about 1–1.5 metres in June, which carry up to twenty large, pendent, fragrant turkscap flowers in pale yellow, spotted purple on the inside.

This Caucasian Lily is a lime-tolerant stem-rooting species which prefers cool growing conditions in semi-shade and seems to do particularly well on heavy, chalky soils which have had leafmould added. I have also seen some fine clumps naturalised in grass, and it is clear that *L. monadelphum* and its allies are best when left undisturbed for as long as possible.

L. pardalinum. The American Panther or Leopard Lily is one of a group of species from the United States, which have curious scaly rhizome-like bulbs that divide and form patches. They prefer damp situations, but not waterlogged, and a semi-shady position with plenty of humus is recommended; since they are not stem-rooting, the bulbs need to be planted only about 5–10 cm beneath the surface. When thriving, it will be found that the clumps require lifting and dividing up every three or four years. It is lime-tolerant so long as its moisture requirements are catered for.

In the case of *L. pardalinum* the stems may grow to two metres or more, bearing whorls of leaves and, in July, several large pendent flowers which have sharply recurved segments, giving a turkscap shape. The colours are very striking, basically a pale reddish-orange but shading to crimson near the tips of the segments and strongly spotted inside with brownish-red.

The very bright colours stand out well against the often drab foliage of evergreens and, if a spot can be chosen where shafts of sunlight break through the shrubs on to the flowers, a clump of *L. pardalinum* can be a most impressive sight.

It is one of the parents of the famous Bellingham Hybrids which are mentioned below under hybrids.

L. pomponium. This attractive but rather rare little Lily from the Maritime Alps is a sun lover and is at its best when planted in a well-drained chalky soil in full sun, where it is sheltered from the north by a wall or evergreen shrub. It is a stem-rooting species, growing to about 65 cm with many narrow leaves and, in June, up to ten pendent turkscap flowers of a brilliant waxy scarlet-red, spotted with black. It is worth a try in a sheltered border with greyish Mediterranean plants such as Cistus, Sage and Lavender.

L. pumilum. This Eastern Asiatic species is often to be found in catalogues under the name *L. tenuifolium.* It is a charming, small Lily only 45–60 cm in height, which has slender stems bearing narrow grassy leaves and five to fifteen pendent scarlet, fragrant turkscap flowers in

June. It is a stem-rooting type which prefers a non-alkaline, well-drained sunny site and its delicate appearance makes it a suitable companion for rock plants, which like similar conditions. Although often not a long-lived plant, it usually produces seeds which can be grown to flowering-sized bulbs in only one or two years. There is an orange-yellow variety of it known as 'Golden Gleam' which is equally attractive.

L. pyrenaicum. This Pyrenean species has been cultivated since the sixteenth century and is one of the easiest of Lilies to grow. It is a stem-rooter, with stout densely leafy stems of 40–120 cm in height, and up to twelve pendent yellow turkscap flowers which are lined and dotted black inside. There is no great preference for soil and position so long as it is reasonably well-drained and not in deep shade, and it is good on alkaline soils. Although not a spectacular Lily, it is worth growing, for it flowers in May or June, making it the earliest species to open, and it is very hardy. The unpleasant scent is a slight disadvantage but interesting, since it is just the same smell as its compatriot *Fritillaria pyrenaica*; this feature is presumably linked to pollination by some insect of the region.

L. regale. Although nowadays a commonly cultivated species, *L. regale* is quite a recently discovered Lily in relation to many others and was introduced to English gardens from China in the early twentieth century. It is one of the best and easiest of the trumpet Lily species and very quick to reach flowering size from seed, usually in only two or three years. The wiry stems usually reach about 1–2 m in height and bear many deep green leaves; then, in July, from one to twenty-five very fragrant, outward-facing trumpet-shaped flowers up to 15 cm long. These are white inside with a yellow throat, and usually purplish-stained on the outside, but there is a var. *album* which is white also on the outside, and a wholly yellow variant has been raised, known as 'Royal Gold'.

L. regale is a stem-rooting type which will tolerate a wide range of conditions, including chalky soils, but does not like deep shade. It associates in sunny borders very well with blue *Agapanthus* and silver-leaved plants such as *Senecio laxifolius*, and can also make a stunning combination with pink H.T. roses.

L. speciosum. This deliciously fragrant Japanese Lily is becoming more and more frequently used as a cut-flower forced to bloom early, but its normal flowering time is in August–October. It can grow to about 1.7 cm in height and carries rather leathery leaves and up to ten pendulous flowers about 15 cm across, which have curled-back wavy segments like large turkscaps, with very long-protruding stamens. The inside of the flower is covered with very prominent papillae, like those of *L. henryi*. In the typical form the ground colour is white suffused with pink and livened by crimson-red of the raised papillae. There are many colour forms now in cultivation and new varieties and hybrids are being raised all the time. Var. *album* is white throughout except for a greeny-yellow median stripe near the base of each petal, and the orange anthers. Var. *rubrum* is stained heavily with a rich, deep carmine colour, with just the margins and tips of the segments white, while 'Grand Commander' is almost wholly bright crimson with very narrow white margins. 'Melpomene' is a well-known cultivar in a very rich, deep carmine-crimson, heavily spotted darker, var. *roseum* is a paler pink and 'Lucie Wilson' is also a rose pink. Other varieties, which might be found in catalogues and which are all excellent, are 'Namazu Beauty' (deep carmine) 'Uchida' (large deep crimson-red), 'Rosemede' (very large flowers, deeply coloured crimson) and 'Ellabee' (pure white).

L. speciosum is a stem-rooting type which likes humid growing conditions but is only really hardy in the south, for its young shoots are susceptible to frost and, in the north, it may bloom too late to be successful. Plenty of humus is essential, with a good deep layer over the bulbs and, if planted in the shade, it should not be too heavy so that at least the upper part of the stems get plenty of light. Like its relative *L. auratum* it is not very tolerant of lime in the soil.

L. speciosum is unfortunately very susceptible to virus diseases; some specialist nurseries, however, are now offering virus-free stocks.

L. superbum. As its name suggests, this North American species is quite a spectacular plant, suitable for growing in a damp, lime-free soil which is rich in peaty humus. It is not stem-rooting so the bulbs, which have a stolon-like behaviour, need not be planted more than about 8–10 cm deep, but it is a very vigorous species, up to two metres or more in height, so will almost certainly require staking. The stems have whorled leaves and, in July or August, produce a pyramid-shaped head of up to forty flowers which are nodding, like large orange turkscaps with reddish-crimson tips to the reflexed segments and conspicuous maroon spots inside. An open patch between Rhododendrons is a suitable position, providing it is supplied with ample moisture during the summer, and it will certainly liven up an area where there is drab evergreen foliage.

L. tigrinum (L. lancifolium). The Tiger Lily from China and Japan needs little introduction and most people will be aware of its ease of cultivation and extraordinary rate of increase by means of the small blackish bulblets in the leaf axils. There are several varieties, but in its common form it has blackish stems up to two metres in height, bearing ten to twenty or more orange pendent turkscap-shaped flowers spotted blackish-purple inside. It is late-summer flowering, from July to September. Var. *fortunei* is rather larger and tends to have more flowers and a distinctive woolly stem; 'Splendens' is also more vigorous and has deeper orange-red flowers. Var. *flaviflorum* is a lemon yellow version, also with dark spots, while 'Flore Pleno' has double orange flowers which are curious rather than

attractive. There are also many hybrids which owe a part of their make-up to *L. tigrinum*, including the Mid-Century Hybrids and the Tiger Lily Hybrids.

L. tigrinum is a stem-rooting Lily which does well if given a rich soil such as one would make up for growing vegetables in the kitchen garden, and it likes a warm, sheltered position in sun. During the growing season an extra mulch of humus is beneficial. Unfortunately it is usually infected with viruses and, although these do not affect its appearance very much, it does mean that other, more susceptible Lilies nearby are likely to become diseased as well; rigorously controlling greenfly will help to reduce the spread of virus, but it is a difficult task.

The orange colour of the Tiger Lily associates well with the purple-leaved form of *Cotinus coggygria* in a surprising way, and it is worth trying a few bulbs in front of one of these shrubs.

Lily Hybrids

There are now a great many hybrids in cultivation; at any one time it is possible to find at least 100 different named cultivars in nursery catalogues and, apart from a few firm favourites, this list is ever-changing. In order to bring some order to this mass of names a classification has been adopted; this forms the basis for exhibiting and judging, and breeders of Lilies are asked to register any new hybrids with the Royal Horticultural Society so that the plants may be described and attributed to their correct group. The groups are mainly formed on the basis of the parentage which, in turn, affects the overall appearance of the hybrid offspring; for example, those Asiatic Hybrids in Division 1(a) have upright flowers in an umbel because of their link with *L. dauricum*, *L. croceum* and *L. concolor*, while those in Division 6(a) are large trumpet Lilies derived from species such as *L. regale*, *L. sulphureum*, *L. sargentiae*, *L. leucanthum centifolium* and *L. brownii*. In many cases it is now very difficult to obtain the original wild species, and several of these are not mentioned in the above species descriptions because of their lack of availability.

Although, to enjoy the Lily hybrids as garden plants, it is not necessary to know their Divisions and parentage, it does make a little more sense if the following named hybrids are arranged so that those which have an overall similarity are grouped together. This is a personal selection and I must stress that in a year or two some new ones will have entered the scene and some of the mentioned ones will have fallen by the wayside.

Asiatic Hybrids with upright flowers in an umbel
In this group there is great activity in the breeding of new varieties and, since they are mostly fairly quick to propagate, they are reasonably cheap to buy. Some varieties force well and are to be seen increasingly in florists' shops as cut-flowers, but they are also excellent garden plants, mostly early flowering. The Mid-Century hybrids are probably the most famous representatives in this group, raised in the mid-twentieth century in the United States, which have been selected and hybridised again and again; they are often sold as a mixed collection or as named varieties, of which 'Enchantment' is the oldest and still one of the most popular. Lilies belonging to the Asiatic Hybrid upright-flowered group mostly flower in June or July. They are hardy, lime-tolerant, stem-rooting Lilies, ideally suited for the mixed border or for pot cultivation on the patio. Full, scorching sun is best avoided, since some of the colours fade, so a position where there is a little shade during the middle of the day is ideal.

'Achilles'—yellow with dark spotting inside
'Alpen Glow'—a pinkish shade
'Chinook'—pale apricot
'Connecticut King'—deep yellow, unspotted
'Corina'—red, spotted dark brown in the centre
'Destiny'—yellow, spotted brown inside

'Enchantment'—orange-red, spotted black
'Festival'—yellow-orange, shading to red on margins and tips of the segments, spotted dark brown inside
'Firecracker'—deep red
'Harmony'—orange, spotted maroon inside
'Manuella'—red with paler margins to the segments, spotted blackish inside
'Mont Blanc'—creamy white with numerous brown-maroon spots inside
'Orange Triumph'—bright orange, spotted purple inside
'Phoebus'—clear yellow, unspotted
'Pirate'—orange-red
'Prominence'—red with small spots inside
'Red Night'—deep cherry-red with dark spots
'Rosita'—a delicate shade of pinkish-purple, spotted blackish inside
'Sterling Star'—white with brown spots inside
'Tabasco'—deep glossy chestnut-red with black spots inside
'Venture'—orange-red.

Asiatic Hybrids with outward-facing flowers
Much the same comments apply to this group as were made above, since the parentage is much the same, and it is mainly the angle at which the flowers are held, facing out horizontally, which differs. They are very hardy and easily cultivated stem-rooting varieties.

'Apricot Beauty'—apricot-orange, conspicuously spotted inside
'Brandywine'—orange, spotted inside
'Corsage'—creamy white centre shading to pink tips, spotted maroon inside
'Early Yellow'—bright golden-yellow
'Fire King'—brilliant orange-red, prominently spotted inside
'Odysseus'—orange
'Orestes'—salmon-orange
'Paprika'—deep red
'Pink Beauty'—deep pink, deeper in the centre
'Prince Constantine'—orange, spotted inside

'Prosperity'—lemon-yellow
'White Tiger'—white with purple spots
'Yellow Star'—yellow with brown spots.

Asiatic Hybrids with pendent flowers

Again, much the same comments about cultivation and constitution as were made above apply to these strong, stem-rooting Lilies which have pendent flowers tending towards the turkscap shape, with swept-back segments.

'Ariadne'—smallish flowers, pinkish-purple at tips, pale within

'Citronella'—bright lemon-yellow, spotted black inside

'Connecticut Yankee'—orange-red, slightly spotted inside

'Discovery'—rose-pink, tipped darker, spotted inside

'Fiesta Hybrids'—a mixed colour race from yellow to orange and red, spotted inside

'Eros'—bright pink, scented

'Harlequin Hybrids'—Turk's Cap-shaped flowers in mixed colours from cream to salmon, pink and yellow, spotted inside

'Hornback's Gold'—soft yellow, spotted inside

'La Boheme'—golden-yellow, spotted blackish-purple

'Lady Bowes Lyon'—deep rich-red, spotted black

'Langtry'—clear yellow, spotted maroon

'Maxwill'—many orange-red flowers, spotted brown; very vigorous

'Pan'—white, sweetly scented

'Pink Giant'—pink with orange centre, spotted brown

'Red Fox'—red suffused darker brownish-red, spotted brown

'Theseus'—crimson-red, scented

'Tiger Hybrids'—a vigorous race based on *L. tigrinum*, mostly dark red

'Viking'—orange-red, an old well-tried variety.

Hybrids of the Martagon Lily

These are mainly hybrids between *L. martagon* and *L. hansonii*, bearing similar racemes of smallish pendent turkscap flowers with their leaves in whorls. They are mostly vigorous stem-rooting Lilies, easily cultivated in any decent soil which is well drained, including alkaline soils if leafmould is dug in. They are resistant to virus diseases and flower rather early, in June or July.

'Backhouse Hybrids'—varying from deep yellow to pinkish, cream or buff, spotted brownish-purple within.

'Mrs. R. O. Backhouse'—a named selection of the above, in orange-yellow, slightly spotted inside and faintly flushed pink outside

'Marhan'—an old hybrid between *L. martagon* var. *album* and *L. hansonii*, orange spotted with brown

L. × dalhansonii—a cross between a dark variety, *L. martagon* var. *dalmaticum* and *L. hansonii*, with deep-maroon flowers shading to orange in the centre, strongly spotted inside

'Jacques S. Dijt'—creamy yellow, spotted purple inside, sometimes seen as 'J.S. Dijt' or L. 'Marhan J.S. Dijt'.

American Hybrids

Many hybrid Lilies have been raised in America, but this group contains those that are crosses between species occurring wild in the United States, especially *L. pardalinum*, *L. parryi* and *L. humboldtii*. They are mostly tall, vigorous plants with their leaves in whorls, not stem-rooting and with the bright flower colours associated with their parents; the flowers are of the turkscap shape, with reflexed segments. These colourful hybrids are best planted in dappled sunlight in a moist, but not stagnant, soil with plenty of leafmould incorporated in it, and are ideal among Rhododendrons or any other dark-leaved shrubs which will act as a foil. They are lime-tolerant plants, providing moisture and humus is available in the soil.

'Bellingham Hybrids'—this is a mixed group of plants, varying in flower colour from yellow to deep orange, heavily spotted orange-red or maroon. They increase quite rapidly to form clumps

'Bullwood Hybrids'—variable in colour from red to orange to peach, spotted darker inside

'Lake Tahoe'—pinkish-red with white and yellow centre, spotted deep red; a most attractive variety

'Shuksan'—a selection of the Bellingham Hybrids; orange flushed with red and spotted darker red.

The Trumpet Hybrid Lilies

This group contains all the hybrids with large trumpet-shaped flowers in a range of colours, usually highly fragrant and vigorous, with stems up to two metres or even more in ideal conditions. They are lime-tolerant, stem-rooting plants, later-flowering than most of the hybrids so far dealt with, in July or August. They have very large bulbs which need to be planted deeply and, if grown in pots, must be fed regularly (see Lilies on the Terrace or Patio, page 113), but they are ideally suited for this purpose and can make a marvellous display. The pinkish-coloured ones are best in partial shade or they may fade, but the whites and yellows can be grown in full sun or semi-shade. I find that they do best if some old, rotted manure is dug into the bottom of the planting hole, or put in the bottom of the pot in the case of container-grown ones, where the strong roots can find it when the plants are growing vigorously. The parentage of these trumpet Lilies is very mixed and there has been a long process of careful selection of thousands of seedlings, but the main species involved were *L. leucanthum*, *L. sargentiae*, *L. sulphureum*, *L. regale* and *L. brownii*.

Many of the hybrids in this group are sold as strains rather than individual clones, so they may vary a little.

'African Queen Strain'—golden-orange to shades bordering on apricot, usually brown on the outside

'Aurelian Hybrids'—an extremely varied group of plants in a wide range of colours and shapes, since the reflexed-petalled *L. henryi* was involved

'Black Dragon'—white trumpets with a brown-purple exterior

'Damson'—deep silvery-pink

'Golden Clarion Strain'—variable yellows from pale lemon to deep gold, with or without a darker exterior

'Golden Splendour'—deep golden-yellow, purple on the outside

'Green Dragon'—soft chartreuse-green, paler inside

'Green Magic'—lemon-yellow, usually flushed green

'Honeydew'—yellow inside, greenish on the exterior

'Limelight'—greenish-yellow outside, yellow inside

'Mabel Violet'—a curious purple shade

'Moonlight Strain'—citron-yellow shades, sometimes darker green outside

'Olympic Hybrids'—variable group from cream to pink or greenish, sometimes darker outside

'Pink Pearl Strain'—pink, darker on the outside

'Pink Perfection'—varying shades of rich pink

'Sentinel Strain'—white with greenish-yellow stain outside.

Hybrids derived from the Asiatic trumpet Lilies but with flowers opening more widely

The same cultivation comments apply here as for the above group, to which they are closely related. The main difference is that the flowers are pendent and are much less funnel-like, the segments opening more widely and recurving, presumably because the reflexed-petalled *L. henryi* has been involved in their breeding.

'Carnival Strain'—these are selections of the Aurelian Hybrids (see in the above group) in shades of yellow, apricot and white.

Hybrids derived from Asiatic Trumpet Lilies but with flattish flowers

These are also Aurelian Hybrids (see above)

in which *L. henryi* is involved as one parent, and here both the funnel shape of the trumpet Lilies and the 'swept-back' turkscap shape of *L. henryi* have been suppressed to give an in-between, flattish flower. Apart from this, the cultural comments made for the above two groups apply and these are lovely Lilies, brightly coloured and not so large as the trumpet types which may be a little 'heavy' for some tastes. The flowers usually have the thick, coloured projections and ridges near the centre which *L. henryi* has.

'Bright Star'—a nearly flat flower with recurved tips; pure white with a pointed orange mark at the base of each segment, giving a star-like orange centre

'Golden Sunburst'—a variable golden-yellow strain, very vigorous and easily cultivated.

Hybrids of the Far Eastern Lily species, known as the Oriental Hybrids

This group is mainly derived from the Japanese Golden-Rayed Lily, *L. auratum* and *L. speciosum*, which have produced hybrids with enormous (up to 20–30 cm across) vividly coloured flowers, often in crimson and carmine tones. They are very vigorous, stem-rooting Lilies which do best on acid soils rich in leafmould, since both the parents are intolerant of lime. A site in dappled sunlight is best, where they will not be too hot and dry, with a good supply of moisture in summer, but at the same time it must be well-drained. The varieties with a lot of white in the flower look well if given a darkish background, such as evergreen shrubs out of flower, but the crimson-carmine ones associate well with silvery-bluish foliage such as the Conifer *Chamaecyparis pisifera* 'Plumosa'. The Oriental Hybrids also do well in pots, but are tall and vigorous, so need large containers to provide sufficient root-run, and enough weight for stability in windy weather. Feeding regularly (see Lilies on the Terrace or Patio, page 113) is essential. The Oriental Hybrids

are late-summer flowering, from July to September.

'Black Beauty'—flower shape like *L. speciosum* with reflexing segments, dark red, with white edges to the segments

'Bonfire'—*L. speciosum*-shaped flower, deep crimson edged silvery-white, spotted darker

'Imperial Crimson Strain'—a variable group in shades of bright crimson, paler at the margins and centre and spotted darker; tips often recurving

'Imperial Gold Strain'—white *L. auratum*-shaped flowers with a gold-yellow stripe along the centre of each segment and spotted red

'Imperial Silver Strain'—pure white with maroon spots within; large wide-open flowers, *L. auratum*-shaped

'Jamboree Strain'—recurving segments like *L. speciosum* in maroon, with silvery-white margins

'Journey's End'—*L. speciosum*-shaped flower with reflexing segments, in rich crimson with a narrow white margin

'Red Band Hybrids'—wide-open *L. auratum*-type flowers in variable shades of bright crimson, sometimes with white margins

'Star Gazer'—wide flowers reflexed at the tips; deep crimson-red spotted darker, with a thin white margin.

LILY PROPAGATION Sooner or later the owner of some Lilies is probably going to have the urge to increase them, although some species and varieties, when growing well, do this of their own accord and form clumps. In this case it is just a matter of digging them up in autumn and splitting the clumps for replanting in newly prepared soil or pots. Others, such as *L. tigrinum* and some of the Asiatic Hybrids, produce many bulblets, either in the axils of the leaves or just above the parent bulb. These can be removed in the autumn and grown on separately from the parents, either planted out in a prepared site, using cultivation methods similar to those of the mature bulbs, or in pots or deep boxes in the protection of an unheated frame. As with mature bulbs, good soil, rich in leafmould, and frequent liquid feeds, encourage growth along more quickly. In the case of the Asiatic Hybrids, such bulblets may flower in their first or second season after detaching from the parent.

Another method of producing bulblets by vegetative means is by removing scales from a large bulb and placing them in a closed polythene bag with a sterile medium such as moist vermiculite and keeping them in a warm place, at about 70°F. Bulblets will form on the broken surfaces of the scales and begin to make roots, and at this stage they can be removed for growing on in boxes of light, sandy leafmould-rich potting soil, planted just below the surface, for the tiny bulbs will not stand deep planting at this stage. The best time to do this is from mid-summer to autumn, scratching away the soil down to the bulbs and removing a few plump scales from each; you can lift them completely, which makes access to the scales easy but of course causes quite a set-back to the mature bulbs. If the scales are taken in summer, the young bulblets might be ready for planting out in the autumn for growing on, but later-scaled ones will need to be kept over the winter in their bags, for spring planting.

There are many variations on this theme and, although the above method is a simple technique for the average gardener, interested in small-scale propagation, these are other ways of inducing Lilies to make a crop of young bulblets. It is best to refer to specialist Lily books or propagation manuals for further ideas.

Seeds present another important method of propagation, and the growing of these is not altogether straightforward, since different species may have different methods of germination. With quite a lot of species, germination

occurs soon after sowing, if conditions are right, and the cotyledons and young leaves are pushed up within a few weeks. Lilies in this group include *L. amabile, L. cernuum, L. concolor, L. davidii, L. duchartrei, L. formosanum, L. longiflorum, L. mackliniae, L. maximowiczii, L. pumilum, L. regale, L. tigrinum* and some of the Trumpet Hybrids and Asiatic Hybrids, such as the Mid-Century group. The seeds of this type can be sown in very early spring, in pots of John Innes Seed Compost. I prefer to sow them very thinly, covering the seeds with coarse grit and placing them in a cold frame, keeping them growing after germination right through until the autumn when they die down naturally. They can then be planted out into a nursery bed for growing on, or into larger pots of standard Lily compost as mentioned on page 114. Some of the Lilies in this group are very quick to reach flowering size, under a year in one or two cases but usually two or three years.

The next type of germination to consider concerns those Lilies in which the seeds lie dormant for a few months before becoming active and pushing up seedling leaves. Much the same treatment is given as for the above group, but sowing can take place whenever the seeds are obtained. Germination may take place at almost any time, following the delay period, and if this happens to be in autumn it is best to protect the seedlings in a cold frame or greenhouse until the spring. After one growing season they can be planted out or grown on in larger pots as above. Lilies in this group include *L. candidum, L. carniolicum, L. chalcedonicum, L. henryi, L. pomponium* and *L. pyrenaicum.*

The third group constitutes those in which germination takes place straight away after sowing but it happens underground, with a small bulb being formed without any leaf growth appearing. Not many of the commonly cultivated Lilies fall into this category, *L. dauricum* being one of the better known. Seeds of the Lilies in this group can be treated in the same way as those of the first, sowing in early spring. Even if nothing appears to have taken place in the seed pot there might well be small bulbs developing below ground, and the first sign of anything above ground is a largish leaf, sometimes in the late summer or autumn following sowing. The young bulbs can be potted on or planted into a nursery bed, as with the other types.

The fourth and final type of germination is where there is a delay before anything happens at all and then a young bulb is produced, with no leaf growth appearing. Obviously this is the slowest and most frustrating type, for there is such a long period of apparent inactivity! I usually sow these in pots in spring and leave them in a frame for the summer, of course keeping them watered. These need a period of several months' warm weather to trigger off the process and, following this, several weeks of cooler weather to encourage the leaf growth. Thus, with my method, it is usually autumn before any aerial growth appears and so they are best kept in a frame or greenhouse for protection in the winter. Some people prefer to sow in the autumn and keep the pots warm indoors for the winter (about 70°F is necessary) to start off the bulb growth, then put them out for a cool period in spring to encourage leaf growth; this then leaves the summer for growing on the young plants ready for autumn planting into a nursery bed or into large containers. Another recommended method is to put the seeds into a polythene bag in damp vermiculite in a warm place in winter (70°F indoors) until germination has taken place and the young bulbs can be seen. These can then be potted in soil and encouraged into leaf growth by a cooler period outdoors in spring. Lilies falling into this group include *L. auratum, L. canadense, L. croceum, L. hansonii, L. martagon, L. monadelphum (L. szovitsianum), L. pardalinum, L. rubellum, L. speciosum* and *L. superbum*.

Apart from increasing Lily species, it can be great fun to try hybridising. If a group such as the Asiatic Hybrids is chosen, it need not be a very long process before flowers are seen, the Mid-Century hybrids, for example, taking only two seasons before producing flowers. The main drawback is that Lily seed capsules can contain an enormous quantity of seeds, and if all these are going to be raised a considerable amount of space and materials is required. On the whole I prefer to leave Lily breeding to the nurserymen who have a few fields to spare, and I concentrate on raising some of the more unusual species from seed obtained by exchange or from one of the specialist Societies or nurseries.

LILIES FOR SPECIAL PURPOSES
With such a large and varied group as the Lilies, it is possible to select species and varieties for different purposes. Here are a few suggestions.

Very fragrant Lilies. Quite a lot of Lilies are scented, some not very pleasantly, but these are particularly good: *L. auratum, L. candidum, L. cernuum, L. hansonii, L. regale, L. speciosum, L. × testaceum,* Trumpet Hybrids, Oriental Hybrids.

Lilies for cool, damp (but not stagnant) soils. The following prefer humus-rich, cool soils which always have plenty of moisture available: *L. auratum, L. canadense, L. maximowiczii, L. pardalinum, L. rubellum, L. speciosum, L. superbum,* American Hybrids, Oriental Hybrids.

Lilies for alkaline soils. Many Lilies will tolerate slight alkalinity, especially if plenty of humus is present, but some, such as the following, seem to do particularly well on calcareous soils: *L. amabile, L. candidum, L. carniolicum, L. chalcedonicum, L. concolor, L. croceum, L. henryi, L. martagon, L. pomponium, L. × testaceum,* Martagon Lily Hybrids.

Lilies for acid conditions. Some Lilies will only grow on acid soils, the following being notable examples. In alkaline areas raised peaty beds might be tried for these, but they must be watered with rain water since the tap water may be alkaline as well: *L. auratum*, *L. canadense*, *L. pardalinum*, *L. rubellum*, *L. speciosum*, *L. superbum*, American Hybrids (e.g. Bellingham Hybrids), Oriental Hybrids.

It will be noticed that this is similar to the list for cool, damp soils and that the species involved are mainly American and Japanese.

Lilies for naturalising. A few Lilies will grow in 'semi-wild' situations but not in too much shade. It is worth trying *L. henryi*, *L. pardalinum* (and American Hybrids), *L. pyrenaicum*, *L. tigrinum*; *L. martagon* sometimes takes to rough grass areas.

Dwarf Lilies for the rock garden. A few Lilies are sufficiently dwarf or slender to look in place in the rock garden and will enjoy the good drainage of such a site: *L. amabile*, *L. carniolicum*, *L. concolor*, *L. mackliniae* (for a cooler position in the semi-shade of rocks or shrubs), *L. pomponium*, *L. pumilum*, *L. rubellum* (for a cool position).

MORAEA

Sadly, the majority of species in this lovely group of Iris-like plants are not hardy, coming from South Africa, and of the few that are, only one or two appear, rarely, in nursery stock lists. These are the Eastern Cape ones, from the summer rainfall region, so that they are at rest in winter although the leaves never entirely die down. The corms are rather like Crocuses, on a large scale, and these push up new tough, long narrow leaves in late spring, followed shortly by the flower stems which can reach a metre or more in height. The few species to be encountered in cultivation are all yellow-flowered and there is little to choose between them as far as ornamental value goes. All look just like yellow Irises, with three large outer segments ('falls') and three small inner ones ('standards') and, although individually fairly short-lived, there is a succession of flowers. *M. spathulata* (*M. spathacea*) is the commonest and this is a bright yellow, sometimes with brownish markings in the centre of

the falls which spread out sideways to give the flower a diameter of about 6–8 cm. *M. huttonii* is similar, but slightly smaller in its flower size, and *M. moggii* is a rather shorter version which is also occasionally to be found in cultivation.

CULTIVATION These yellow Moraeas do well in warm, sunny borders which are well supplied with moisture in the summer months, so a site along a south- or west-facing wall or fence is ideal. When growing well, the corms usually divide to produce clumps and, although these can be dug up and divided in spring, I find that they are really best if left undisturbed. Plenty of seeds are normally produced and self-sown seedlings may well appear, but plants can be raised separately in pots if propagation is required. From an early spring sowing, germination usually takes place during spring, and if the young seedlings are kept actively growing through the first summer they will be ready to plant out the following spring, preferably as a complete pot ball without breaking them up into separate corms; the initial sowing should therefore be thin. It is best not to try to keep them in pots for more than a year, since the young corms naturally pull themselves down to a great depth (20 cm is not unusual) and they may well go out through the hole in the bottom of the pot into the plunge material underneath! Needless to say, therefore, when planting Moraea corms they should be placed at least 10 cm deep in heavy soils or 15 cm in sandy ones.

Silver-leaved *Santolina*, *Nepeta* (Catmint) and Lavender make ideal sun-loving companions for the yellow Moraeas which will overtop these low, bushy plants.

NECTAROSCORDUM

In some catalogues and books this small group of about four species is included with *Allium*, but there are good botanical reasons for

133
134

135
136

37
138

133 *Trillium grandiflorum* in a damp semi-wild setting. **134** *Trillium grandiflorum* 'Flore Plena' in a peat garden. **135** *Trillium essile* 'Rubrum', a lovely foliage plant for a cool spot. **136** *Tulipa* (Lily Flowered) 'China Pink' with *Silene dioica* at Kew. **37** *Tulipa fosteriana* 'Orange Emperor' is superb with back-lighting. **138** *Tulipa* (Darwin Hybrid) 'Golden Apeldoorn' with orget-me-Nots and Bowles' Golden Grass.

139

140

141

142

143

144

139 *Tulipa greigii* 'Red Riding Hood' has striking leaves and flowers.   140 *Tulipa kauffmanniana* 'Stresa', one of the varieties of the early Water Lily Tulip.   141 *Tulipa linifolia*, a wild species from Central Asia. Needs a hot sunny position.   142 *Tulipa tarda* in a rock garden. One of the dwarfest species.   143 *Tulipa* (Lily Flowered) 'West Point' with *Brunnera macrophylla* at Kew.   144 *Zephyranthes candida* in a warm sunny bed in autumn.

keeping it separate. Of one thing there is no doubt, it certainly is related, and you have only to bruise a bulb or leaf to detect the characteristic smell, in this case not appetising!

Two species are cultivated, *N. siculum* (*N. dioscoridis*) and *N. bulgaricum*, but they are very similar in overall appearance and in gardens have probably hybridised, making the distinctions unclear. The first is to me the most attractive since it has more colour in the flowers. It is a tall plant, up to a metre in height when in flower, producing first a basal tuft of long, sharply-angled leaves, then stiff stems in May or June which are terminated by a large but loose umbel of flowers. The individual flowers are very distinctive and need not be confused with any *Allium*, being more like small Fritillaries. They are bell-shaped and carried on long arching stalks which turn upwards, becoming stiffly erect by the time the seeds are ripe. The individual flowers are about 2–2.5 cm long in an attractive mixture of soft green and pinkish-purple, each petal edged with white. *N. bulgaricum* is very similar in overall appearance, but has whitish or creamy flowers tinged with green, lacking the purplish suffusion of *N. siculum*. Variations have occurred in gardens and some forms, presumably of *N. siculum*, have rich plum-coloured flowers.

A useful attribute of either species is that they dry off extremely well for winter decorations, the stems remaining very stiff with their distinctive upright seed capsules and, being so tall, they make a useful centrepiece for a dried arrangement.

CULTIVATION   Nectaroscordum is of the easiest cultivation and will do well in any undisturbed border in sun or semi-shade, preferring soil which does not dry out excessively in summer. It can in fact be a little too successful, and I prefer to grow it in a patch of rough grass, although in this situation it means that mowing must be delayed until the beginning of July at the earliest.

If they are planted in a border among other perennials such as Hellebores, hardy Geraniums and Hostas, try to choose a spot where a patch of sun will fall on the flowers, preferably from behind, for the interesting colours can be greatly enhanced with back-lighting. The best results are obtained by planting several bulbs close together to form a compact clump. These are obtained in the autumn and should be planted about 10 cm deep.

Propagation is taken care of naturally, since offset bulbs are produced quite readily, and seeds in great abundance. In fact it is wiser to cut off the fruiting stems just before the seeds are shed and, if they are to be kept for winter decoration, hang upside down in a dry place with a container beneath to catch the seeds.

NOMOCHARIS

This small group of beautiful Chinese bulbous plants is closely related to *Lilium* but, for most people, much more difficult to cultivate than the Lilies; they really only thrive in the damper or cooler parts of the country and are especially successful in Scotland. The scaly bulbs and leafy stems, up to about a metre in height, are similar in appearance to those of many Lilies, but the flowers are rather different, being flattish or saucer-shaped, about 6–8 cm across, with broad-overlapping segments. A few species can be obtained from specialist alpine plant nurseries, not usually from the 'dried bulb' firms since these are plants which will definitely not tolerate being lifted and dried. *N. aperta* has pale pink flowers blotched with reddish-purple towards the base and a darker blackish-purple eye right in the centre, while *N. mairei* is even more heavily spotted and blotched on a whitish ground, and three of the segments have fringed margins. *N. pardanthina* is pink and usually only slightly spotted near the centre and *N. farreri*, sometimes regarded as a variety of this, is similar but with a paler, almost white ground colour. *N. saluenensis* is one of the best-known species in cultivation, with large saucer-like flowers, very variable in shade of pinkish-purple and degree of spotting, but always with a dark reddish-purple eye in the centre. They all flower in mid to late summer, usually July or August.

CULTIVATION Nomocharis need cool, moist, acid growing conditions and are thus best in a semi-shaded peat garden or in light woodland, in deep, humus-rich soil. If possible they are best obtained in spring as pot-grown plants which can be knocked out of their containers and planted directly into the soil with little disturbance, about 6–8 cm deep. In the drier parts of the country they must be kept moist in summer, and frequent spraying is necessary during hot, dry spells if they are to survive. Top-dressing with leafmould is beneficial each spring before growth commences. Propagation is by seed which should be sown thinly in pots in autumn or spring, in a cold frame. I find it best to grow these undisturbed in their pots for at least one year before planting the whole 'pot ball' out into the position where they will hopefully flower after two or three more years.

ORNITHOGALUM

The Star of Bethlehem is, of course, mainly associated with spring, loved for its starry white flowers which open wide in the sun but almost disappearing from view when they close because of the green outside. There are many species in Europe and Asia and some of these are to be found on page 80 in the Spring Section. A few of the taller northern hemisphere species do, however, flower in early summer, although they are surpassed by some of the South African species, most of which are not hardy but which can be grown in the summer garden and lifted for safe storage in the winter.

O. arabicum is a very striking early-summer species from the Mediterranean area, with stout stems up to 45 cm in height, carrying up to twelve large creamy-white saucer-shaped flowers about 4–5 cm in diameter. The most noticeable feature is the sharply contrasting blackish ovary in the centre, making it the most attractive of the taller ones.

O. thyrsoides is the only other summer species which is generally available from nurseries and this, being South African, is not hardy. It grows perfectly well, however, if planted out in spring and lifted for dry storage in a frost-free place for the winter. This has 30–40 cm spikes of clean white flowers which open in long succession and last in good condition for ages, even when cut, so that it makes a very good florists' subject and is sold under its vernacular name of Chincherinchee.

CULTIVATION Both these species can be obtained in spring for planting as soon as the danger of hard ground frosts is over. A well-drained, sheltered, sunny position is best and heavy, damp, cold soils must be broken up by adding sand and humus. An alternative method of growing these is to start them into growth in pots in a cool greenhouse, about five bulbs to a 10–15 cm diameter pot; then, when the weather has begun to warm up reliably, usually during May, carefully knock out the whole pot of bulbs and plant it in the open garden. They must not be forced too much beforehand and, ideally, by planting time the tips of growth should just be through the surface. The planting depth for these Ornithogalums is about 5–8 cm and about the same apart.

The white flowers show up best against a darkish background and, if a 'sun-trap' site can be chosen, where something like a dark blue-green Conifer gives protection from behind, the spikes will stand out well. The purple-leaved form of *Cotinus coggygria* also makes a suitable background companion.

Propagation can be by seed, if produced, or by small offset bulbs which can be detached at replanting time in the spring.

POLIANTHES

Only one species, *P. tuberosa*, the Tuberose, is cultivated to any extent, although there are several others which have less showy flowers. This one has a long history in gardens, at least 400 years, and a mystery surrounds its origins for it has never been rediscovered in the wild. Almost certainly it comes from Central America, since all the related species occur in Mexico.

P. tuberosa grows to about 50–100 cm in height, with several long basal leaves and a loose spike of very fragrant, tubular white flowers, which are almost wax-like in the texture of their five spreading lobes. The tubers are normally offered in the spring catalogues since these are summer growers and are not hardy enough to be planted out in the autumn. It seems to be more frequently on sale in its double form, known as 'The Pearl', which has extra lobes in the centre, but occasionally the single can be located and personally I find this more attractive.

CULTIVATION   Although generally recommended for pot cultivation, it is worth trying to grow Tuberose in a warm, sunny, protected place such as at the foot of a south wall. They like a rich soil and it was recommended in the eighteenth century, when the plant was very popular, that a lot of old manure should be dug into the soil. Sandy soils, heavily manured, were considered to be the most successful. The tubers are planted, with the crowns only just below the surface, in mid-spring when serious frosts are usually past; right through the growing and flowering season plenty of water must be supplied. Flowering time is usually in mid-summer, but it is important to keep the plants growing on after this, with liquid feeds once a fortnight into the autumn. Once the leaves have begun to die back, the tubers can be lifted and stored in nearly dry sand in a frost-free, but not warm, place. In very mild areas they can be left in the ground through the winter, with the crowns covered over with bracken or sacking—anything in fact that will keep out frosts.

In pots, since they are vigorous plants, it is enough to have just three tubers in a deep pot at least 15 cm in diameter, in compost such as John Innes no. 2 with some leafmould added, for these plants enjoy extra humus. They can be started off in a cool greenhouse in early spring, and then stood out on a terrace in May or June for flowering, with plenty of water and liquid feeds every two weeks, replacing them inside in the autumn and drying them off for the winter months. Repotting should be carried out every year in early spring.

P. tuberosa can be propagated by removing any offset tubers at replanting or repotting time, and these should be grown on separately from the parent tubers in similar rich, well-drained soil.

RHODOHYPOXIS

Few of the summer bulbs are dwarf plants, but Rhodohypoxis is a real miniature, reaching only about 5 cm in height when in flower. Only one species, *R. baurii*, is generally cultivated, and this is a plant of damp places in the high mountains of the Eastern Cape and Lesotho, the Drakensberg. Here, they receive frosts in the winter months and are thus fairly hardy, although will not tolerate severe frosts which make the ground solid for weeks on end.

The tiny blackish corms start to grow in late spring and produce narrow grey-green, hairy leaves followed shortly by curiously shaped flowers in a wide range of colours, from white through pinks to various shades of red. Each short stem usually has only one flower, but a long succession comes from each corm, so the flowering period may last right through the summer, with a peak about June. The upward-facing flowers are about 2.5–3 cm across and are curious in that there is no open centre, so that the stamens are hidden and the visible portion of the flower consists of six petals converging and pressing together at their bases. Although it is usual to find only mixed colours on offer in nurseries, there are named varieties and occasionally some of these are to be found in catalogues, sometimes in the spring collections rather than autumn catalogues.

CULTIVATION Rhodohypoxis can be grown outside successfully in areas where the ground does not freeze to a great depth; in such districts a layer of dry, loose peat or bracken will help to provide protection, or they must be grown in pots which can be placed in a frost-free place for the winter. The corms can be obtained and planted in spring, at a depth of about 2–4 cm, and they require a light soil which has sand and humus present and which does not become too dry and hot; hence it is often necessary to water them during the summer months. During winter, however, they are dormant and need to be kept on the dry side, so it may be necessary to provide some protection from excess water in high-rainfall districts. Their dwarf stature makes them ideal for a rock garden where the sandy-peaty soil can be easily provided and winter drainage is good in the raised pockets. They are also particularly attractive for growing in a sink or trough garden where soil conditions are under easy control.

Propagation is normally by division since, when growing well, the corms increase quite rapidly. This can be done in spring, just before active growth commences, or after the main flush of flowers is over in summer. In the latter case the dividing and replanting is done quickly to avoid drying out, and the plants watered in well afterwards; treated in this way they will grow on without a check. Seeds can be obtained but are not easy to find in the tiny capsules, but if they can be located it is a good way to raise new varieties. They should be sown straight away in summer, in pots or boxes of sandy/peaty compost, and after germination kept in growth for as long as possible. Protection in winter must be provided for the young seedlings, but they can be planted out at the start of the second growing season.

Full sun is necessary for Rhodohypoxis and it is ideal if this can be combined with protection from cold north and east winds in winter, thus preventing the worst of the frosts. A wall, fence or hedge provides such protection and on a rock garden one might choose the sunny side of a shrub to give some degree of shelter. The very brightly coloured forms of Rhodohypoxis need placing carefully, where they will not clash with other showy flowers, and they can be enhanced by grey foliage plants such as *Artemisia schmidtiana* 'Nana' and dwarf forms of Lavender.

SCILLA

The main entry for the Squills is, of course, in the Spring Section, for it is the early dwarf blue-flowered species which are the charmers of this genus. There is, however, one early summer flowering species which is worthy of mention, *S. peruviana*. This is a native of southern Europe, not Peru (one of those nomenclatural errors!), and is quite a striking species when in flower, although its many long leaves are a disadvantage. These are produced in autumn and are a littly 'tatty' at the tips by flowering time in May or June. The stems rise to about 20–30 cm and carry a broad, conical-shaped raceme of many flattish, starry steely-blue flowers, or white in the albino form 'Alba'.

CULTIVATION *S. peruviana* has large bulbs which should be planted in the autumn in the sunniest position you can find, at the foot of a south-facing wall or fence if possible. This is important, since it does not flower very freely in cool situations. The bulbs are best planted with their tips only just below the surface. If drainage is good the type of soil is not too important and for preference should not be too rich, otherwise excessive leaf growth will result. If there is a tendency to flower rather shyly, then a dressing of sulphate of potash or a potash-rich fertiliser may help, applied in autumn or early spring.

Propagation is by division of established clumps which build up quite rapidly of their own accord.

SPARAXIS

The Harlequin Flower. These colourful species of South African members of the Iris family are not normally suitable for outdoor cultivation, since they come from the winter rainfall region and begin their growth cycle during our autumn, only to succumb in the winter. The corms can, however, sometimes be obtained in spring and these should be planted about 5–7 cm deep in a well-drained sunny, sheltered position in late March or early April, for flowering in summer. They grow to about 15 cm in height with narrow, erect Iris-like leaves, and bear spikes of flattish flowers about 3–5 cm across in an amazing array of bright colours, in the mixtures which are usually on sale. They range from white to peach, orange and red, usually with a yellow throat and sometimes also with a purple-red zone around the yellow centre. They are fairly cheap and can thus be replaced each year, or the corms can be lifted and stored over winter in a frost-free place, but it is not easy to stop them sprouting into growth before the spring and I prefer to leave this to the nurseryman!

TIGRIDIA

Tiger Flower, Mexican Shell Flower. Although there are several colourful species of Tigridia, mostly from Central America, only one, *T. pavonia*, is in general cultivation and readily obtainable. This is, however, by far the most spectacular and has a long history of cultivation, firstly by the Aztecs who used the bulbs as a food, and in European gardens certainly since the early nineteenth century. Horticulturists have raised and named many varieties differing widely in colour, from white to yellow, orange-red and crimson, plain or heavily red-blotched inside, but it is unusual to find these on sale separately nowadays, a mixed selection being the usual nurseryman's offering.

T. pavonia has a fan of erect pleated leaves and a central flower stem about 30–45 cm in height, which produces several flowers in succession. Each one lasts only a few hours, in the morning, but is very showy, about 10–15 cm across, with three large widely-spreading outer segments and three small inner ones; the inner segments and the base of the outer ones are curved, forming a bowl-shaped centre which in most varieties carries prominent red blotches, although there are some forms in which the centre is devoid of marks. The flowering time is late summer.

CULTIVATION   Being a native of Mexico, *T. pavonia* is not very hardy in this country, but since the bulbs are dormant in the winter they can be lifted in autumn when the leaves are dying back and stored safely in a frost-free place in a slightly damp peat-sand mixture, just moist enough to stop them shrivelling. Planting out in spring should be delayed until the soil has begun to warm up—not before the end of April and usually about mid-May. The soil needs to be light and well-drained, sand and peat being added to heavy clays, and during growth plenty of water must be given and ideally a liquid fertiliser every other week. The bulbs are placed about 5–7 cm deep in the soil.

Propagation is by seeds which are freely produced, many in each capsule. These can be sown in March to May in any commercial seed compost, and given protection from frost in the early stages. Once germination has taken place, the young seedlings can be planted out into the garden or retained in pots for the first year, planting out the following May. In ideal conditions *T. pavonia* may flower the same year that the seeds are sown, but two years is the usual time taken to reach flowering size.

In most parts of the country Tigridias are treated as tender plants and need to be placed in a warm, sunny position with protection from cold winds, such as a fence, wall or dense shrub might provide. However, in mild climates they can be planted in any sunny situation and left undisturbed to increase or seed at will. Being very gaudy, they look best if there is little competition from other flowers, so some neighbours with fairly uniform appearance are best. Grey-leaved plants are ideal, such as sage (*Salvia officinalis*) in its green, purple or variegated-leaved forms, *Cistus*, *Senecio* or a Rosemary bush which will provide flowers early in the year before the Tigridias are planted. All these plants require similar sunny places.

There are about 30 species in all, with a great range of flower colour, such as white, yellow, orange, blue and purple, some of them strikingly bicoloured. None is as colourful and large as *T. pavonia* and as yet this is the only one obtainable from nurseries.

TULIPA

Although Tulips are mainly associated with spring, there is one unusual, very late-flowering species which opens its blooms in late May or early June. *T. sprengeri* is small compared with the large spring-bedding varieties, but it is a graceful species with intensely coloured flowers, making it ideal for growing among other small plants. Surprisingly, although it is hardy and easy to cultivate, and will seed itself when doing well, it is clearly very rare in the wild in Turkey, for its whereabouts have never been rediscovered since the original collection in the last century.

T. sprengeri is about 35–45 cm in height when in flower, with unobtrusive narrow, shiny leaves and solitary bright scarlet flowers about 7–10 cm in diameter when fully open. The exterior of the segments, and hence the bud, is overlaid with a buff-gold colour, so it is the half-open stage which is especially attractive, when the gold outside is opening to reveal the red interior.

CULTIVATION It is difficult to know what to recommend as the best method of growing *T. sprengeri*, for it seems to do well in most situations. I have seen it growing in semi-shaded grass on a chalky soil, in a partially shaded peat garden with Hellebores and Erythroniums and in a hot, sunny situation against a south wall; in fact it seems to tolerate any, except waterlogged, soils and most aspects providing there is at least dappled sunlight. The flower colour goes particularly well with grey leaves and I think the most attractive planting I have seen was between greyish *Cistus*, *Dianthus* and a Rosemary bush in a warm, sunny border.

The bulbs can be obtained in autumn, sadly rather expensive in spite of the ease of propagation by the plentifully produced seeds, and should be planted at least 10 cm deep. Seeds are best sown directly into the ground where they are intended to flower, rather than raised separately in pots, but care must be taken not to cultivate the places where they are germinating; flowering is usually about three to four years after sowing.

WATSONIA

These are interesting and beautiful plants, not unlike Gladiolus and, like them, originating from South Africa, but unfortunately they are very little-known in cultivation and are only occasionally offered in nursery catalogues. There are a considerable number of species which fall into different types of growth pattern depending upon their place of origin, since some occur in the winter rainfall area of South Africa, the S.W. Cape, and others in the summer rainfall, eastern Cape, region. Mostly they are rather tender plants, but in southern and western districts they are well worth a try in a sheltered, sunny position.

Most species have long spikes of flowers which are often individually smaller and more densely arranged than on a Gladiolus spike, the most noticeable difference being that the flowers are nearly regular in shape, with six more or less equal petals. The leaves are rather tough and leathery and the plants may be evergreen or deciduous in winter, depending upon the species. Most Watsonias are fairly tall plants, the flower stems reaching a metre or more in height. *W. pyramidata* (*W. rosea*) is sometimes available and this is one of the more attractive species, with pinkish-mauve flowers about 5–6 cm across in late summer. *W. ardernei* has branching stems with white flowers which have the segments widely spreading at the mouth of the tube, giving a diameter of about 5 cm. *W. beatricis* is a bright orange with unbranched stems, the flowers also flared at the mouth, but *W. foureacei* has more tubular, less-flared flowers about 6–7 cm long, in a deep reddish-purple. These and others, ranging in colours from bluish-mauve to salmon-pink and scarlet-orange, can occasionally be found and are worth looking out for.

CULTIVATION It is best to treat all Watsonias as tender plants and give them protection in the winter. The site should be sheltered and sunny but, since most of them are in active growth in summer, they require plenty of moisture as well, so it may be necessary to keep them watered in situations which receive very hot sun. Whether they are evergreen ones or species which die down in winter, it is a good idea to place loose bracken or something similar over the plants to keep out the worst frosts. Those that die down for the winter can be lifted and placed in boxes of sand in a frost-free place until the spring. The corms, looking like those of Gladiolus, are usually offered in spring bulb catalogues and should be planted about 15 cm deep as soon as serious frosts are past. Like so many other 'bulbs' for spring planting, they can be potted up earlier in the year, then kept in a cool greenhouse for planting out in April or May. Propagation is usually simple because the parent corms divide naturally or produce offsets from time to time.

Watsonias associate well with such plants as *Cistus* and Rosemary which enjoy the same sunny conditions and, being woody and evergreen, provide extra protection for them in winter.

ZANTEDESCHIA

These well-known South African Arum Lilies are mostly greenhouse plants requiring a winter temperature of not less than 50°F (10°C), but the white-flowered *Z. aethiopica* is hardier and will survive lower temperatures. There is a form of this called 'Crowborough' which can be grown in the milder counties in the open border or at the edge of a garden pool.

Arum Lilies have a tuberous stock, giving rise to bold, broadly arrow-shaped leaves which are overtopped in late summer by the familiar large white funnel-like spathes surrounding a yellow pencil-shaped spadix. Although it is naturally more or less evergreen, in most winters it is likely to get frosted and will die back to ground level, but normally reappears unharmed with the warmer weather.

CULTIVATION *Z. aethiopica* 'Crowborough' is usually to be found in the catalogues of hardy plant nurseries, but occasionally bulb firms offer it as well. It is best planted in spring in a sunny or partially shaded position, in soil which has been enriched with old rotted manure which will give it the rich diet it needs and help to retain moisture, a necessary factor in the successful cultivation of the Arum Lily.

In cold winters, cover the crowns with bracken, leaves or loose peat. It looks especially good at the edge of a pond where the white spathes are reflected in the water. It will take a depth of 15–30 cm of water if it is planted actually in the pond. Propagation is by division of established clumps in early spring.

ZIGADENUS

The North American species of this small genus are the most attractive, which should not be taken to mean that they are spectacular! These are greenish-flowered bulbs, producing racemes of smallish starry flowers which, although not striking, may find a place on a rock garden or peat garden where the finer detail can be appreciated. *Z. elegans* and *Z. glaucus* are very similar to each other, producing linear basal leaves and, in mid-summer, flower stems about 30–60 cm in height carrying the many pale green flowers which are individually about 1.5–2 cm in diameter. On closer inspection these can be seen to have darker green glistening nectaries at the base of each segment. The Californian *Z. fremontii* is perhaps the best, with creamy-green flowers up to 2.5 cm in diameter, also bearing conspicuous nectaries, and there is a dwarf 10–15 cm form of this, var. *minor*, which is a useful early summer bulb for the rock garden.

CULTIVATION Zigadenus are easily cultivated and will grow well in ordinary garden soil in sun or partial shade. *Z. fremontii* will take a drier position than the others, and the dwarf form can be planted on a raised pocket of a rock garden where its flowers show up better. The taller ones can be grown in a mixed border, but if there are too many showy plants around they will be completely overshadowed. They are, however, useful for planting amid such perennials as Hellebores and Pulmonarias which have finished their flowering much earlier. Several bulbs should be placed close together for the best effect, and these need to be about 5–7 cm deep, planted in autumn or spring depending upon when they can be obtained, for these are plants which are usually sold in pots by nurseries specialising in hardy herbaceous perennials or alpines rather than dried bulbs.

For propagation purposes the bulbs increase vegetatively slowly, so that clumps can be lifted and divided periodically, but it is quicker to grow new ones from seeds which are freely produced. Clumps are best divided in early autumn and the seeds best collected and sown as soon as ripe, planting the young bulbs out about a year after germination.

BULB NURSERIES AND SPECIALIST SOCIETIES

Any specialities are noted in brackets

Nurseries

Amand, J., Beethoven Street, London W10. (*A good range.*)

Avon Bulbs, Bradford-on-Avon, Wiltshire. (*A good range and some rarities.*)

Blom, Walter, & Son, Coombelands Nurseries, Leavesden, Watford, Herts. (*A wide range.*)

Broadleigh Gardens, Barr House, Bishops Hull, Taunton, Somerset. (*A good range of dwarf bulbs, some rarities.*)

Bowlby, Rupert, Gatton, Reigate, Surrey, RH2 0TA. (*Mainly dwarf bulbs, some rarities.*)

Cambridge Bulbs, 40 Whittlesford Road, Newton, Cambridge. (*Rare bulbs, especially Crocus, Fritillaria, Iris.*)

Carncairn Daffodils Ltd, Carncairn Lodge, Broughshane, Co. Antrim, N. Ireland. (*Narcissus.*)

Cornish Bulb Co., 13a Church Street, Falmouth, Cornwall. (*Narcissus.*)

De Jager & Sons, The Nurseries, Marden, Kent. (*A wide range.*)

Fox, Derek, Bullwood Nursery, 54 Woodlands Road, Hockley, Essex. (*Lilium.*)

Highland Liliums, Kiltarlity by Beauly, Invernesshire. (*Lilium.*)

Hoog, M. H., Koninginneweg 86, Pf 3217, N 2001, Haarlem, Holland. (*A wide range, many rarities.*)

Jefferson-Brown, M., Maylite, Martley, Worcester. (*Narcissus, Lilium.*)

Kelways Nurseries, Langport, Somerset. (*A wide range.*)

Linfield Nurseries, Holly Road, Barton-under-Needwood, Staffs. (*Lilium.*)

Parker-Jervis, J. and E., Martens Hall Farm, Longworth, Abingdon, Oxon. (*Galanthus, Colchicum.*)

Potterton & Martin, The Cottage Nursery, Moortown Road, Nettleton, near Caistor, N. Lincs. (*A good selection of dwarf bulbs.*)

Tile Barn Nursery, Standen Street, Iden Green, Benenden, Kent. (*Cyclamen.*)

Van Tubergen, Oldfield Lane, Wisbech, Cambs. (*A wide range.*)

Wallace & Barr, The Nurseries, Marden, Kent. (*A wide range.*)

Societies with seed lists or annual bulb auctions or systems of exchange

Alpine Garden Society, Lye End Link, St. Johns, Woking, Surrey.

British Gladiolus Society, 10 Sandbach Road, Thurlwood, Rode Heath, Cheshire.
British Iris Society, 67 Bushwood Road, Kew, Richmond, Surrey.
Cyclamen Society, 7 Montreal Road, Ilford, Essex.
Daffodil Society, 1 Dorset Cottages, Birch Road, Copford, Colchester, Essex.
Royal Horticultural Society, Vincent Square, London SW1.
RHS Lily Group, 21 Embrook Road, Wokingham, Berks.

FURTHER READING

General books on bulbs
Dwarf Bulbs by Brian Mathew, 1973, B. T. Batsford.
Larger Bulbs by Brian Mathew, 1978, B. T. Batsford.
The Bulb Book by Martin Rix and Roger Phillips, 1981, Pan Books.
Growing Bulbs by Martin Rix, 1983, Croom Helm.
Collins' Guide to Bulbs by Patrick M. Synge, second edition 1971, Collins.
The Bulb Book by P. Schauenberg, 1965, Frederick Warne.

Specialist subjects
The Iris by Brian Mathew, 1982, B. T. Batsford.
The Crocus by Brian Mathew, 1982, B. T. Batsford.
Lilies by Patrick M. Synge, 1980, B. T. Batsford.
A Handbook of Crocus and Colchicum by E. A. Bowles, new edition 1985, Waterstone.
A Handbook of Narcissus by E. A. Bowles, new edition 1985, Waterstone.
Cyclamen by R. D. Meikle and C. Grey-Wilson, 1975, Alpine Garden Society.
Snowdrops and Snowflakes by F. C. Stern, 1956, Royal Horticultural Society.
Fritillaries by C. Beck, 1953, Faber & Faber.
The Genus Tulipa by A. D. Hall, 1940, Royal Horticultural Society.
Growing Lilies by D. Fox, 1985, Croom Helm.
Miniature Daffodils by A. Gray, second edition 1961, Collingridge.
Lilies of the World by H. D. Woodcock and W. T. Stearn, 1950, Country Life.
The Daffodil by M. J. Jefferson-Brown, 1951, Faber & Faber.
The International Lily Register, 1982, Royal Horticultural Society.

Propagation
Bulb Production, M.A.F.F. Bulletin 62.

Pests and diseases
Collins' Guide to the Pests, Diseases and Disorders of Garden Plants by S. Buczacki and K. Harris, 1981, Collins.
Diseases of Bulbs, 1959, M.A.F.F./A.D.A.S.

INDEX OF BULB NAMES

Acidanthera 93–5
  A. bicolor 95
  cultivars 95
Allium 22, 52–3, 95–6, 128–9
  A. aflatunense 96; *A. albopilosum* 95; *A. azureum* 95; *A. caeruleum* 95; *A. callimischon* 22–3; *A. christophii* 95; *A. dioscoridis* 96; *A. elatum* 95; *A. flavum* 96; *A. giganteum* 95–6; *A. karataviense* 52–3, 96; *A. moly* 96; *A. neapolitanum* 53; *A. oreophilum* 53, 96; *A. ostrowskianum* 53, 96; *A. pulchellum* 96; *A. rosenbachianum* 96; *A. siculum* 96; *A. sphaerocephalon* 96; *A. stipitatum* 96; *A. triquetrum* 53
Amaryllidaceae 12, 22, 26 *see also Amaryllis*
Amaryllis 12, 21, 23–4, 99
  A. belladonna 22–3, 26, 33–5
  varieties 23
Anemone (Ranunculus family) 12, 14, 37–8, 42, 52–5, 97
  A. apennina 54, 65, 85; *A. blanda* 37–8, 48, 54; *A. coronaria* (Poppy Anemone) 53–5, 97; *A. fulgens* 54–5; *A. hepatica* 31, 55; *A. nemorosa* (Wood Anemone) 16, 53–5, 65, 85; *A. pavonina* (Peacock Anemone) 53, 55; *A. ranunculoides* 53, 55
  varieties 38, 53–5, 97
Anomatheca 97
  A. cruenta 97; *A. laxa* 97
Arisaema 97–8
  A. candidissimum 97–8; *A. consanguineum* 98
Arisarum 55
  A. proboscideum 55
Arum 13, 38–9, 55–6, 97
  A. creticum 55–6; *A. dioscoridis* 56; *A. italicum* 38–9, 56
Autumn Crocus 24, 26 *see also Colchicum autumnale*
Autumn Daffodil 34 *see Sternbergia*

Bluebells 51, 69, 82–3 *see Scilla*
Brimeura amethystina 69
Brodiaea 98–9
  B. lactea 98; *B. laxa* 98
  varieties 98
Bulbocodium 56–7
  B. vernum 56

Calochortus (Lily family) 57
  C. albus 57; *C. luteus* 57

Camassia 99
  C. esculenta 99; *C. leichtlinii* 99; *C. quamash* 99
  varieties 99
Cardiocrinum 99–100
  C. giganteum 99
Chincherinchee *see Ornithogalum*
Chionodoxa (Glory of the Snow) 52, 57–8, 68, 81
  C. forbesii 57–8; *C. gigantea* 58; *C. luciliae* 57–8; *C. sardensis* 57–8; *C. siehei* 57; *C. tmoli* 57; *C. tmolusi* 57
Chionoscilla allenii 58
Colchicum (Lily family) 15, 17, 22, 24–6, 56, 58–9
  C. agrippinum 24–5; *C. autumnale* 24–5; *C. bifolium* 58; *C. bivonae* 25; *C. bowlesianum* 25; *C. byzantinum* 25; *C. cilicicum* 25; *C. luteum* 58; *C. nivale* 58; *C. sibthorpii* 25; *C. speciosum* 21, 25–6; *C. szovitsii* 58
  varieties 25–6
Convallaria (Lily of the Valley) 16
Corydalis 59–60
  C. ambigua 59; *C. bulbosa* 59; *C. cashmeriana* 59; *C. caucasica* 59; *C. cava* 59; *C. diphylla* 59; *C. solida* 59, 60; *C. transsilvanica* 59
  varieties 59–60
Crinum (Amaryllidaceae family) 93, 100
  C. × powellii 26, 100
Crocosmia (Montbretia) 100, 101
  C. aurea 100; *C. × crocosmiflora* 100; *C. masonorum* 100–1; *C. pottsii* 100
  varieties 100
Crocus (Iris family) 12, 14, 16, 22, 24, 26–9, 36, 39–41, 46, 52, 58, 60–2, 93
  C. ancyrensis 39–49, 61; *C. angustifolius* 61; *C. asturicus* 28; *C. aureus* 39, 66; *C. banaticus* 27; *C. biflorus* 60–2; *C. cancellatus* 27; *C. chrysanthus* 40, 60–2; *C. cilicicus* 27; *C. corsicus* 61; *C. etruscus* 61; *C. flavus* ('Large Yellow') 39–40, 60–2; *C. fleischeri* 61; *C. goulimyi* 27–8; *C. hadriaticus* 28; *C. imperati* 61; *C. korolkwii* 61; *C. kotschyanus* 28; *C. laevigatus* 28, 37, 39, 40; 'Large Dutch' 60; *C. longiflorus* 22, 28; *C. medius* 28; *C. minimus* 61; *C. niveus* 28; *C. nudiflorus* 27–8; *C. ochroleucus* 27–8; *C. olivieri* 61; *C. pulchellus* 28; *C. salzmannii* 28; *C. sativus* 27–8; *C. serotinus* 22, 28–9; *C. sieberi* 39, 61; *C. speciosus* 21, 27, 29; *C. tommasinianus* 36, 39, 40, 61; *C. tournefortii* 29, 40–1; *C. vernus* (Dutch Crocus) 60–2; *C. zonatus* 28

varieties 39–40, 60–1
Curtonus 101
  C. paniculata 101
Cyclamen (Primula family) 12, 14, 16, 22, 29–31, 36, 41–2, 52, 62–4
  C. atkinsii 41; *C. balearicum* 63; *C. cilicium* 30; *C. coum* 36–7, 39, 41–2, 49, 63; *C. creticum* 63; *C. europaeum* 30; *C. graecum* 30; *C. hederifolium* 29–32, 62; *C. ibericum* 41; *C. libanoticum* 63; *C. mirabile* 30; *C. neapolitanum* 29, 62; *C. orbiculatum* 41; *C. persicum* 29; *C. pseudibericum* 63; *C. purpurascens* 30; *C. repandum* 63; *C. vernum* 41; wild 21
  varieties 30, 42
Cypella 101–2
  C. herbertii 101–2

Daffodil 15, 16, 18, 21, 47, 52, 74, 80, 93 *see also Narcissus*
Dierama 102
  D. pulcherrimum 102
  varieties 102
Dracunculus (Arum family) 102–3
  D. vulgaris 102–3

Eranthis (Winter Aconite) (Ranunculus family) 13, 42–3, 64
  E. cilicica 42; *E. hyemalis* 42–3; *C. × tubergenii* 42
Erythronium (Dog's Tooth Violet) 12, 17, 48, 51–2, 64–5, 67
  E. californicum 64; *E. dens-canis* 64–5; *E. hendersonii* 65; *E. oregonum* 64; *E. revolutum* 64; *E. tuolumnense* 64–5
  varieties 64–5
Eucomis (Pineapple Flower) (Lily family) 93, 103–4
  E. autumnalis 103; *E. bicolor* 103; *E. comosa* 103; *E. punctata* 103; *E. undulata* 103; *E. zambesiaca* 103

Freesia 104
Fritillaria 15, 16, 52, 65–8, 129
  F. acmopetala 66; *F. assyriaca* 66; *F. camtschatcensis* 66–7; Crown Imperial 65–7; *F. imperialis* 66–7; *F. meleagris* (Snakeshead Lily) 66–7; *F. pallidiflora* 66; *F. persica* 66–7; *F. pontica* 66–7; *F. pyrenaica* 66, 120; *F. uva-vulpis* 66–7
  varieties 66

Galanthus (Snowdrop) 31–2, 43–4, 68, 72
  G. caucasicus 43–4; *G. corcyrensis* 44; *G. elwesii* 44; *G. ikariae* 44; *G. latifolius* 44; *G. nivalis* 31, 44; *G. octobrensis* 31; *G. reginae-olgae* 31–2, 43–4, 68

varieties 44
Galtonia 93, 104
  G. candicans 104
Gladiolus 11–12, 13, 94–5, 105–8
  Butterfly 105, 106–7; *G. byzantinus* 105; *G. cardinalis* 108; *G. × colvillei* 108; *G. communis* 105–6; *G. imbricatus* 105–6; *G. italicus* 105–6; Large-Flowered 105, 106–7; Miniature 105, 106; *G. nanus* and hybrids 105–6, 108; *G. papilio* 105–6; Primulinus 105, 106–8; *G. purpureo-auratus* 105–6; *G. saundersiae* 105–6; *G. segetum* 105–6; *G. tristis* 108; *G. undulatus* 105
  classification 106
  varieties 105–8
Grape Hyacinth *see Muscari*

Hermodactylus (*Iris tuberosa*) 68
  H. tuberosus 68
Hyacinthus 12, 68–9
  H. amethystinus 69; *H. orientalis* 68–9
  varieties 69

Ipheion 12, 69–70
  I. uniflorum 51, 69
  varieties 70
Iridaceae 12 *see also Iris*
Iris 12–14, 16, 22, 44–7, 70–2, 108–10
  I. aucheri 70–1; *I. bakeriana* 46, 70; *I. bucharica* 70–1; *I. danfordiae* 45–6; Dutch Iris 108–10; *I. graeberiana* 70–1; *I. histrio* 46; *I. histrioides* 45–6, 52; Juno Irises 13, 70–1; *I. latifolia* (English Iris) 108–9; *I. lusitanica* 109; *I. magnifica* 70–1; *I. orchioides* 70; *I. persica* 70; *I. reticulata* 15, 19, 44–7, 52, 68, 70; *I. sindjarensis* 70; *I. stylosa* 45; *I. tingitana* 109; *I. unguicularis* 23, 32, 34–7, 44–5, 68, 74; *I. warleyensis* 71; *I. × warlsind* 71; *I. winogradowii* 45–6; *I. × xiphioides* 108–9; *I. xiphium* (Spanish Iris) 108–9
  hybrids and varieties 45–6, 109–10
Ixia (South African Corn Lily) (Iris family) 110
Ixiolirion 72
  I. montanum 72; *I. pallasii* 72; *I. tataricum* 72

Jonquil 48, 79 *see also Narcissus jonquilla*

Leucojum (Snowflakes) (Amaryllis family) 32, 43, 47, 52, 72–3
  L. aestivum 72–3; *L. autumnale* 32; *L. hiemale* 72; *L. nicaeense* 72–3; *L. roseum* 32; *L. vernum* 47, 72–3
  varieties 72
Liliaceae 12, 22 *see also Lilium*

Lilium 12, 15, 16, 18, 32–3, 93–4, 110–28
  L. amabile 115, 126–8; American Hybrids 123–4, 128; Asiatic Hybrids 121, 122–3; *L. auratum* 22, 32, 111, 114–15, 121, 125, 127–8; Aurelian Hybrids 124–5; Bellingham Hybrids 119, 123–4, 128; *L. brownii* 121, 124; *L. bulbiferum* 116; *L. canadense* 115, 127–8; *L. candidum* (Madonna Lily) 93, 110–11, 113, 115–16, 126–7; *L. carniolicum* 115–16, 126–8; *L. cernuum* 115–16, 126–7; *L. chalcedonicum* (Scarlet Martagon) 116, 126–7; *L. concolor* 116–17, 121, 126–8; *L. croceum* (Orange Lily) 116–17, 121, 127; *L. dauricum* 117, 121, 126; *L. davidii* 117, 126; *L. duchartrei* 117, 126; *L. formosanum* 117–18, 126; *L. henryi* 118, 120, 124–8; *L. × hollandicum* 116–17; *L. humboldtii* 123; *L. lancifolium* 121; *L. leichtlinii* 119; *L. leucanthum centifolium* 121, 124; *L. longiflorum* (Easter Lily) 118, 126; *L. mackliniae* 118, 126, 128; *L. × maculatum* 117; *L. martagon* 119–20, 123, 127–8; Martagon Hybrids 122, 127; *L. maximowiczii* 119, 126–7; *L. monadelphum* 119, 127; *L. nansonii* 118, 123, 127; Oriental Hybrids 125, 127–8; *L. pardalinum* (Panther or Leopard Lily) 119, 123, 127–8; *L. parryi* 123; *L. pomponium* 126–8; *L. pumilum* 119, 126, 128; *L. pyrenaicum* 120, 126, 128; *L. regale* 120–1, 124, 126–7; *L. rubellum* 127–8; *L. sargentiae* 121, 124; *L. speciosum* 22, 32, 120–1, 125, 127–8; *L. sulphureum* 121, 124; *L. superbum* 121; *L. szovitsianum* 119, 127; *L. tenuifolium* 119–20; *L. × testaceum* 116, 127; *L. tigrinum* 32, 121, 123, 125–6, 128; Trumpet Hybrids 124–5; *L. unicolor* 117; *L. willmottiae* 117
  buying and planting 112
  propagation 125–7
  soils and sites 112
  varieties 115, 117, 119–20, 122–5

Mariposa Tulip 57
Meadow Saffron 25 *see also Colchicum autumnale*
Montbretia *see Crocosmia*
Moraea 93, 128
  M. moggii 128; *M. spathacea* 128; *M. spathulata* 128
Muscari (Grape Hyacinth) 33, 51–2, 68, 71, 73–4, 80
  M. armeniacum 73–4; *M. azureum* 73; *M. botryoides* 73–4; *M. comosum* 73–4; *M. latifolium* 73; *M. neglectum* 73–4; *M. moschatum* 73–4; *M. racemosum* 73; *M. tubergenianum* 73
  varieties 73–4

Narcissus 12, 47–9, 52, 54, 74–80
  N. asturiensis 48–9, 78–9; *N. bulbocodium* 48–9, 56, 77, 79–80; *N. canaliculatus* 78–9; *N. cantabricus* 47–8, 77; *N. clusii* 77; *N. cyclamineus* 36, 48, 75–9; *N. jonquilla* 76, 78–9; *N. juncifolius* 78–80; *N. lobularis* 78; *N. minimus* 78; *N. nanus* 78; *N. poeticus* 75–80; *N. pseudonarcissus* (Lent Lily) 74, 78–80; *N. rupicola* 78–9; *N. tazetta* 48, 74–80; *N. triandrus* (Angel's Tears) 76, 78–80
  classification of 74–9
  Divisions 1–4 75; Divisions 5–8 76; Divisions 9–11 77–9
  hybrids and varieties 47–9, 75–9
Nectaroscordum 96, 128–9
  N. bulgaricum 129; *N. dioscoridis* 129; *N. siculum* 129
Nerine 21–3, 33, 99
  N. bowdenii 33–4, 74
Nomocharis 129–30
  N. aperta 129; *N. farreri* 129; *N. mairei* 129; *N. pardanthina* 129; *N. saluenensis* 129

Ornithogalum (Star of Bethlehem) 51–2, 80–1, 130
  O. arabicum 130; *O. balansae* 80–1; *O. narbonense* 81; *O. nutans* 80–1; *O. pyramidale* 81; *O. pyrenaicum* 81; *O. thyrsoides* 81, 130; *O. umbellatum* 80–1
  varieties 81

Polianthes 131
  P. tuberosa 131
Primula family 12, 22
Puschkinia 81
  P. libanotica 81; *P. scilloides* 81

Ranunculus family 12 *see also Anemone, Eranthis*
Rhodohypoxis 93, 131–2
  R. baurii 131
Romulea 81–2
  R. bulbocodium 82; *R. ramiflora* 82

Saffron Crocus 28
Scilla (Squills) 12, 33–4, 46, 49–52, 57, 68, 81–3, 132–3
  S. amoena 82; *S. autumnalis* 33; *S. bifolia* 49–50, 58, 83; *S. bithynica* 82; *S. campanulata* 83; *S. hispanica* 83; *S. lilio-hyacinthus* 82; *S. mischtschenkoana* 49; *S. non-scripta* 83; *S. nutans* 83; *S. peruviana* 132; *S. siberica* 49–50, 82; *S. tubergeniana* 39, 49, 82–3
  varieties 49, 82, 132
Snowdrop (*Galanthus q.v.*) 17, 21, 31–2, 36–9, 42–3, 47, 55, 61, 64, 67–8

Snowflake 43, 47 *see also Leocojum*
Sparaxis (Harlequin Flower) (Iris family) 133
Sternbergia (Amaryllis family) 23, 34–5
   S. candida 34; *S. clusiana* 34–5; *S. fischeriana* 34; *S. lutea* 21–2, 34–5; *S. sicula* 34–5

Tecophilaea 12, 51, 83–4
   T. cyanocrocus 83
   varieties 84
Tigridia (Tiger Flower) 93, 101–2, 133–4
   T. pavonia 12, 133–4
Trillium 14, 52, 55, 65, 84–5
   T. chloropetalum 85; *T. erectum* 85; *T. grandiflorum* 84–5; *T. sessile* 85
   varieties 85
Triteleia 98–9
   T. hyacinthina 98; *T. ixioides* 98; *T. laxa* 98; *T. × tubergenii* 98
   varieties 98
Tulipa 12, 13, 17, 52, 85–92, 134
   T. acuminata 89–90; *T. aucheriana* 90; *T. batalinii* 90; *T. clusiana* 90–1; Cottage 87; Darwin 87, 89; Early Double 86–7; *T. eichleri* 90; *T. fosteriana* 86, 88–9; *T. greigii* 80, 86, 89; *T. hageri* 90; *T. kauffmanniana* 86, 89; Late

Double 89; Lily-Flowered 88; *T. linifolia* 90–1; Mendel and Triumph 87; Multiflowered 88; *T. orphanidea* 90; Parrot and Fringed 88; *T. praestans* 90; *T. pulchella* 90; Rembrandt 88–9; *T. saxatilis* 90–1; Single Early 86; *T. sprengeri* 90–1, 134; *T. sylvestris* 90–1; *T. tarda* 90–1; *T. turkestanica* 90; *T. urumiensis* 90; *T. viridiflora* 87–8; *T. whittallii* 90
   classification of 86–90
   hybrids and varieties 86–90

Watsonia 134–5
   W. ardernei 135; *W. beatricis* 135; *W. foureacei* 135; *W. pyramidata* 135
Winter Aconite (*Eranthis q.v.*) 12, 37–9, 42–3, 61, 64

Zantedeschia (Arum Lily) 135–6
   Z. aethiopica 135
Zephyranthes 21, 23, 35
   Z. candida 22, 34–5, 74; *Z. citrina* 35; *Z. grandiflora* 35
Zigadenus 136
   Z. elegans 136; *Z. fremontii* 136; *Z. glaucus* 136

GENERAL INDEX

acid soil, bulbs that like 24, 26, 30, 32, 40, 43, 45, 69, 74, 79, 82, 97, 111, 120, 125, 127–8, 130
alkaline soil, bulbs that like 24–6, 30, 34, 37, 40, 43, 45, 47, 67, 69, 71, 74, 79, 82, 90–1, 97, 108, 111–12, 118, 123–4, 127

bird damage to bulbs 61
Botrytis (grey mould) 19
bulbs 13–15, 43, 57
    areas producing 12, 29 *see also* specific species
    definition of 12, 16
    feeding of 18
    dormant 17, 22, 29, 37, 42
    problems with 18–19 *see also* specific species

cold frame and greenhouse, bulbs needing 29, 34, 66, 70, 73, 75, 84, 89, 117, 126
companion planting *see* specific species
container cultivation 93–5, 103, 113–14, 124–5, 127, 131
corms 13–16, 24, 27–8, 30, 36, 40, 56, 58, 60–2, 94–5, 106
crossing 40, 44, 49, 77, 86, 117, 129
cultivation *see* specific species

deep planting 46, 55–6
diseases 18–19, 115, 121
dormancy 17 *see also* specific species
drainage 17, 34, 38, 41, 47, 49, 54, 62–3, 65, 71, 96, 98, 100, 110, 112
drought, effect on bulbs 17 *see also* specific species

fertilisers 18, 28, 33, 35, 41, 80, 92, 113–14
frost damage 23, 25, 31, 41–2, 45–6, 54, 63, 94–6
fruiting stage 22, 27 *see also* seeding
fungicides 19, 47

greenhouses, bulbs needing *see* cold frame
grey mould *see* Botrytis

hardy bulbs 27, 33, 39, 41, 81–2, 96, 98, 100–1, 103–7, 110, 118, 122
hybridisation *see* crossing

Ink Disease 19, 47
International Lily Register 111
lifting bulbs *see* specific species

moist, cool positions, bulbs liking 28, 38, 43, 47–8, 50, 103, 108, 127–31
mouse-resistant bulbs 61

naturalising (bulbs suitable for) 29, 38, 48, 50, 52–4, 58, 79, 81–2, 93, 96, 99, 128

over-drying 30, 37, 42–3, 47

peat gardens, bulbs suitable for 52, 55, 59, 65, 67, 85, 98, 117, 136
pests and pesticides 18 *see also* bird damage, slugs
planting depths *see* specific species
planting out *see* specific species
'plumping up' bulbs 37–8, 42
propagation *see* specific species

rhizomes 14, 16, 45, 53–5, 84
rock gardens, bulbs suitable for 22, 31–2, 41, 46–7, 49, 51–3, 55, 58–9, 62–3, 65, 67, 72–3, 77–9, 82, 95–7, 132, 136
Royal Horticultural Society 19, 111, 121

seeding 29, 31–2, 39–42, 44–5, 47, 49–50, 53, 56–8, 60, 63, 65, 67, 71–4, 80–1, 85, 96–9, 101–2, 104, 118, 126, 128, 133
shady sites, bulbs liking 27, 67, 85, 113
    semi-shade 17, 24, 27, 29, 37–44, 47–8, 50, 52–6, 58–9, 63, 65, 79, 81, 98–9, 115, 118–19, 129, 135
siting bulbs *see* specific species
slugs 18, 71
soil types *see* alkaline soils, acid soils, specific species
storage, dry 94, 130 *see also* specific species
sunny situations, bulbs needing 21, 27–8, 30, 32–5, 37, 39–41, 46, 48–9, 53–4, 58, 61–2, 67, 71, 79, 81–2, 95–8, 100–1, 104, 128–9, 132, 135

tubers 13–14, 16, 30, 37–9, 41–2, 53, 55–6, 59, 63, 65, 68, 85